WALKING ON DARTMOOR

40 WALKS IN DARTMOOR NATIONAL PARK INCLUDING A TEN TORS WALK

by Steve Davison

JUNIPER HOUSE, MURLEY MOSS,
OXENHOLME ROAD, KENDAL, CUMBRIA LA9 7RL
www.cicerone.co.uk

© Steve Davison 2023
First edition 2023
ISBN: 978 1 78631 108 5
eISBN: 978 1 78362 966 4
Reprinted 2025 (with updates)

Printed in Singapore by KHL Printing using responsibly sourced paper.
A catalogue record for this book is available from the British Library.

This replaces Cicerone's *Walking on Dartmoor* guide by John Earle ISBN 9781852843601.

© Crown copyright and database rights 2023 OS AC0000810376
All photographs are by the author unless otherwise stated.

Cicerone's EU representative for GPSR compliance is Easy Access System Europe, Mustamäe tee 50, 10621 Tallinn, Estonia. Email gpsr.requests@easproject.com.

Updates to this guide

While every effort is made by our authors to ensure the accuracy of guidebooks as they go to print, changes can occur during the lifetime of an edition. Any updates that we know of for this guide will be on the Cicerone website (www.cicerone.co.uk/1108/updates), so please check before planning your trip. We also advise that you check locally about such things as transport, accommodation and shops. Even rights of way can be altered over time. We are always grateful for information about any discrepancies between a guidebook and the facts on the ground, sent by email to updates@cicerone.co.uk.

Register your book: To sign up to receive free updates, special offers and GPX files where available, create a Cicerone account and register your purchase via the 'My Account' tab at www.cicerone.co.uk.

Front cover: Cadover Cross, a Medieval wayside cross on Wigford Down (Walk 19)

CONTENTS

Map key 4
Route summary table 7

INTRODUCTION 11
Geology and landscape 12
Habitats and wildlife 13
A brief history. 15
When to walk and equipment 16
Getting to and staying in Dartmoor. 17
Bases 19
Maps and GPS 19
Safety 20
Waymarking and access 21
Using this guide 22

NORTH-EAST. 25
Walk 1   Drewsteignton and Fingle Bridge. 26
Walk 2   Chagford and Meldon Hill 30
Walk 3   Moretonhampstead and Mardon Down. 35
Walk 4   Trenchford and Tottiford Reservoirs and Christow 40
Walk 5   North Bovey and Easdon Tor 45
Walk 6   Challacombe, Grimspound and Water Hill 51
Walk 7   Lustleigh Cleave, Hunter's Tor and River Bovey 56
Walk 8   Widecombe in the Moor, Hamel Down and Bowerman's Nose. . . 61
Walk 9   Hound Tor and Haytor Rocks 66
Walk 10   Buckland Beacon and Rippon Tor 71

SOUTH-EAST. 77
Walk 11   The stepping stones walk. 78
Walk 12   Dartmeet figure-of-eight 83
Walk 13   Dart Valley via Bench Tor and Sharp Tor 88
Walk 14   Ryder's Hill and Snowdon. 95
Walk 15   River Avon and Eastern White Barrow 100
Walk 16   Old tramways and Three Barrows 105
Walk 17   Butterdon Hill, Ugborough Beacon and Sharp Tor. 110
Walk 18   Erme Valley and Stalldown Barrow 115

SOUTH-WEST		121
Walk 19	River Plym and Dewerstone Rock	122
Walk 20	Drizzlecombe and Gutter Tor	126
Walk 21	Burrator Reservoir, Meavy and Sheeps Tor	132
Walk 22	Down Tor, Nun's Cross and Fox Tor	137
Walk 23	Leeden Tor, Sharpitor and Leather Tor	143
Walk 24	Devonport Leat and Black Tor	147
Walk 25	Great Mis Tor and Lich Way	152
Walk 26	Longaford Tor, Rough Tor and Beardown Tors	159
Walk 27	Foggintor, King's Tor and Merrivale	164
Walk 28	Cox Tor, Great Staple Tor and Pew Tor	170

NORTH-WEST		175
Walk 29	Peter Tavy and White Tor	176
Walk 30	Postbridge and Bellever Tor	181
Walk 31	Postbridge to Fur Tor	186
Walk 32	Fernworthy Reservoir, Grey Wethers and Watern Tor	193
Walk 33	Fernworthy Reservoir, Scorhill and Kestor Rock	198
Walk 34	Willsworthy, Tavy Cleave and Hare Tor	203
Walk 35	Great Links Tor and Widgery Cross	208
Walk 36	High Willhays via Yes Tor and Black-a-Tor Copse	213
Walk 37	Belstone, Cullever Steps and West Mill Tor	219
Walk 38	Steeperton Tor, Hangingstone Hill and Oke Tor	225
Walk 39	Cosdon Hill and Belstone Cleave	230

TEN TORS		237
Walk 40	Ten Tors two days	238

Appendix A	Useful contacts	252
Appendix B	Glossary	253
Appendix C	Further reading	254

Route symbols on OS map extracts

route

alternative route

(SF) start/finish point

(SF) alternative start/finish point

route direction

for OS legend see printed OS maps

SCALE: 1:50,000

GPX files
for all routes can be downloaded free at
www.cicerone.co.uk/1108/GPX

Honeybag Tor and Dartmoor pony (Walk 9)

A woodland stream near Christow on the way to Bowden Farm (Walk 4)

ROUTE SUMMARY TABLE

Walk	Walk title	Start/finish (grid ref)	Distance km (miles)	Ascent (m)	Time (hrs)	Page
North-east						
1	Drewsteignton and Fingle Bridge	Drewsteignton (SX 736 909)	9.5 (6)	340	3	26
2	Chagford and Meldon Hill	Chagford (SX 702 874)	10.5 (6½)	430	3½	30
3	Moretonhampstead and Mardon Down	Moretonhampstead (SX 753 859)	15.5 (9¾)	610	5	35
4	Trenchford and Tottiford Reservoirs and Christow	Trenchford Reservoir (SX 804 823)	12.5 (7¾)	335	3½	40
5	North Bovey and Easdon Tor	North Bovey (SX 740 838)	11.25 (7)	355	3½	45
6	Challacombe, Grimspound and Water Hill	Warren House Inn (B3212) (SX 676 811)	12 (7½)	300	3½	51
7	Lustleigh Cleave, Hunter's Tor and River Bovey	Trendlebere Down (SX 784 793)	14 (8¾)	565	4½	56
8	Widecombe in the Moor, Hamel Down and Bowerman's Nose	Widecombe in the Moor (SX 718 768)	15.5 (9¾)	450	4½	61
9	Hound Tor and Haytor Rocks	Hemsworthy Gate (B3387) (SX 741 761)	12 (7½)	400	3¾	66
10	Buckland Beacon and Rippon Tor	Hemsworthy Gate (B3387) (SX 741 761)	8.5 (5¼)	225	2½	71
South-east						
11	The stepping stones walk	Dunnabridge Pound (SX 642 746)	11.25 (7)	340	3½	78
12	Dartmeet figure-of-eight	Dartmeet (SX 672 732)	13.25 (8¼)	450	4	83
13	Dart Valley via Bench Tor and Sharp Tor	New Bridge (SX 711 709)	18 (11¼)	670	5½	88

Walk	Walk title	Start/finish (grid ref)	Distance km (miles)	Ascent (m)	Time (hrs)	Page
14	Ryder's Hill and Snowdon	Holne (SX 706 695)	13.25 (8¼)	490	4	95
15	River Avon and Eastern White Barrow	Shipley Bridge (SX 680 628)	12 (7½)	315	3½	100
16	Old tramways and Three Barrows	Shipley Bridge (SX 680 628)	15.75 (9¾)	365	4½	105
17	Butterdon Hill, Ugborough Beacon and Sharp Tor	Ivybridge Station (SX 647 565)	16.5 or 12 (10¼ or 7¾)	450 or 360	5 or 3½	110
18	Erme Valley and Stalldown Barrow	Ivybridge (SX 635 566)	17.75 or 21 (11 or 13)	460 or 500	5 or 6	115

South-west

Walk	Walk title	Start/finish (grid ref)	Distance km (miles)	Ascent (m)	Time (hrs)	Page
19	River Plym and Dewerstone Rock	Shaugh Bridge (SX 533 636)	6.75 (4¼)	220	2	122
20	Drizzlecombe and Gutter Tor	Ringmoor (SX 558 666)	12 (7½)	300	3½	126
21	Burrator Reservoir, Meavy and Sheeps Tor	Norsworthy Bridge (Burrator Reservoir) (SX 569 693)	13.25 or 7.5 (8¼ or 4¾)	400 or 230	4 or 2¼	132
22	Down Tor, Nun's Cross and Fox Tor	Norsworthy Bridge (Burrator Reservoir) (SX 569 693)	15.25 or 9.25 (9½ or 5¾)	370 or 235	4½ or 2¾	137
23	Leeden Tor, Sharpitor and Leather Tor	Sharpitor car park (B3212) (SX 560 708)	9.25 (5¾)	280	2¾	143
24	Devonport Leat and Black Tor	Princetown (SX 590 734)	12.5 (7¾)	245	3½	147
25	Great Mis Tor and Lich Way	Princetown (SX 590 734)	21.25 (13¼)	540	6¼	152
26	Longaford Tor, Rough Tor and Beardown Tors	Two Bridges (SX 609 750)	13.25 or 14.25 (8¼ or 9)	340 or 350	4 or 4¼	159
27	Fogintor, King's Tor and Merrivale	Four Winds car park (B3357) (SX 560 749)	13 (8)	300	3¾	164
28	Cox Tor, Great Staple Tor and Pew Tor	Pork Hill car park (B3357) (SX 530 751)	9 (5¾)	280	2¾	170

Route summary table

Walk	Walk title	Start/finish (grid ref)	Distance km (miles)	Ascent (m)	Time (hrs)	Page
North-west						
29	Peter Tavy and White Tor	Peter Tavy (SX 521 779)	11.5 (7¼)	380	3½	176
30	Postbridge and Bellever Tor	Postbridge (SX 649 788)	11.75 or 10.5 (7¼ or 6½)	365 or 310	3½ or 3	181
31	Postbridge to Fur Tor	Postbridge (SX 649 788)	19.25 (12)	480	5½	186
32	Fernworthy Reservoir, Grey Wethers and Watern Tor	Fernworthy Reservoir (SX 669 839)	17.25 or 10 (10¾ or 6¼)	480 or 280	5 or 3	193
33	Fernworthy Reservoir, Scorhill and Kestor Rock	Fernworthy Reservoir (SX 669 839)	18.5 or 15 (11½ or 9¼)	515 or 445	5½ or 4½	198
34	Willsworthy, Tavy Cleave and Hare Tor	Willsworthy car park (A386) (SX 517 834)	13 or 15 (8 or 9¼)	300 or 350	3¾ or 4¼	203
35	Great Links Tor and Widgery Cross	Lydford (A386) (SX 525 853)	12.5 or 15.75 (7¾ or 9¾)	400 or 470	3¾ or 4¾	208
36	High Willhays via Yes Tor and Black-a-Tor Copse	Meldon Reservoir (SX 561 918)	14 or 10.5 (8¾ or 6½)	470 or 445	4¼ or 3½	213
37	Belstone, Cullever Steps and West Mill Tor	Belstone (SX 621 938)	14.5 (9)	435	4¼	219
38	Steeperton Tor, Hangingstone Hill and Oke Tor	Belstone (SX 621 938)	18.5 or 13 (11½ or 8)	535 or 350	5½ or 3¾	225
39	Cosdon Hill and Belstone Cleave	South Zeal (SX 652 934)	14.5 (9)	470	4½	230
Ten Tors						
40	Ten Tors two days	Belstone (SX 621 938) or Okehampton railway station (SX 592 944)	58 (36)	1600	2 days	238

Honeybag Tor (Walk 9)

INTRODUCTION

Dartmoor National Park logo

Dartmoor, a National Park since 1951, is a wild, and at times isolated, upland area tucked in the south-western corner of Devon, in South West England. Home to a diverse range of wildlife, this is a landscape dominated by an expansive high granite plateau, clothed in blanket bogs and grass moors, crowned with fascinating tors and incised by tumbling streams crossed by ancient clapper bridges. Several millennia ago, our ancestors left behind a fascinating treasure trove, from intriguing stone rows (60 per cent of all the stone rows in England are found on Dartmoor), to fascinating stones circles and burial cairns (there's over 1500 of them), to numerous hut circles (over 5000). But there are also the stark ruins of Dartmoor's mining heritage, and picturesque villages and hamlets that are home to interesting old churches and cosy pubs. Oh, and there's the odd legend or two, from infamous mires to Bowerman the Hunter, who was cast in stone for disturbing a coven of witches.

Here you can wander along tree-shaded river valleys or stand on High Willhays, which, at 621m (2039ft), is not only a mountain but also the highest point in Southern England. On a clear day there are great views out over Devon's rural landscape from many of Dartmoor's summits. To the west is Cornwall and Bodmin Moor, while from the more easterly tops you can see as far as Portland in Dorset.

Yes, the weather can be inclement at times, low cloud and mist can obscure the views and the high rainfall leads to numerous bogs and mires, but this climate also brings with it fascinating woodlands clothed in moss and lichen like some enchanted land. When the mist rolls in, the tors take on an other-worldly character – it was here that Sir Arthur Conan Doyle gained inspiration for his Sherlock Holmes novel *The Hound of the Baskervilles*. As you walk past mist-shrouded tors your pulse might start to race; was that a spectral hound you glimpsed or just your imagination running wild?

The joys of walking on Dartmoor are many. Stop a while on a craggy tor and admire the wonderful views while listening to nature's music, from skylarks singing high above to the wind whispering over the moor. Take your time, wander past ancient sites – from stone circles to stone rows that seem to be marching over the moor – and wonder as to their purpose, or cherish the little insights gained from chatting to a farmer with years of local knowledge. But, most of all, enjoy and respect Dartmoor.

GEOLOGY AND LANDSCAPE

The story of Dartmoor's geology starts over 400 million years ago, when the area that now forms Dartmoor was covered by a shallow, warm sea. This was the Devonian and Carboniferous period (300 to 420 million years ago), when large quantities of sand and mud were deposited; these became sedimentary rocks such as sandstone and slate, which can be found round the edges of Dartmoor.

About 280 million years ago tectonic activity caused the sedimentary rocks to be squeezed and crumpled. Below, a large mass of molten rock, or magma, rose up, baking the surrounding rocks. This molten rock cooled relatively slowly to form coarse-grained granite – a form of igneous rock – which consists of three main minerals: quartz, feldspar and mica. The intense heat and pressure generated by the molten rock produced rich mineral deposits, including tin, copper and iron. The same mass of granite that forms Dartmoor can be found further west at both Bodmin Moor and Land's End, and on the Isles of Scilly.

Contraction of the granite mass as it cooled caused vertical joints or factures to be formed. Over time, the erosion of the overlying sedimentary rock allowed the granite to expand upwards, causing horizontal joints or factures. Hydrothermal activity (heated water) later passed through these joints, leading to a weakening of the rock. This process is known as kaolinisation, where the feldspar which makes up between 30 to 40 per cent of the granite is partially decomposed to form white clay, or kaolin. The next stage of tor formation occurred during the Tertiary period, some 30 to 60 million years ago, the granite was exposed to a hot and wet subtropical climate, and rainfall containing acids from rotting plants seeped through the granite, further weakening the feldspar.

The final phase of granite erosion occurred during the Pleistocene period between 12,000 and 2 million years ago. This was a time of ice ages and glaciers, and, although the ice sheets never reached Dartmoor, the area suffered periglacial conditions. Water inside cracks in the exposed granite was subjected to freeze-thaw conditions which caused the water to expand, fracturing the rock; all of these processes led to the formation of Dartmoor's characteristic tors. The rocks that broke off were transported down the slope as the soil thawed in the summer months, while the ground below remained frozen; this is known as solifluxion, or soil flow. This caused the slopes below the tors to be littered with debris, or clitter. Both tors and clitter are two of the main characteristics of the Dartmoor landscape.

Following the end of the last ice age, the climate was warmer than today and the land was densely wooded. But by 6000 years ago the forests were in retreat as a result of both natural causes and human intervention; rainfall started to increase and the climate began to cool. This was when blanket bogs – another characteristic of Dartmoor – began to develop.

HABITATS AND WILDLIFE

For many people, the highlight of walking is admiring the views, but another important part of the joy of

Bloody-nosed beetle (Timarcha tenebricosa)

walking is catching sight of local wildlife. Dartmoor contains a number of important habitats that are home to a range of plants and wildlife, from numerous lichens to wild daffodils, from beetles to endangered butterflies, and from rare birds to the iconic Dartmoor pony.

Blanket bog – this is the term given to the mantle of peat, ranging from 0.5 to 7 metres in thickness, which covers gentle slopes (typically 15 degrees or less) above 400m. Many of Devon's rivers start in these blanket bogs, as the sphagnum moss soaks up rainfall; the peat is also a vital carbon store. Over time these have been damaged by drainage, cutting and erosion, although action is being taken to safeguard the habitat by reducing water run-off. Species include deer grass, hare's tail cotton grass, cross-leaved heath, round-leaved sundew and bog asphodel; birds such as dunlin and golden plover nest on the higher blanket bogs.

Upland heath – covers most of the open moor that is not covered by blanket bogs. Plants include heather, bilberry, cross-leaved heath, gorse, purple moor grass and bristle bent grass; birds include raven, meadow pipit, stonechat and red grouse. Other inhabitants include the adder, common lizard and butterflies such as the brown fritillary and green hairstreak.

Grass moor – often the product of heavy animal grazing, is dominated by several species of grass; other plants include tormentil, bedstraw, milkwort and areas of bracken. This is an important habitat for several species of butterfly including the pearl-bordered fritillary.

Valley mires – areas of waterlogged peat in valley bottoms and natural basins where peat has accumulated. Characteristic plants include cotton grass, mosses and sedges, bog bean, round-leaved sundew and bog asphodel. This is an important habitat for dragonflies, snipe and curlew.

Upland oakwoods – situated above 250m, these rare, high-level oak woods – such as Wistman's Wood, Black-a-Tor Copse and Piles Copse – are home to stunted oak trees festooned with mosses, lichens and ferns as they grow among moss-covered boulders. These woods are home to birds such as the pied flycatcher, wood warbler, redstart and buzzard, and butterflies such as the speckled wood, purple hairstreak and silver-washed fritillary; this is also a great habitat for the dormouse.

Rhos pasture – found in wet valley bottoms away from the open moor, usually adjacent to wet woodlands of willow and alder. Species include rushes, purple moor grass, devil's-bit scabious and heath spotted orchid, along with snipe, foxes, roe deer and several species of butterfly.

Rocky outcrops – Dartmoor's characteristic tors, clitter and former quarries can be home to as many as 60 species of lichen. There are also rare ferns and birds such as the peregrine falcon and ring ouzel.

Rivers and streams – these provide habitats for spawning salmon and sea trout, birds such as the dipper, grey wagtail, kingfisher and heron, and mammals such as the otter.

A BRIEF HISTORY

Humans arrived in Dartmoor and the surrounding area soon after the last ice age ended about 12,000 years ago. These earliest inhabitants were nomadic hunter-gatherers who roamed over the forested landscape. As time progressed, people started clearing areas of forest so that animals could be encouraged to graze, making it easier to hunt them. By the Neolithic period (6000 years ago) the population was growing and larger areas of forest were being cleared for grazing livestock. This was the period when Dartmoor's oldest monuments, including stone rows, stone circles and standing stones (menhirs), were constructed. The discovery of bronze brought with it more change; the climate was warmer and more people settled on the high moor. Much more of the forest was cleared to allow the land to be used for pasture and growing crops, and fields separated by stone banks, or reaves, were formed. Other artefacts from this period include hut circles and stone burial cairns.

During the Iron Age people left the high moor in favour of lowland areas brought about by a change in climate as well as economic and social changes. During this period defended hillforts such as Cranbrook Castle were built to protect people and animals. There is little evidence of activity on the moor following the Roman Conquest (AD43), and for the next 1000 years.

Ditsworthy Warren House starred in Steven Spielberg's film War Horse (Walk 20)

After the Norman Conquest in the 11th century, castles were built at Lydford and Okehampton; the weather was warmer and farmers settled higher on the moor. Hamlets, such as the one near Hound Tor, were formed, although these were later abandoned due to the climate becoming harsher and as a result of the plague (Black Death). It was during this period that we get the first written evidence of tin extraction on the moor, although this had probably been going on for some period of time, as bronze is an alloy of copper and tin.

In more modern times, as the demand for tin, copper and lead increased, larger underground mines were constructed. From the late 18th century through to the end of the 20th century, granite was quarried as a building material, and a number of famous London landmarks are constructed from Dartmoor granite. China clay was also mined on the moor to make pottery, bricks and pipes. During the 19th and 20th centuries reservoirs were created to supply drinking water for expanding towns outside Dartmoor and, following the First World War, commercial conifer plantations were established. Since the early 1800s Dartmoor has been used for military training, and the first purpose-built artillery range was established south of Okehampton; today the military still uses parts of northern Dartmoor for live firing.

In 1951 Dartmoor became a National Park. Today the Park is home to around 35,000 people and has a mainly rural economy ranging from farming and forestry to tourism and recreation.

WHEN TO WALK AND EQUIPMENT

Firstly, the walks in this guidebook can be undertaken year-round; however, the seasons do bring with them different expectations. The weather is influenced by a west or south-west airflow, bringing in moist Atlantic air masses. On reaching higher ground, such as Dartmoor, these air masses release their rain. For example, Princetown (the highest settlement on Dartmoor at 435m) receives over twice the average annual rainfall of places on the fringes of the moor, and many of Devon's rivers rise on Dartmoor. These higher areas are also cooler (by 2 or 3°C) and they typically suffer stronger winds.

October to the end of March is generally the wettest period with the lowest temperatures, and snow may be encountered, especially high up. Daylight hours are also much shorter during this period. During the winter months, spells of rain can make the ground quite wet and river crossings difficult (see the Safety section). However, walking on a clear, frosty or snowy winter's day can be magical. April through to the end of September is typically the driest and warmest period; however, the weather can be very unpredictable, so always be prepared. Late spring and summer bring colourful flowers and abundant birdsong, while cool autumn nights clothe the countryside in shades of russet, gold and brown.

Always choose clothing suitable for the season and terrain, and remember the weather can change very quickly on Dartmoor. Good waterproof boots and a waterproof outer layer are always advisable, and a map and compass should always be carried. Trekking poles can be useful for both probing boggy ground and as an aid for river crossings; gaiters can also be very useful when walking through long vegetation; and in winter it can be worth carrying a headtorch. It is also worth carrying a small first-aid kit, including a tick remover (see Safety).

Although some of the walks pass places where there are pubs, cafés, or shops, there is no guarantee that these will be open when required. Therefore, always carry enough food and water with you, plus some emergency rations.

GETTING TO AND STAYING IN DARTMOOR

There are several ways of getting to Dartmoor:

Rail: There are railway stations at Exeter, Newton Abbot, Totnes, Okehampton, Ivybridge and Plymouth; for information contact National Rail Enquiries on 03457 48 49 50 or www.nationalrail.co.uk.

Coach: long distance coach services operate to several towns and cities close to Dartmoor; try either National Express (0871 781 8181; www.nationalexpress.com) or Megabus (https://uk.megabus.com).

Siward's Cross and Nun's Cross Farm (Walks 22 and 24)

Road: Dartmoor is within easy reach from the M5 motorway in Devon via the A30 and A38.

Getting around

Dartmoor is surrounded by a good road network including the A30 along the northern edge, the A386 along the western edge and the A38 on the eastern side. The B3212 crosses Dartmoor from Dunsford to Yelverton; another route crosses from Ashburton to Tavistock. Extending off these main routes is a network of narrow lanes. The speed limit on all parts of the open moor is 40mph, reducing to 30mph in places. On the open moor, ponies, sheep and cattle roam freely so extra care is required, especially at night. All accidents with stock animals must be reported to the Livestock Protection Officer (see Appendix A). Only park in designated car parks and never block access points.

Some of the walks may be accessed by using public transport (buses or trains); see Appendix A for contact details. Train services operate to both Okehampton and Ivybridge, where a few of the walks in this book may be started. A brief list of bus routes that may be of use are given below, but please bear in mind that bus routes can change or be withdrawn, and that services may not operate on Sundays.

178: Newton Abbot to Okehampton via Lustleigh, Moretonhampstead, Chagford and South Zeal (Country Bus Devon)

173: Exeter to Moretonhampstead via Chagford and Drewsteignton (Stagecoach)

118: Okehampton to Tavistock via Mary Tavy and the Dartmoor Inn on the A386 (Stagecoach)

271 – Haytor Hoppa: Newton Abbot via Bovey Tracey, Widecombe in the Moor, Haytor Visitor Centre, Manaton and Hemsworthy Gate; Saturdays only from May to November (Country Bus Devon)

171/172: Newton Abbot to Tavistock via Moretonhampstead (171), Postbridge (171), Dartmeet (172), Two Bridges, Princetown and Merrivale (Country Bus Devon)

98: Tavistock to Yelverton via Princetown and Merrivale; limited service via Two Bridges and Postbridge (Oakleys Coaches)

Dartmoor online

For up-to-date information on how to get there, public transport, accommodation and other visitor information, visit www.visitdartmoor.co.uk. For information about the National Park, visit www.dartmoor.gov.uk.

Protecting the countryside

While you are out enjoying these walks, please respect the countryside and follow the Countryside Code:

Be safe – plan ahead and follow any signs

Leave gates and property as you find them

Protect plants and animals, and take your litter home

Keep dogs under close control
Consider other people

BASES

The main bases within the National Park that offer a range of facilities – such as shops, pubs and accommodation – are Princetown, Widecombe in the Moor, Chagford, Moretonhampstead, Ashburton, Buckfastleigh, Yelverton, Horrabridge and Lydford. Adjacent to the National Park there are several larger towns including Okehampton and Ivybridge (both of which have rail services), Tavistock and Bovey Tracey.

Accommodation

There is a wide range of accommodation both within and just outside the National Park. Designated campsites range from simple, rustic farm-based sites to larger ones that include caravan parks with a range of facilities. There are a number of hostels including Youth Hostel Association hostels at Bellever (www.yha.org.uk/hostel/yha-dartmoor) and Okehampton (www.yha.org.uk/hostel/yha-okehampton-bracken-tor). Other accommodation includes guest houses, pubs with rooms and hotels.

Wild camping

For information on where wild camping is currently allowed visit the Dartmoor National Park website at www.dartmoor.gov.uk/about-us/about-us-maps/camping-map; please follow the latest advice provided by the Dartmoor National Park Authority (DNPA). Wild camping brings responsibilities, and campers should always ensure they have as little impact on the environment as possible; leave no trace, do not light fires, take all rubbish away with you and bury faeces well away from any water courses.

MAPS AND GPS

A good map preferably at a scale of 1:25,000, along with a compass, is essential for navigating your route in Dartmoor, especially in poor visibility. Two companies provide maps covering Dartmoor: the Ordnance Survey® and Harvey Maps.

Ordnance Survey (www.shop.ordnancesurvey.co.uk)

1:50,000 Landranger® maps 191 (Okehampton & North Dartmoor) and 202 (Torbay & South Dartmoor)

1:25,000 Explorer® map OL28 (Dartmoor) and OL44 (Torquay and Dawlish; Walk 4 only)

Harvey Maps (www.harveymaps.co.uk)

1:40,000 British Mountain Map: Dartmoor

1:25,000 Superwalker maps: Dartmoor South and Dartmoor North

Maps are also available to download to a handheld GPS device or smartphone with GPS (there are a number of apps available). These devices can prove very useful; however, batteries can run out of power, so always carry a map and compass. Even if you don't have maps on your phone, there is a free app – OS Locate – that is worth downloading, as this can give you a grid reference that you can use to find your location on a paper map.

SAFETY

Parts of the high moor can seem quite remote; it is always a good idea to let someone know where you will be walking. It is also worth noting that mobile phone signals are very poor in some parts.

Some of the walks involve crossing streams or rivers where there are no footbridges, or using stepping stones (which may be slippery). In normal weather these should not cause any problems; however, if water levels are high after rainfall, you are strongly advised not to attempt to cross, but to turn back and save the walk for another day. You may find trekking poles useful for river crossings.

Ticks (small blood-sucking parasite) are present on Dartmoor; you can reduce the risk of tick bites by:
- wearing trousers
- tucking trousers into your socks, or wearing gaiters
- staying on paths where possible

If you do find a tick on you, either remove it with fine tweezers or use a tick removal tool (follow the manufacturer's guidance). If you get bitten by a tick and subsequently develop a circular rash, seek medical advice (www.nhs.uk/conditions/lyme-disease).

Cattle will be present on many of the walks. Try not to walk between cows and young calves; if you feel threatened, move away calmly, do not panic or make sudden noises, and if possible find an alternative route.

The stepping stones at Week Ford cross the West Dart River near Huccaby (Walk 12)

Always take care when crossing or walking along roads. Use pavements where they are provided, or walk on the right (facing oncoming traffic) if there is no pavement, taking extra care on blind corners.

In case of a serious accident, call 999 or 112 (the European emergency number) and ask for the police, ambulance or fire service depending on the nature of the accident.

The Dartmoor Search and Rescue Group (www.dartmoor-rescue.org) comprises four teams (Tavistock, North Dartmoor, Ashburton and Plymouth) that provide a search and rescue service for Dartmoor and the surrounding area. These volunteer organisations rely on donations and they deserve your support.

WAYMARKING AND ACCESS

Large parts of Dartmoor are classed as open access land where you can freely roam. This includes military ranges, except when closed for live firing. For this reason, rights of way are usually only marked outside the main open access areas. However, walking along tracks and paths is much easier, and during the bird nesting season (from March to end of July) it is important to try and stay on existing routes so as not to disturb ground-nesting birds.

Rights of way are marked as follows:
- Footpaths Yellow Arrow – walkers only
- Bridleways Blue Arrow – walkers, cyclists and horse riders
- Restricted byways Purple Arrow – same as for a byway except no motorcycles or vehicles
- Byways Red Arrow – walkers, cyclists, horse riders, motorcycles and vehicles

Military ranges

The Ministry of Defence Dartmoor Training Area comprises three live firing ranges on the north moor: Okehampton, Willsworthy and Merrivale. These are clearly marked on OS 1:25,000 mapping.

The boundaries of these live firing areas are marked on the ground by a series of red and white posts with warning notices. The public has access to these moorland areas, except when live firing exercises are in progress. The warning signals are red flags by day and red lamps by night; these indicate that live firing is taking place within the range boundaries. When the warning signals are displayed, you must not enter the range. The following walks include sections within the live firing ranges:

Okehampton – Walks 36, 37, 38 and 40

Willsworthy – Walks 34 and 40

Merrivale – Walks 25, 26 (extension only) and 40

For the latest firing timetable, visit: www.gov.uk/government/publications/dartmoor-firing-programme or phone 0800 458 4868.

Military firing range – a red flag (or red light at night) means do not enter

USING THIS GUIDE

Routes are listed under four headings based on geographical location within the National Park (North-east, South-east, South-west and North-west). The routes vary in length from 6.75 to 21.25km (4¼ to 13¼ miles), along with a two-day, 58km (36 mile) challenge.

The lower-level walks exploring the river valleys and villages should be suitable for most walkers; however, the longer walks are designed for the more adventurous walker. These routes explore the more remote, high-level moor and require better planning, equipment and navigational skills; navigating on the open, often featureless, moor in mist and low cloud can be quite challenging.

A box at the start of each route gives key information such as the start/finish point, the walk distance (km/miles rounded to the nearest 0.25km or ¼ mile), the amount of ascent and an estimate of the time it will take to complete the walk; this information can also be found in the Route Summary Table at the start of the book. Brief descriptions of the terrain and details of pubs and cafés are also provided. Many of the walks follow sections of good path and tracks, and some also involve lane walking. Higher moor paths can be rather indistinct and can cross boggy ground (do not attempt to cross any mires); these high-level walks may also involve stream or river crossings. Low visibility and bad weather can make the walk more demanding.

USING THIS GUIDE

Each route begins with a short introduction providing a brief summary of the walk and identifying any major points of interest, including villages. The walk is then described. Throughout the text you will find key landmarks highlighted in bold type; there is also additional information provided about the places of interest passed on the route.

The maps in this guide are extracts from the Ordnance Survey 1:50,000 Landranger series maps. The routes have been marked on to the maps, along with any shortcuts and extensions. These maps have a scale of 2cm to 1km.

However, you are strongly advised to carry the Ordnance Survey 1:25,000 Explorer map (Dartmoor OL28 and Torquay and Dawlish OL44) or Harvey Maps equivalent with you when undertaking any of these walks, and also to take a compass and know how to use it; mist and low cloud can make navigation very difficult, especially over featureless terrain. These larger-scale maps offer a much higher level of detail, which will make navigation on the ground easier. Please note that the OS 1:25,000 map may indicate fractionally different heights compared to the OS 1:50,000 extracts used in this guidebook.

Times and distances

The distances quoted in the text have been measured from OS Explorer maps; note that the heights quoted on the maps are in metres and the grid lines are spaced at intervals of 1km. Distances are given in metric first, with approximate imperial conversions rounded to the nearest ¼, ½, ¾ or whole number. Estimated walking times are based on a walking speed

The western and highest of the three outcrops that make up Beardown Tors (Walk 26)

of 4km per hour (2½ miles per hour), plus 10 minutes per 100m (300ft) of ascent. These are the figures I use when walking on Dartmoor, but – of course – some people walk faster and some slower. The estimated walking times should be treated as the minimum amount of walking time required to undertake the route, and they do not include any time for rests, lunch, photography, consulting the map or guidebook, or simply admiring the view. Poor weather, or walking over boggy ground, can also make the walk take much longer.

GPX tracks
GPX tracks for the routes in this guidebook are available to download free at www.cicerone.co.uk/1108/GPX. If you have not bought the book through the Cicerone website, or if you have bought the book without opening an account, please register your purchase in your Cicerone library to access GPX and update information.

A GPS device is an excellent aid to navigation, but you should also carry a map and compass and know how to use them. GPX files are provided in good faith, but in view of the profusion of formats and devices, neither the author nor the publisher accepts responsibility for their use. We provide files in a single standard GPX format that works on most devices and systems, but you may need to convert files to your preferred format using a GPX converter such as www.gpsvisualizer.com or one of the many other apps and online converters available.

Long distance routes
Finally, if you want a much longer walk, there are two routes available, both of which intersect with some of the walks in this guidebook:

The Dartmoor Way – a 173km (108 mile) circular route round Dartmoor and the Dartmoor Way High Moor Link from Tavistock to Buckfast (www.dartmoorway.co.uk and see *Walking the Dartmoor Way* by Sue Viccars, published by Cicerone).

The Two Moors Way – a 188km (117 mile) north–south coast-to-coast path through Devon from Lynmouth to Wembury, crossing both Exmoor and Dartmoor (www.twomoorsway.org and see *Walking the Two Moors Way* by Sue Viccars, published by Cicerone).

Boundary stone on Hamel Down looking towards Haytor Rocks (Walk 8)

NORTH-EAST

WALKING ON DARTMOOR

WALK 1
Drewsteignton and Fingle Bridge

Start/finish	Drewsteignton village car park (SX 736 909)
Distance	9.5km (6 miles)
Ascent	340m
Time	3hrs
Terrain	Low-level, but hilly walking on good paths and tracks through woods and some fields
Maps	OS Explorer OL28 (Dartmoor)
Refreshments	Drewe Arms (01647 281377) and village shop/tearoom at Drewsteignton; Fingle Bridge Inn (01647 281287); café at Castle Drogo (National Trust)
Public transport	Buses between Exeter and Moretonhampstead or Chagford stop at Drewsteignton and Castle Drogo

From Drewsteignton the walk sets out along the Two Moors Way for a while before joining with the Dartmoor Way to arrive at Sharp Tor with views of the wooded Teign valley; from here a detour leads to Castle Drogo. The walk continues along the Hunters Path just below Castle Drogo before dropping down to the River Teign. The route then follows the tree-shaded river downstream to Fingle Bridge, home to the Fingle Bridge Inn. The final section meanders through woods back to Drewsteignton.

From the far end of the car park at Drewsteignton turn right along a path. Pass a thatched cottage and at the next cottage turn right following the tarred path through the churchyard, passing left of the **church**.

The **Church of the Holy Trinity** in Drewsteignton dates mostly from the 15th century. The thatch-roofed Drewe Arms was known as the Druids' Arms; the name was changed in the 1920s when Julius Drewe built Castle Drogo (see later). For 75 years the pub was kept by Mabel Mudge, who retired in 1994 at the grand age of 99.

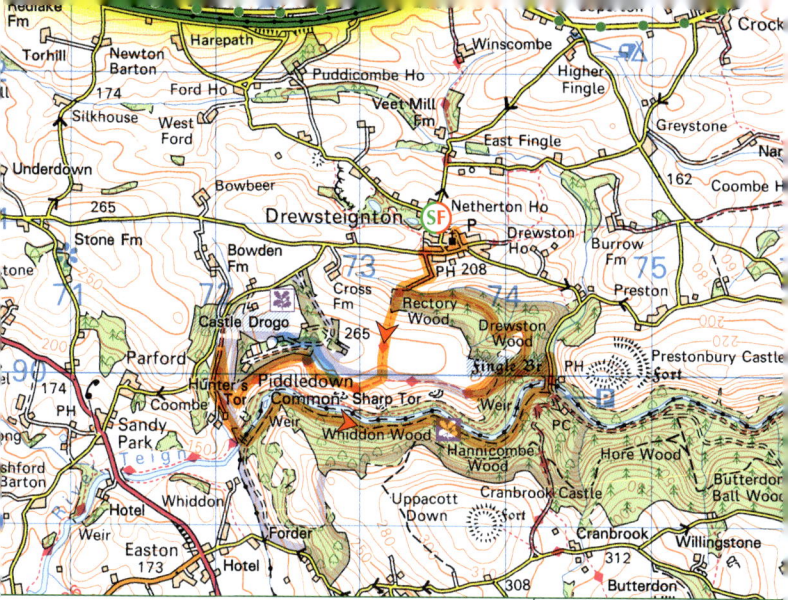

Keep ahead through the village square, passing the pub and village shop/tearoom (both on your right), then turn left along the road. Fork right at the junction (direction Whiddon Down) for 120 metres, then turn left at the fingerpost and the Two Moors Way stone. ▶ Follow the track downhill as it swings right.

Go through a gate at the bottom to enter **Rectory Wood**. Keep right at the junction and at the next junction turn left (Piddledown and Two Moors Way); straight on is a more direct route via steep steps. Having turned left, go right at the next junction and follow the track as it soon swings left to another junction. Turn right and keep ahead past some beech trees. Go through a gate and follow the right-hand fence through two fields. Exit through a gate and keep ahead to a path T-junction.

Turn right along the Hunters Path (now following the Two Moors Way and Dartmoor Way) for 350 metres to a signed junction at **Sharp Tor**. ▶ To visit Castle Drogo turn right (see detour route), otherwise go straight on along the Hunters Path to the next junction; the castle detour rejoins here from the right.

The commemorative stone is one of four placed along the route when it opened in 1976; the others are located at Ivybridge, Morchard Bishop and Lynmouth.

Take a break and enjoy the views over the Teign Valley, but be careful, it's a steep drop.

Detour to Castle Drogo

Head north up the steps (signed to Castle Drogo). Go through a gate and keep ahead to a junction with a stony path. Turn right uphill then go left along the drive and fork right, following the signs for the castle entrance. Retrace your steps back along the drive, turn right down the stony path and keep right (straight on) at the junction. Follow the path as its swings right down steps and through a gate to rejoin the Hunters Path and turn right (adds 1.1km/¾ mile).

The early 20th-century **Castle Drogo** – said to be the last castle built in England – was built by Sir Edwin Lutyens (1869–1944) for Julius Drewe (1856–1931), founder of the Home and Colonial Stores, which, in the 1920s, was one of the UK's largest retail chains. Drewe chose the site because he mistakenly believed that his ancestors had connections with the nearby village of Drewsteignton. The castle was given to the National Trust in 1974.

Looking west along the Hunters Path near Sharp Tor

WALK 1 – DREWSTEIGNTON AND FINGLE BRIDGE

Main route
Keep along the wide path below Castle Drogo to a junction near Hunter's Tor where the main route goes right. ▶ Follow the path, with the castle up to the right, go through a gate and turn left down a tarred track (signed Fisherman's Path and River Teign) for 375 metres to a junction. Fork left along the track (Gibhouse and footpath) and, just before the cottage, fork left down a narrower path to a junction. Turn left and immediately turn right across the footbridge – known as the **Iron Bridge** – over the River Teign. ▶

Cross the wall via the stone steps and turn left along the track with the wall on your left. Go through a gate where the route splits. Either fork right along the track or fork left to pass the Hydro Turbine building before rejoining the track and continuing through Whiddon Wood.

> The wall once formed part of the boundary of **Whiddon Deer Park** which was enclosed in the mid 16th century to contain a herd of fallow deer. Julius Drewe had two water-driven turbines installed on the River Teign to provide electricity for his newly built castle.

Keep along the riverside track through Hannicombe Wood to a junction at **Fingle Bridge** and turn left over the bridge, with the Fingle Bridge Inn on the right. ▶

> The 17th-century **Fingle Bridge** which straddles the River Teign is a fine example of a three-arched packhorse bridge; on the south side of the river is a National Trust car park and toilets.

Head northwards along the lane (parking on right) for 140 metres and then turn sharp left to follow a bridleway (Dartmoor Way) up through Drewston Wood for 600 metres to a junction. Turn sharp right (almost doubling back) and follow the bridleway (Hunters Path to Drewsteignton) as it contours round the hill. Go through a gate and keep ahead at the crossing track. Cross a

---

Side notes:

Take a quick 120-metre detour by keeping left and going through a gate to Hunter's Tor, where there is another great view. Return to the junction and turn left.

The path along the north bank of the river is the Fisherman's Path that also leads to Fingle Bridge.

The path joining from the left is the Fisherman's Path from the Iron Bridge.

WALKING ON DARTMOOR

stream, continue to a track junction and keep right. At the next junction, keep left (straight on) to another junction and fork right. Follow the level track to a junction passed earlier in the walk and turn right through the gate.

Follow the track uphill as it later swings left up to the road in **Drewsteignton**. Turn right, then left at the junction and shortly turn right into the square. Enter the churchyard and turn left along the path, then down some steps back to the car park.

WALK 2
Chagford and Meldon Hill

Start/finish	Chagford car park off the High Street (SX 702 874)
Distance	10.5km (6½ miles)
Ascent	430m
Time	3½hrs
Terrain	Low-level sections on paths and lanes; higher sections over Meldon Hill involve two steep descents and two stream crossings
Maps	OS Explorer OL28
Refreshments	Several pubs and cafés in Chagford
Public transport	Chagford has bus links to Moretonhampstead, Okehampton, Newton Abbot and Exeter

From bustling Chagford the route follows the Dartmoor Way to Chagford Bridge before then following the Two Moors Way to Rushford Bridge. The walk then starts rising through fields and woods to arrive at Week Down with its ancient wayside cross. The next stop is Nattadon Common before the route heads steeply downhill and then up to the top of Meldon Hill. After admiring the great panoramic view it's a rather steep descent back to Chagford.

Turn left out of the car park in Chagford, keep left and then bear right along the High Street with the **Church of**

WALK 2 – CHAGFORD AND MELDON HILL

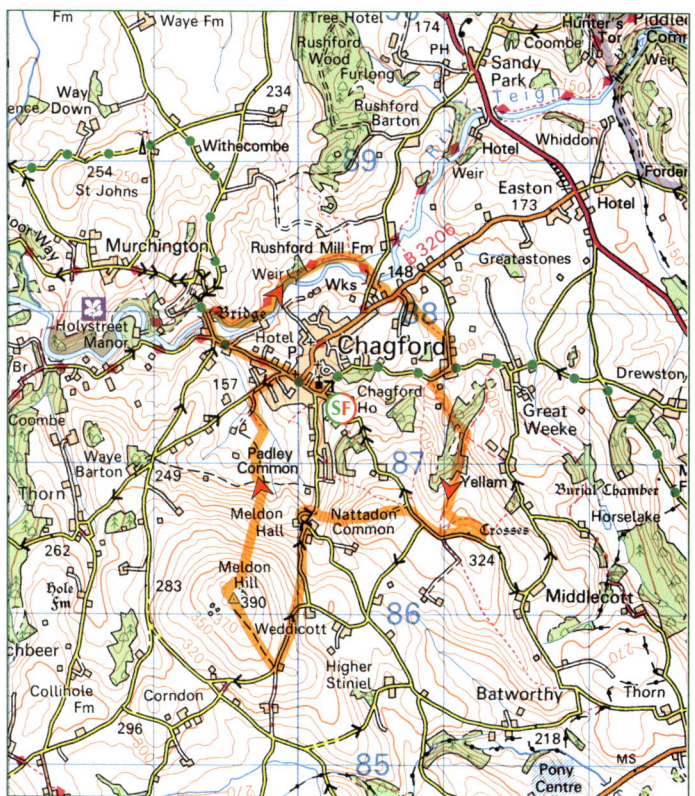

St Michael the Archangel on the right and the Globe Inn on the left. Continue past the thatch-roofed Three Crowns to the square and the octagonal-shaped Market House. Keep ahead along Mill Street to a junction and fork right (Gidleigh and Throwleigh); the left-hand fork is the return route. Continue along the lane following the Dartmoor Way down to a cross-junction (Factory Cross) and turn right. Immediately after crossing the late-16th-century, three-arched **Chagford Bridge** over the River Teign, turn

CHAGFORD

Church of St Michael the Archangel at Chagford

Chagford, a former 'Stannary Town' where smelted tin was brought for assaying and taxation, is home to a range of services. The unusual octagonal Market House, built in 1862 and known locally as 'the Pepperpot', can be found in the square. The fairly large 15th-century Church of St Michael the Archangel is also worth a visit. Take a look at the roof bosses, which include one depicting the 'tinners' rabbits' – each rabbit has two ears, but there are only three ears between them.

right through a gate; the walk now follows the Two Moors Way for 1.4km (1 mile).

Continue through a gate and pass some oak trees on top of stone walls before passing another gate. Continue alongside the river for 450 metres, passing through three gates, and enter a small wood with a weir on the right. The route now bears left away from the river, following a leat on the right instead (this provided water to Rushford Mill). Cross a stile and continue through two fields separated by a gate. Keep ahead at the junction through another gate (signed for

Rushford Bridge) and cross a footbridge. Head diagonally left across the field, go through the hedge gap and continue across the field and through a gate to join a lane.

Turn right over **Rushford Bridge**, re-crossing the River Teign, and immediately turn left over a stile. Follow the enclosed path, go through a gate and bear slightly right across the field. Go through a gate and continue to the road (B3206). Cross over and turn left for 75 metres to a junction and turn right along the lane (Broomhill). At the split, keep ahead following a signed path through the gate and continue between fences to a stile.

Keep ahead south-eastwards across the field to the corner and cross a stile. Continue south-eastwards across the field and leave through a gate in the corner. Follow the track to a lane and turn right to a junction (Westcott Cross) beside Westcott Farm. Turn right up the lane (Chagford direction) for 150 metres to a path junction at the right-hand bend, just after a field gate on the left. Bear left and immediately turn left through a gate following a path signed for Yellam and Week Down. Continue up the track as it curves left past some trees and then, as its curves right towards a barn, fork left on a path to a gate.

Go through the gate and down some steps, then follow the path through the trees. Ford the stream, go up some stone steps and continue steeply up through the wood to a four-way junction just after crossing a stile. Turn right (signposted for Week Down), pass two gates and follow the old walled track (bridleway) uphill to the open ground of Week Down. Keep ahead for 20 metres and turn left up a path, then follow a wider path as it curves right up towards a lane at the top left corner beside a cattle grid. ▸ To continue the walk, turn right (west) parallel with the lane to Week Down cross.

A hundred and twenty-five metres east (left) along the lane is a wayside cross known as the Shorter Cross on the north side of the lane.

The **medieval cross** at the top edge of Week Down lies along the route between Moretonhampstead and Chagford; the views from here include Nattadon Common and Meldon Hill (west), Cosdon

Hill (north-west) and Castle Drogo (north). Shorter Cross, which could be of Saxon origin, is unusual in that it consists of a plain granite pillar with a Latin cross carved in relief.

To the south-west is Meldon Hill, the next stop on the walk, where there is an even better view.

Continue parallel to the lane to a signed path junction and keep ahead along the lane for 275 metres before bearing left over the open ground of **Nattadon Common**, following the wall on the left. Where this goes left, keep ahead to the summit (333m). ◄

Continue westwards down a narrow path passing Nattadon Tor (rocky outcrops) and zig-zagging through trees to cross a small footbridge over a stream. Keep ahead and ford another stream then follow a stony path down beside the small cascade to join a lane. Turn left up the lane past **Meldon Hall** (right) to a junction and turn right. Follow the lane uphill for 350 metres and turn right over a stile, then head diagonally left up through the field. Cross a stile on the right a short way from the field corner and continue across to the corner of the next field. Leave over a stile and turn right up the lane for 400 metres to a building on the left. Turn right and follow the

Looking north-west from Meldon Hill towards Cosdon Hill

wide grassy path north-north-west up to the trig point on **Meldon Hill**.

> **Meldon Hill** (390m) is crowned by several tors that are all worth exploring for their slightly different views. From the trig point the view includes Cosdon Hill (north-west), Castle Drogo (north-east), Haytor Rocks (south-east), Fernworthy Forest (south-west) and Kestor Rock (west) with Watern Tor/Hangingstone Hill in the distance. On the northern tor there is also a good example of a rock basin.

From the trig point head over to the northern tor, pass round to the right-hand side and take the path steeply downhill aiming for Chagford. At the bottom of the slope continue along the left-hand side of Padley Common and keep ahead with the cricket ground on the left. Turn left through a gate. Shortly go through another gate and then bear right along the concrete track to a road. Turn right up to the junction passed earlier and retrace the outward route back to the square and on to the car park.

WALK 3
Moretonhampstead and Mardon Down

Start/finish	Moretonhampstead car park on Station Road (A382) (SX 753 859)
Distance	15.5km (9¾ miles)
Ascent	610m
Time	5hrs
Terrain	A long hilly walk on paths, tracks and lanes, with sections of riverside, woodland and open moor
Maps	OS Explorer OL28
Refreshments	Several choices in Moretonhampstead; the Fingle Bridge Inn (01647 281287) at Fingle Bridge
Public transport	Moretonhampstead has bus links to Exeter, Tavistock and Newton Abbot

A rollercoaster of a walk offering wooded valleys, Iron Age hill forts and views. From Moretonhampstead the route heads north skirting past Butterdon Hill before visiting Cranbrook Castle hill fort for a great view. Then it's a steep descent to Fingle Bridge, home to the Fingle Bridge Inn before following the tree-shaded River Teign downstream for a while. Leaving the river behind, the route heads up to the earthworks of Wooston Castle before meandering through peaceful woods dipping through another valley on the way. A quick trip over Mardon Down, passing a stone cairn circle and a stone circle, offers more views before the final section heads back down to Moretonhampstead.

MORETONHAMPSTEAD

Bustling Moretonhampstead, which dates back to Saxon times, was mentioned in the Domesday Book as 'Mortone'; the 'Hampstead' part was added in the 15th century. The town was granted a charter by King John in 1207 to hold a weekly market with a rent of one sparrowhawk per year (there is a sparrowhawk sculpture in the square); the market ended in 1939. The 'calculating boy' George Parker Bidder (1806–78) was born here and became a well-respected engineer. St Andrew's Church and the almshouses date from the 15th century, although the latter were refurbished in 1637. The remains of a medieval cross can be found on Cross Street. Facilities include pubs, cafés, shops, bus links and a tourist information centre.

Exit the car park, turn left up Station Road and keep ahead at the crossroads beside the square on the left (anyone using public transport starts from the square); the almshouses and **stone cross** are to the right along Cross Street. At the next junction turn right into Fore Street and immediately go left along Lime Street passing the memorial to George Parker Bidder. ◄ Continue down Lime Street, cross the stream and, after the driveway on the left, turn left through a gate.

At the east end of Fore Street is St Andrew's Church.

Follow the left-hand field edge, go through a gate and keep ahead (stream on left) before crossing a footbridge and continuing with the stream on your right. Go into the next field and head diagonally left up to a path junction at the

WALK 3 – MORETONHAMPSTEAD AND MARDON DOWN

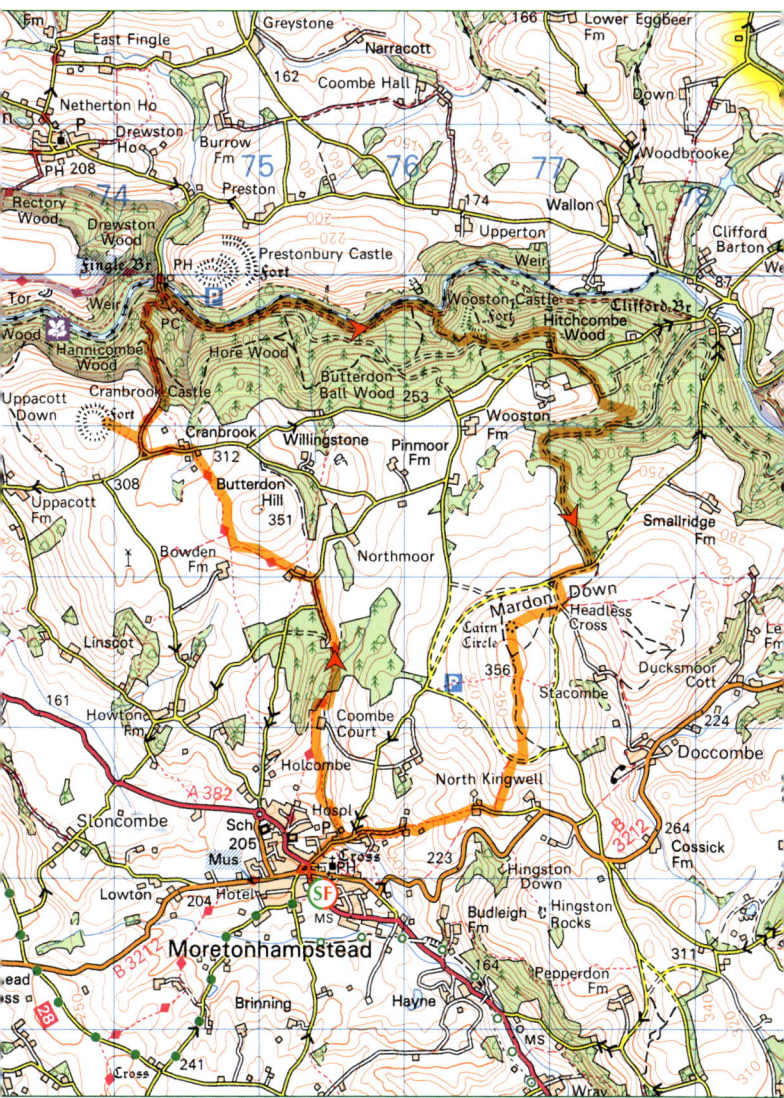

top right corner and leave through a gate. The walk now follows the Dartmoor Way for 4.4km (2¾ miles) to Fingle Bridge. Turn left up some steps and follow the enclosed route. Go through a gate and continue, later with a fence on the left (Coombe Court is hidden in the trees on the right). Keep ahead through the trees with a stream on the right. Go through a gate and continue up through the wood to a track junction at Hill Farm Cottages and bear right (straight on).

Keep right (straight on) along the lane to a right-hand bend and turn left along the track (Dartmoor Way and bridleway). Keep ahead between walls with cottages on either side and follow the bridleway as it curves right. Go through the gate and follow the left-hand wall clockwise round the west side of **Butterdon Hill**.

Keep following the wall as it swings right (northwards). Pass a standing stone (SX 748 884) and in 75 metres go left over a stile. Follow the left-hand boundary down through three fields to join a lane at **Cranbrook**. Turn left for 350 metres and at a slight left bend, turn right on a track (byway and Dartmoor Way); after 125 metres a gate on the left gives access to Cranbrook Castle.

> The earthworks of the Iron Age hill fort of **Cranbrook Castle** have a commanding view. To the west is Cosdon Hill and the high tops above Okehampton. Swinging right is Castle Drogo, Drewsteignton (north), then Prestonbury Castle above Fingle Bridge round to Butterdon Down (south-east).

Continue along the track, soon heading northwards steeply downhill towards Fingle Bridge, ignoring all side routes; the track swings right at SX 742 898 where there is a seat (left) with a view along the valley towards Castle Drogo. Continue down the track as it swings left to a track junction and turn sharp right (south-east). The track (Dartmoor Way) to the left leads over the 17th-century Fingle Bridge to the Fingle Bridge Inn (100 metres each way).

Continue past the parking area (toilets) and follow the track for 2km (1¼ miles), keeping the River Teign on the left. ◄ Turn right at a footpath sign for 'Wooston

Shortly after the car park, on the left, are the remains of the water-powered Fingle Mill, used as a fulling mill (to clean and soften wool) and for milling flour.

The riverside Fingle Bridge Inn at Fingle Bridge

Castle' just after crossing a stream (SX 7619 8976). Head uphill, curving left to a track and keep ahead; a path on the left leads through the earthworks of **Wooston Castle Iron Age Hill Fort**, where there is a view west along the River Teign valley.

Follow the track eastwards for 550 metres to a junction and turn right (south), signed 'Sawmill Car Park', passing the sawmill shed to join a minor road; to the right is the car park. Turn left for 15 metres, then fork right along a track past a gate, heading south-east through the trees. Follow the track as it swings left and descends for 200 metres to a junction (SX 7758 8910), then go sharp right down to another junction. Turn right, cross the stream to a junction and fork right (west) following the track uphill for 1.3km (¾ mile), then pass a couple of gates to join a minor road.

Turn right to a junction and go left to a small parking area on the left at Mardon Down. Turn right up past the standing stone – marked on the map as a 'Headless

The late Neolithic/ early Bronze Age stone circle – the largest on Dartmoor, although only twenty stones remain – has a great view including Cosdon Hill (west), Hamel Down (south-west) and Haytor Rocks (south).

Cross'. Keep right at the split to reach a **cairn circle** (remains of a Bronze Age burial cairn) on the right. Follow the main path as it curves left (south) and keep ahead for 475 metres, ignoring all crossing routes and passing the Giant's Grave (little remains of this stone burial cairn) to reach the stone circle. ◄

Continue southwards (Haytor Rocks is visible ahead and slightly right) and, as the track starts to descend and curve left, go straight on down to a minor road. Turn right for 40 metres to a bridleway sign and turn left down to a gate. Follow the enclosed bridleway, go through a gate and turn right down the lane to its end at a house entrance (Yarningdale – private). Fork left (straight on) down the track for 50 metres to a junction and fork right through a kissing gate. Follow the old sunken path downhill, later passing a house (left) and go through a gate.

Turn right along the track, keeping ahead at a junction to join a minor road. Bear left (straight on) and continue up to the junction in **Moretonhampstead** beside the George Parker Bidder memorial and retrace your steps back to the start.

WALK 4
Trenchford and Tottiford Reservoirs and Christow

Start/finish	Trenchford Reservoir car park (SX 804 823)
Distance	12.5km (7¾ miles)
Ascent	335m
Time	3½hrs
Terrain	Low-level walking on paths, tracks and lanes, waterside paths and fields
Maps	OS Explorer OL44
Refreshments	The Artichoke Inn (01647 253194) and community shop at Christow
Public transport	Buses between Bridford and Exeter stop at Christow

WALK 4 – TRENCHFORD AND TOTTIFORD RESERVOIRS AND CHRISTOW

From the car park the walk follows the shorelines of Trenchford Reservoir and Tottiford Reservoir before heading down to Moor Barton. The route continues down through woods and then along Bennah Hill to Christow, home to the thatch-roofed Artichoke Inn. Then it's a steady climb beside a lovely wooded stream before passing Bowden Farm and Clampitt Plantation for a quick visit to Kennick Reservoir. The final section goes through pine plantations before heading back to the car park.

From the information board at Trenchford Reservoir car park, follow a path northwards gently down through trees, crossing a footbridge on the way and then following the

The path to the left is the return route.

water's edge. Bear right across a footbridge at the head of the reservoir to a junction and turn right. ◀ Follow the path along the north shore of **Trenchford Reservoir** (water on your right) for 1km to the dam and go through a gate to join a lane.

> The three adjacent **reservoirs** of Trenchford, Tottiford, and Kennick (the latter is visited near the end of the walk) were created to supply drinking water to the Torbay area of Devon. Tottiford, the oldest reservoir in Dartmoor, was built in 1861, followed by Kennick in the early 1880s and then Trenchford in the early 1900s.

Turn right, crossing the dam, to a junction and turn left. Then fork left to follow the waterside path, keeping **Tottiford Reservoir** on the left for 1km to a four-way junction (raised path and footbridge to left). Turn right following a path up through the trees. Keep right (straight on) at a junction and follow the wide path as it swings right and left. Go through a gate and turn right along the lane for 25 metres.

Turn left at the bridleway sign, go through the gate and follow the enclosed route downhill. Go through a gate and continue down the track passing some gates and buildings at **Moor Barton**. Continue up the surfaced track and head eastwards, later curving left to a lane.

Following the track from Moor Barton

WALK 4 – TRENCHFORD AND TOTTIFORD RESERVOIRS AND CHRISTOW

Cross straight over and follow the hedge-lined byway for 150 metres. Turn right along the tree-shaded path (signed for Christow and Bennah Hill) to a gate and cross the ladder stile. Follow the right-hand field edge and leave through a gate. Keep ahead down the wide grassy strip through the wood, curving left. At the end, turn right for 25 metres and then turn left through a gate. Continue across the field and through a gate. Turn right down the track (Brennah Hill – this is no longer a minor road as marked on the map), enjoying the views across the Teign Valley.

At the T-junction turn right down the lane as it curves left past a thatched cottage at **Brennah** and keep left at the junction to a Y-junction. ▶ Fork left down to a junction beside the Artichoke Inn (right) in **Christow** and keep left (500 metres down to the right is the shop, car park and toilets).

> The village of **Christow**, on the eastern edge of the national park, is home to the 17th-century, thatch-roofed Artichoke Inn and the mainly 15th-century Church of St James the Apostle. Inside the church there is a 12th-century Norman font and several monuments, including one to Admiral Edward Pellew, 1st Viscount Exmouth and his son, the 2nd Viscount, both of whom died in 1833.

Follow the lane for 100 metres, turn left at the footpath sign (just before the crossroads) and follow the enclosed path up beside a stream. Cross a stile and continue up through the woods with the stream on your right, crossing another stile and a ladder stile on the way. On reaching a wall, turn right across the stream and go over the ladder stile beside the gate. Turn left up the left-hand field edge. Cross a stile and continue up through the wood, now with the stream on your left, then cross a stile at the top to join a track.

Turn right (bridleway to Bowden) following the track as it curves left and rises, with a hedge on the right. At the top go through a gate and follow the concrete track

To visit the church, fork right down the lane to a T-junction, turn right to the church on the left (200 metres further down the lane is the community shop), then turn around and keep right at the junction up to the pub, then turn right.

past Bowden Farm then turn right (north-west) along the track for 100 metres; here there is a choice. Either keep ahead along the track (permissive footpath only) and then turn left along the lane, or alternatively turn left through the gate and follow the bridleway as it soon swings right across the field to a gate and then turn left along the lane.

Continue up the lane, keeping ahead at the first junction, then fork right at the next junction following the narrow lane uphill; this soon becomes a track. Keep ahead past a house and then Beacon Farm (both on right) and drop slightly to a T-junction. ◀ Turn left along the track (bridleway) to a junction and turn right. At the next junction, where the track swings left, go straight on along the path (signed for Kennick Reservoir) for 500 metres.

Bear right (straight on) along the lane to **Kennick Reservoir** (right) and turn left through a gate just before the dam. Follow the path beside the fence on the right down to a 3-way junction. Turn right, cross a footbridge

On the right is a plaque for the 'Society of Friends Quakers Clampitt Burial Ground 1674–1740'.

Kennick Reservoir

and bear left to another 3-way junction. Turn right up through the trees (Trenchford direction) and continue to a lane. Cross diagonally left, go through the gate and follow the path signed for Trenchford Reservoir.

At a junction with a track turn left (path sign), then right at the next junction following the path down to a junction (with a footbridge ahead) and turn left to another junction. Turn right across the footbridge and retrace the outward route back to the car park.

WALK 5
North Bovey and Easdon Tor

Start/finish	North Bovey village car park (SX 740 838)
Alt start/finish	Manaton car park (SX 750 812)
Distance	11.25km (7 miles)
Ascent	355m
Time	3½hrs
Terrain	Low-level paths, tracks and lanes with higher open moor section over Easdon Tor; the Horsham Steps option requires care
Maps	OS Explorer OL28
Refreshments	Ring of Bells Inn (01647 440375) at North Bovey; Kestor Inn (01647 221626) off route at Water
Public transport	None

From North Bovey the route heads along the Bovey valley to Foxworthy. Here you can cross the River Bovey either by a bridge or via the fascinating Horsham Steps – a pile of giant-sized boulders – but only use this option if the river levels are low. Next stop is Manaton with its thatched cottages before heading along lanes and tracks up to Easdon Tor for a great view. From here it's an easy downhill wander back to North Bovey.

Exit the car park in North Bovey and turn right, then right again, with the village green and ancient cross on the left.

NORTH BOVEY

Church of St John the Baptist at North Bovey

Picturesque North Bovey is home to a tree-shaded village green complete with a medieval wayside cross in the south-west corner, overlooked by 17th-century thatched cottages and a thatched pub, the Ring of Bells Inn. There is also the Church of St John the Baptist, which dates from the 13th and 14th centuries. Go inside to see the 15th-century, carved-wood rood screen and a range of roof bosses including one with three rabbits with conjoined ears, a symbol of the Trinity and an emblem of 14th-century tin miners (see also Chagford).

A track on the right leads to the picturesque stepping stones across the River Bovey.

Keep ahead to another junction, with the **Ring of Bells Inn** opposite, and turn right (Dartmoor Way). Follow the lane downhill, which soon becomes a track. ◄ Continue eastwards along the track (later tarred) for 1.6km (1 mile) crossing the Dickford Water on the way, to a T-junction at **Barnecourt**.

Turn right for 300 metres and then turn left along a concrete track (Foxworthy Bridge and Lustleigh Cleave) to a junction (Walk 7 joins from the left). Fork right past a gate and follow the track southwards (bridleway to Foxworthy Bridge), later passing a gate. Continue down to another gate and turn left along the surfaced track at **Foxworthy**,

WALK 5 – NORTH BOVEY AND EASDON TOR

where there are several thatched cottages. Turn right down to the River Bovey; here, you have a choice.

To continue without Horsham Steps
Keep ahead across Foxworthy Bridge, then fork left up through the trees (signposted to Hammerslake and Horsham). Join a surfaced track, turn left for 40 metres and then turn left again. Go through a gate to enter the **East Dartmoor National Nature Reserve** (now following the Dartmoor Way), heading south-south-east through Neadon Cleave to a junction, then turn right uphill. ▶

The path from the left is the route up from Horsham Steps.

The alternative route crosses the River Bovey at Horsham Steps

Alternative via Horsham Steps

Retrace steps for 20 metres and turn right (south-east) along the track (bridleway to Hammerslake). Just before Foxworthy Farmhouse fork right and, at the entrance to Foxworthy Mill, keep left through the trees for 100 metres to a waymarked junction. Turn right down the meandering path to the River Bovey. The route now crosses the river via the jumble of massive boulders, known as Horsham Steps at SX 759 817. The river normally flows under the boulders, which are mossy and can be slippery; take care and do not attempt to cross when the river is in flood. Once on the other side, turn left (river on left), soon following the path as it swings right up to a junction where the main route joins from the right, then go straight on.

WALK 5 – NORTH BOVEY AND EASDON TOR

The **East Dartmoor National Nature Reserve** – which consists of three adjacent sites (Bovey Valley Woods, Trendlebere Down and Yarner Wood) – offers a mix of woodland, heathland and wetland habitats with an abundance of wildlife, from kingfishers to dormice.

Continue steeply uphill and leave the East Dartmoor National Nature Reserve through a gate. Continue along the enclosed path, later going right and left, then passing a cottage. Bear left down the track and follow this to the right to a signed track junction.

Fork right (west) and follow the enclosed track (bridleway to Manaton); the left fork is followed by Walk 7. ▶ Pass a gate on the way; soon houses can be seen on the right and the track later joins a lane. Turn left and head towards the village green in **Manaton** (75 metres to the left is a car park (SX 750 812) – alternative start). ▶

Head across the village green and enter the churchyard via the lych gate. Follow the path just left of the **church** and leave through the gate to a path junction. Keep ahead (west) along the enclosed path. Go through a gate and continue through the field with a wall and trees on the right, then cross a stile in the far-right-hand corner.

Turn right along the lane to a junction and keep ahead for a further 75 metres before turning left over a stile in the hedge. Head diagonally right (north-west) across the field, cross a track and over a stile in the hedge. Keep ahead through the next field and leave via another stile in the hedge.

Turn left along the lane for 450 metres to a junction and fork right. Follow the lane up past Barracott and Boodown Farm (both on right). Keep ahead along the track (byway), go through a gate on to the open moor and turn right. Follow the wall on the right up to the corner and then fork diagonally left (north-north-west) up to the ridge. Turn left to the trig point on **Easdon Tor**; the onward route heads diagonally right from here.

Detour to Kestor Inn: keep left (straight on) to a 4-way junction and turn right (Dartmoor Way) to a lane, bear left and then right to the pub; retrace steps to the junction and turn left towards Manaton (1km each way).

Thatched cottages and the 15th-century St Winifred's Church overlook the village green. Visit the church to see the lovely 16th-century wooden rood screen.

View to the north-west from Easdon Tor

Easdon Tor (439m) offers some great views, including Cosdon Hill (north-west) and the high tors above Okehampton, Hamel Down (south-west) and Haytor Rocks (south-south-east) with the sea in the distance. Situated about 100 metres south of the trig point is Whooping Rock. Some say the name comes from the sound of strong winds blowing past the rock, while others say that it was a place to cure children of whooping cough; take your pick.

From the trig point follow a path north-north-west downhill. Leave through a gate and keep ahead to a junction with a byway. Turn right along this for 800 metres (½ mile) over the rise then down to a lane and turn right downhill. ◄

On the way, look left to see the early 20th-century Bovey Castle (hotel), built for Viscount Hambleden (Frederick Smith), grandson of William Henry Smith, founder of W H Smith newsagents.

Keep right at the junction (Olde Yarde) down to Bovey Bridge. Go straight on and, as the lane curves left, fork right up the enclosed track (footpath). At a gate ahead which leads into the churchyard, go right and left following the enclosed path to a lane in **North Bovey**, almost opposite the car park.

WALK 6
Challacombe, Grimspound and Water Hill

Start/finish	Warren House Inn car park on B3212 (SX 676 811)
Distance	12km (7½ miles)
Ascent	300m
Time	3½hrs
Terrain	Paths and tracks including over open higher-level moor, low cloud may require map and compass over Hookney Tor and Water Hill
Maps	OS Explorer OL28
Refreshments	Warren House Inn (01822 880208) on the B3212
Public transport	Buses between Newton Abbot and Tavistock stop at the Warren House Inn (B3212)

From near the Warren House Inn the walk loops round Challacombe Down passing the ruins of a medieval village before heading to the impressive Bronze Age settlement of Grimspound. From here it's off to Hookney Tor and then on to Birch Tor. The route then heads down to the ancient Bennett's Cross, passing some old gerts, before heading to Hurston stone row. From here the route heads south up to Water Hill before heading down to the car park. For a shorter walk there are a couple of shortcuts described.

From the back of the car park (road behind you) take the track eastwards for 550 metres. As the track swings left (north), fork right (straight on) down the narrow bridleway passing some ruins of the former **Birch Tor and Vitifer Tin Mine**. Cross the stream to a junction, turn right (south-east) and then keep right (south) at the split. ▶ Follow the track southwards, passing through a gate on the way. At the junction keep left (straight on) along the valley, passing the ruins of the Golden Dagger Tin Mine. Keep ahead through a gate and follow the track up over Challacombe Down as it curves left round

To miss out Challacombe bear half-left on a bridleway heading south-south-east and then east-north-east past an old mine to a junction near Headland Warren Farm (minus 3.1km/2 miles).

WALKING ON DARTMOOR

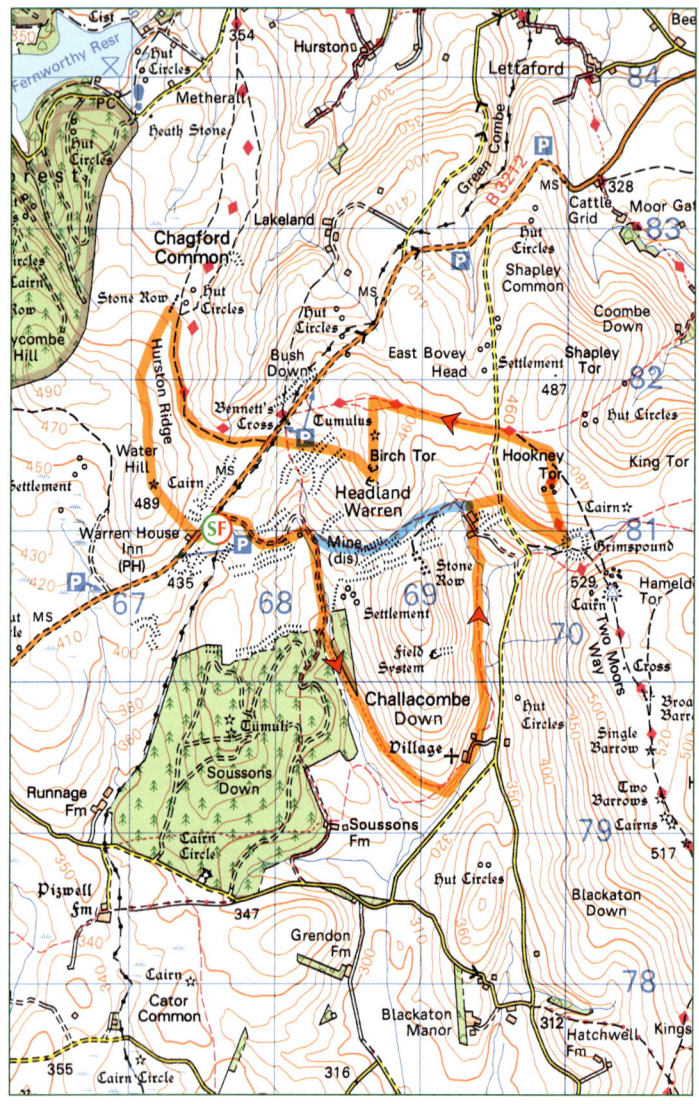

One of the ruined houses at the former medieval village of Challacombe

the slope and then heads northwards. Continue through a gate and follow the track past Challacombe Farm. ▶

Keep ahead and, where the concrete track curves right, go straight on through a gate and continue past Challacombe Cottages (left). Go through a gate and continue northwards (look out for the pair of slotted granite gateposts on the way). Go through a gate at a wall and continue towards Headland Warren Farm. Pass through gates to reach a tarred drive. The right of way passes in front of the house; however, we follow the permissive route up to the right through a gate. Then bear left alongside the fence round the property to reach a signed junction on the far side. ▶ Turn right (east) up a narrow route to the minor road. Cross over and bear right on a narrow path contouring round the hill to **Grimspound** (which is just across the stream). The onward route turns left (north) just before the stream and follows the Two Moors Way up to Hookney Tor.

Grimspound is an impressively large Bronze Age settlement built around 3500 years ago, which

Just to the north of the farmhouse is the site of the medieval village of Challacombe, known as Chalvecombe in 1481, where you can explore several ruined buildings, including a longhouse.

The shortcut missing out Challacombe rejoins the main walk here from the left.

contains the remains of 24 stone roundhouses within a large boundary wall; head north up the slope for 150 metres towards Hameldown Tor for a good aerial view of the site. Views from Hookney Tor (497m) include Grimspound and Hameldown Tor to the south; to the south-south-west is Challacombe Down and to the west is Birch Tor (next stop on the walk); to the left of Birch Tor is the Warren House Inn.

From **Hookney Tor** there are several paths. Stand facing north (Grimspound behind you) and head north along the Two Moors Way, soon passing through an old wall. Here the route splits three ways. Bear half-left (west-north-west) following the middle route (Two Moors Way) downhill. Cross the minor road and continue in the same direction following the Two Moors Way up to the brow of the hill. Here, turn left (south) along the ridge to Birch Tor (487m). ◀

Turn sharp right (north-west) to follow a narrow path gently downhill, later passing just right of a stone-walled

> From here views include Soussons Wood (south) and the Warren House Inn on the B3212 (south-west).

Bennett's Cross looking back to Birch Tor

enclosure and dipping through some impressive old mining gerts – once part of the Vitifer Mine that closed in 1925 – to arrive at a car park with **Bennett's Cross** 20 metres over to the right.

> **Bennett's Cross** is an ancient, if rather misshapen, wayside cross that has more recently been used as a boundary stone between the parishes of Chagford and North Bovey, and as a boundary marker for Headland Warren. It has been suggested that the cross may actually be a Christianised prehistoric standing stone.

Cross straight over the road and follow the path (Two Moors Way) westwards. ▶ Keep to this as it curves to the right heading north of west and then north to reach the southern end of a stone row.

> The late Neolithic double **stone row** consists of 99 stones with a cairn at the southern (upper) end and a blocking stone at the northern (lower) end. In the area are the remains of Bronze Age reaves and hut circles.

Turn hard left (almost doubling back) and head south-south-west and then south up Hurston Ridge to the large cairn (originally a Bronze Age burial cairn) on **Water Hill** (489m). ▶ Head diagonally left (south-east) down to the B3212 beside the 19th-century **Warren House Inn**, the highest pub in Southern England at 434m. Cross over and turn left back to the car park on right.

To miss out this last section you could turn left from the car park and follow a path parallel to the road back to the start (minus 1.3km/¾ mile).

Views include Birch Tor, Hookney Tor, Grimspound and Hameldown to the east, and the distinctive Kestor Rock to the north.

WALK 7
Lustleigh Cleave, Hunter's Tor and River Bovey

Start/finish	Trendlebere Down lower car park (SX 784 793)
Distance	14km (8¾ miles)
Ascent	565m
Time	4½hrs
Terrain	Lower-level but hilly route mainly through woodland on paths, tracks and lanes with a section of riverside path
Maps	OS Explorer OL28
Refreshments	The Cleave pub (01647 277223), Primrose Tearoom (01647 277365) and village shop at Lustleigh; Kestor Inn (01647 221626) off route at Water
Public transport	Buses between Newton Abbot and Chagford via Moretonhampstead call at Lustleigh (SX 786 815)

The route sets out along the Old Manaton Road before crossing a packhorse bridge over the River Bovey for a stiff climb to Lustleigh. The route then meanders through woods up to Sharpitor and follows the eastern side of Lustleigh Cleave to Hunter's Tor. After dropping down to cross the River Bovey at Foxworthy the route meanders along the wooded west side of the cleave before rejoining the Old Manaton Road back to the start.

From the back of the car park follow the narrow path north downhill, then bear left down the track (Old Manaton Road) for 750 metres (½ mile) to a junction just after passing a large boulder. Turn right, go through a gate (East Dartmoor National Nature Reserve – Hisley Wood) and cross the River Bovey via the **old packhorse bridge** (Hisley Bridge) to a split junction. ◄ Go left for 50 metres up to a junction and turn sharp right (south-east) following the track (bridleway) up through Hisley Wood (Woodland Trust). Later the route swings sharp left (north-north-west) and continues to climb, passing below Gradnor Rocks.

The East Dartmoor National Nature Reserve (NNR) includes Bovey Valley Woods, Trendlebere Down and Yarner Wood, offering a mix of woodland, heathland and wetland habitats with an abundance of wildlife.

Leave the wood and follow the enclosed bridleway. Pass through a gate and continue towards Higher Hisley. Do not go through the gate ahead but turn right between farm buildings and then left to a gate. Follow the enclosed bridleway to a track and turn right down to a lane. Turn left and then immediately right down the lane at **Rudge**.

Hisley Bridge – an old packhorse bridge over the River Bovey

Once level with a house (left), turn right down the bridleway. Turn left along the lane following it as it curves left, and bear right at the junction up to a crossroads in Lustleigh beside the village shop. Turn right passing the **church** (left), Primrose Tearoom and picturesque village green (right) and then the Cleave pub (right).

The Church of St John the Baptist in **Lustleigh** dates from the 13th century. Call in to see the Datuidoc's Stone, an early Christian (AD550–600) sculptured gravestone. For a while the village had a railway connection, when a branch line from Newton Abbot to Moretonhampstead opened in 1866, but this closed in 1964.

Keep right at the first junction then turn left at the next beside the War Memorial. Head up the lane for 50 metres and, as it curves right, fork left along a track to its end, then bear right along an enclosed path. Go through a gate and follow the right-hand path straight on through the field, passing left of a large boulder (part of

WALK 7 – LUSTLEIGH CLEAVE, HUNTER'S TOR AND RIVER BOVEY

Pathfields Tor). In the next field fork left (signed to Lower Combe). Go through a gate and follow the enclosed path; keep ahead as a path joins from the right and shortly go through a gate to join a surfaced track (path junction).

Turn left and, as the track splits, go straight on along the narrow path. Cross a clapper bridge and continue up through the wood past the large boulders to a stile. Turn left along the lane for 40 metres, then turn right following an enclosed bridleway between two house entrances. After passing a gate, fork right (straight on) signed for Hunter's Tor, heading up the wooded bridleway. Keep ahead as a path joins from the right and pass the outcrops of Hammerslake Tor and then Sharpitor. ▶ On reaching the top, a brief view opens out to the south-west.

Head north-west along the bridleway with a stone wall over to the right, passing the rocks of Harton Chest. ▶ Continue along the bridleway with views to the south-west over Lustleigh Cleave as the trees are left behind, passing Foxworthy Tor to reach **Hunter's Tor**.

> **Lustleigh Cleave** follows the line of the Sticklepath fault that formed during the early part of the Tertiary period (65 to 50 million years ago). The fault runs north-west to south-east from Bideford to Torbay, cutting across the north-east corner of Dartmoor. Hunter's Tor offers a great view; to the south is Haytor Rocks, moving right is Hound Tor (south-west), then Bowerman's Nose with Hamel Down behind, and to the north-west is Bovey Castle with Cosdon Hill in the distance. Just to the east of the tor are the remains of an Iron Age hill fort.

Go through a gate in the wall and bear right (north-east) down the bridleway, keeping to this as it turns sharp left and continues to descend. Go through a gate and follow the right-hand boundary, passing left of Peck Farm to a gate. Follow the surfaced track to a junction (the track to the right is Walk 5). Turn left past a gate and follow the track (bridleway to Foxworthy Bridge) southwards, later passing a gate. Continue down to another gate and turn

---

There used to be a logan stone (or rocking stone) at Sharpitor called the Nut Crackers.

The boulders offer a great view across Lustleigh Cleave, but be very careful as there are some steep drops.

Thatched houses at Foxworthy

Left leads down to Horsham Steps, a jumble of massive boulders under which the River Bovey usually flows (see Walk 5 for directions to use this instead of Foxworthy Bridge).

To visit the Kestor Inn turn right at the four-way junction (Dartmoor Way) to a lane, bear left and then right to the pub; retrace steps (400 metres each way).

left along the surfaced track to a cluster of thatched cottages at **Foxworthy**.

Bear right and cross Foxworthy Bridge over the River Bovey, then fork left up through the trees (signed to Hammerslake and Horsham). Turn left along a surfaced track for 40 metres, then turn left again. Go through a gate to enter the **East Dartmoor National Nature Reserve** (now following the Dartmoor Way), heading south-southeast through Neadon Cleave to a junction. ◀ Turn right uphill, go through a gate and follow the enclosed path as it soon swings right and left and then passes a cottage. Bear left down the track and follow this to the right to a signed three-way junction (the right-hand fork is Walk 5).

Take the left-hand track (bridleway) south-eastwards for 650 metres towards Water. At the four-way track junction (buildings ahead), turn left and follow the track as it swings right and then left. ◀

Go through a gate (East Dartmoor NNR) and follow the bridleway down through the trees. At a junction keep ahead down the bridleway (signed Clam Bridge for Lustleigh Cleave) to the River Bovey and a **footbridge** beside the old Clam Bridge made from two old tree trunks. Do not cross the footbridge but turn right (south-east) along the path (signed for Old Manaton Road and Trendlebere Down) through Houndtor Wood keeping the river on your left for 1.5km (1 mile). Follow the path as it goes sharp right, then left across a footbridge over the Becka Brook. Turn left (south-eastwards) along the track (Old Manaton Road) for 350 metres to a junction passed earlier and then retrace the outward route back up to the car park.

WALK 8
Widecombe in the Moor, Hamel Down and Bowerman's Nose

Start/finish	Widecombe in the Moor village green car park (SX 718 768)
Distance	15.5km (9¾ miles)
Ascent	450m
Time	4½hrs
Terrain	Long walk on paths, tracks and lanes; navigating on the open high-level moor sections over Hamel Down could be difficult in low cloud; long descent on lane near end of walk
Maps	OS Explorer OL28
Refreshments	The Old Inn (01364 621207), The Rugglestone Inn (01364 621327) and Café on the Green (01364 621720) in Widecombe in the Moor
Public transport	Limited Haytor Hoppa bus service calls at Widecombe in the Moor

From picturesque Widecombe in the Moor the walk heads up and then along the broad ridge of Hamel Down, offering some great views on the way to Hameldown Tor. Then it's off down to the poignant Jay's Grave before heading to the unusual granite stack of Bowerman's Nose. The final port of call is the impressive rocky mound of Hound Tor before heading back down to Widecombe.

WIDECOMBE IN THE MOOR

Widecombe in the Moor is home to a fair on the second Tuesday of September immortalised in the folk song 'Widecombe Fair' along with 'Old Uncle Tom Cobley and All'. The 14th-century Perpendicular-style Church of St Pancras is known locally as the 'Cathedral of the Moor'; the lofty tower was added in the 16th century. The Church House, with its loggia on granite posts, dates from the 16th century.

WALK 8 – WIDECOMBE IN THE MOOR, HAMEL DOWN AND BOWERMAN'S NOSE

At the village green in Widecombe in the Moor face the church with your back to the Café on the Green and turn right (west) along the tarred path. Keep ahead along the road (Natsworthy direction) for 125 metres and turn left up the tarred track (footpath for Grimspound via Hameldown). At buildings on the left, bear right (straight on) along the track and through a gate on to the open moor. Follow the track left and right uphill to a junction. Keep right, following the Two Moors Way with the wall on your right; the walk now follows the Two Moors Way for 3.6km (2¼ miles) to Hameldown Tor. At the wall corner, keep ahead (northwards) up the broad ridge to **Hameldown Beacon** (517m), beside a wall on your left.

> Dotted along **Hamel Down** are the remains of several Bronze Age cairns, or burial mounds. Atop of these are boundary stones to mark the Duke of Somerset's Natsworthy Manor land, carved with the initials 'DS' and the date '1854'. The first stone on Hameldown Beacon is also carved with the words 'Hamilton Beacon'. The others are engraved 'Two Burrows', 'Single Burrow' and 'Broad Burrow'.
>
> The views as you walk along the ridge, culminating at the trig point, are impressive. Looking south and moving clockwise you can see Eastern White Barrow (the double cairn that looks a bit like a submarine, south-south-west) and the mast near Princetown (west-south-west); to the west is the whitewashed Warren House Inn, Cosdon Hill (north-north-west), Castle Drogo (north-north-east), Easdon Tor (east-north-east) and Haytor Rocks (south-east); and on a clear day you can see the Isle of Portland across Lyme Bay in the east, 100km (62 miles) away.

Keep ahead to the corner of the wall and **Two Barrows**. Continue northwards, passing Single Barrow, to reach Broad Barrow (532m). Here the route splits; take the left-hand fork heading slightly west of north to the trig point on **Hameldown Tor** (529m). ▶ Turn right (east) at the trig point following a path and keep ahead at the

After 220 metres, some 70 metres to the left of the path are the remains of Hamel Down Cross, a medieval wayside cross; further on from the trig point is Grimspound Bronze Age settlement (see Walk 6).

Heading towards Natsworthy Gate

To shorten the walk you can follow the Two Moors Way south along the road back to the start (reduces walk by 4.7km/3 miles).

junction down to a War Memorial (the large boulder and plaque commemorates the loss of the crew of a Second World War bomber).

Continue downhill bearing right (south-east), soon following the boundary and trees on your left. Cross a stream and go through a gate to a minor road at Natsworthy Gate. ◄ Turn left and almost immediately turn right through a gate (signposted to Jay's Grave). Follow the enclosed bridleway for 1.2km (¾ mile) and go through a gate to **Jay's Grave**.

Jay's Grave is a reminder of the sad story of Kitty Jay, a young unmarried housemaid, who was betrayed after getting pregnant and took her own life in despair. Back then it was usual practice for suicide victims to be buried at a crossroads.

Cross over the road and keep left of the fence, heading eastwards over the open moor of Cripdon Down (fence on right). Later bear slightly left as the fence falls away to the right and go through a gate in the wall ahead.

Bowerman's Nose

Continue downhill, cross the minor road and bear half-left following a path north-eastwards up to the distinctive granite stack of **Bowerman's Nose**.

> Legend has it that Bowerman the Hunter was out hunting on the moor with his hounds when he disturbed a coven of witches. Seeking revenge, they turned the hunter and his hounds to stone. Bowerman became the granite stack known as **Bowerman's Nose** and the dogs became **Hound Tor** (see later).

Turn right and head south-east over the rocks to the main tor (397m) on Hayne Down. Descend slightly to a junction and turn right (west) back to the minor road. Turn left through the gate and follow the road southwards to a junction. Turn left for 25 metres to another junction (car park to the left) and head south-east over the moor towards **Hound Tor**, passing just to the right of the impressive rock stacks.

WALKING ON DARTMOOR

On the way, 50 metres over to the right amongst the heather, are the remains of a Bronze Age cairn circle and cist (SX 7410 7876).

From the south side of the tor head south-south-west to rejoin the minor road and go straight on. ◄ Follow the road downhill (at the dip, a gate on the left gives access to Devon Wildlife Trust's Emsworthy Mire Nature Reserve). After the cattle grid, fork right and follow a grassy path west-south-west, keeping left at a split with Bell Tor up to the right to join a minor road near Bonehill Rocks.

Turn right down the road for 1.4km (1 mile) to a T-junction with the B3387 at **Widecombe in the Moor**. Turn left for 15 metres, then turn right through a gate. Follow the path through the meadow, with the East Webburn River on the left. Leave through a gate to join a minor road. ◄

A hundred and fifty metres to the left is The Rugglestone Inn.

Turn right along the road and soon go right up some steps and through a gate. Head through the field, aiming for the church, and go through a gate to enter the churchyard. Keep ahead, then turn left past the church (right) and leave through the lych gate. Continue past the Church House (right) to a junction with the Old Inn opposite and turn right back to the village green.

WALK 9
Hound Tor and Haytor Rocks

Start/finish	Hemsworthy Gate car park on B3387 (SX 741 761)
Distance	12km (7½ miles)
Ascent	400m
Time	3¾hrs
Terrain	Open moor walk on paths, tracks and lanes, several ups and downs; low cloud/mist may require map and compass navigation
Maps	OS Explorer OL28
Refreshments	None on the walk; off route is the Rock Inn (01364 661305) and the Moorland Hotel (01364 661142) at Haytor Vale
Public transport	Limited Haytor Hoppa bus service stops at Hemsworthy Gate

WALK 9 – HOUND TOR AND HAYTOR ROCKS

From Hemsworthy Gate it's a short climb to Top Tor, the first of many tors on the route that offer lots of great views. From here its north over Bonehill Down to visit Bonehill Rocks, Honeybag Tor, Chinkwell Tor and Bell Tor. Then it's off to the impressive Hound Tor, before passing the ruins of a medieval village. After a steep descent through trees to cross the clapper bridge over the Becka Brook, the route heads up to Smallacombe Rocks. After crossing the old granite tramway, the next stop is Haytor Rocks. Having soaked up the views it's an easy walk westwards passing Saddle Tor back to Hemsworthy Gate.

From the car park beside Hemsworthy Gate head slightly north of west up the path to the summit of **Top Tor** (432m). Turn right following a path north-north-west down to a road (B3387) and car park. Cross straight over and continue in the same direction over Bonehill Down aiming for Chinkwell Tor. Pass just right of Bonehill Rocks and then bear left parallel with the minor road down to a parking area just before the wall.

Turn right across the road and follow the track with a wall on the left, keeping to the track as it curves left. ◀ Continue along the level track for 1.3km (¾ mile) and, just after passing a wall and trees on the left, turn right up a narrow path to a col. Turn left to **Honeybag Tor** and then double back to the col and keep ahead (south) up **Chinkwell Tor**.

For a shorter walk (minus 2.5km/1½ miles) bear right (east-north-east) for 375 metres to a junction and keep ahead. The main walk joins from the left.

Honeybag Tor (445m) and **Chinkwell Tor** (458m) lie at the northern end of Bonehill Down and both offer a great view including Hound Tor (east-north-east), Haytor Rocks (east-south-east), Rippon Tor (south-south-east), Widecombe in the Moor (south-west) and Hamel Down (north-west).

Head south-south-east to a junction just left of Bell Tor and fork left. Pass just left of a pond (often dry) to a

Hound Tor

WALK 9 – HOUND TOR AND HAYTOR ROCKS

junction and bear left (east-north-east) for 450 metres to a lane. Turn left along this, passing the cattle grid, and continue for 400 metres, soon heading uphill. (A gate on the right in the dip gives access to Devon Wildlife Trust's Emsworthy Mire.) At the top of the rise, just after a gate on the right (Holwell Lawn), fork half-right (north-north-east) over the open moor to **Hound Tor** (414m). ▶

On nearing the tor, 50 metres over to the left among the heather, are the remains of a Bronze Age cairn circle and cist (SX 7410 7876).

> Legend has it that a local hunter known as Bowerman was out hunting on the moor with his hounds when he disturbed a coven of witches. Seeking revenge they turned the hunter and his hounds to stone – the dogs became **Hound Tor** and the hunter became **Bowerman's Nose** (Walk 8). The legend is said to have inspired Sir Arthur Conan Doyle while writing his Sherlock Holmes novel *The Hound of the Baskervilles*.

On nearing the tor bear right and then bear right again (tor behind you) and head south-east down the slope following the path through the bracken, aiming towards Greater Rocks. On reaching a junction of ways beside an old boundary wall (SX 745 787) bear left (east) and continue gently downhill. Pass just right of the ruins of **Hundatora**, go through an old boundary and continue; Greater Rocks are over to the right.

> The atmospheric remains of **Hundatora** (recorded in the Domesday Book) – Hound Tor medieval village – includes the ruins of several 13th-century longhouses and barns; the village was abandoned in the late 14th or early 15th century.

Go through a gate and follow the bridleway down through the trees, passing two more gates on the way. Keep ahead, crossing the clapper bridge over the Becka Brook and continue along the boulder-strewn route through the trees to a bridleway sign and junction (the bridleway heads north-east). Go straight on (east-south-east) following a path uphill as it curves right (south) and continues up to **Smallacombe Rocks**. ▶

Views west across the valley include Chinkwell Tor, Honeybag Tor and Hound Tor (all visited earlier); moving right, Hameldown Tor, King Tor and Easdon Tor can be seen.

From Smallacombe Rocks there are a number of routes. Take the one heading south, aiming for Haytor Rocks on the skyline. Cross straight over the granite tramway and follow the narrow path uphill to the col between the two large outcrops of **Haytor Rocks**. ◄

For a pub visit at Haytor Vale, head east down to and then alongside the B3387 to a junction. Turn right, then fork left to the Rock Inn; retrace steps (2.7km/1¾ miles return).

> **Haytor Rocks** (457m), one of Dartmoor's best-known and most-visited tors, offers some great views: to the west is the large mast at Princetown, while nearer and to the north-west are Hameldown Tor, Chinkwell Tor and Hound Tor. To the south-east is the Teign valley with the sea beyond, while further right is the South Hams region (south). The granite tramway, built using granite rails to guide the wheels of horse-drawn wagons, was opened in 1820 to transport granite from the quarries at Haytor down to Ventiford Quay on the Stover Canal, to the south-east of Bovey Tracey.

Turn right and pass just to the left (south) of the second large outcrop, with flat outcrops in the heather on the left. Follow the path down a short steeper section and continue south-westwards, keeping left at the split, aiming for **Saddle Tor** (428m). ◄ Continue between the two outcrops and head down to a car park (SX 748 761); from here you can visit Emsworthy Mire Nature Reserve. To continue the walk, bear right (west) alongside the road (B3387) for 650 metres to **Hemsworthy Gate**. Go through the gate beside the cattle grid and keep ahead across the minor road back to the car park.

The views from Saddle Tor are similar to those from Haytor Rocks, except that from here you can get a good view of the Haytor Rocks as well.

Detour to Devon Wildlife Trust's Emsworthy Mire Nature Reserve

Head north-north-west away from the car park (SX 748 761) keeping the wall on the left to a gate and reserve map. Keep ahead through two gates a few metres apart and then follow the wall on the right for 175 metres. Cross a footbridge to a marker post and turn right between the stone walls towards Emsworthy barn. The walled fields around the barn offer a great display of bluebells in early summer. To return, retrace steps (1.2km/¾ mile return).

WALK 10
Buckland Beacon and Rippon Tor

Start/finish	Hemsworthy Gate car park on B3387 (SX 741 761)
Alt start/finish	Cold East Cross car park (SX 740 742)
Distance	8.5km (5¼ miles)
Ascent	225m
Time	2½hrs
Terrain	A shorter walk on paths over medium-level open moor
Maps	OS Explorer OL28
Refreshments	None on the walk; nearby is Widecombe in the Moor or Haytor Vale
Public transport	Limited Haytor Hoppa bus service stops at Hemsworthy Gate

An easy half-day walk to the east of Buckland in the Moor visiting several tors and offering some great views. From Hemsworthy Gate the route heads up Top Tor and continues past Pil Tor and Tunhill Rocks before heading south over Buckland Common to reach Buckland Beacon and the Ten Commandment Stone. After admiring the views, the route heads to Welstor Rock before heading north to Cold East Cross and then up to Rippon Tor. From here it's an easy descent back to the start.

From the car park beside Hemsworthy Gate head slightly north of west up the slope following a good path to the summit of **Top Tor** (432m). Bear left (south-west) and soon pass between the two rock outcrops of **Pil Tor** (417m). Head west-south-west to Tunhill Rocks and admire the panoramic view.

> The view from **Tunhill Rocks** includes Buckland Beacon (south), Brent Moor (south-west) and the church at Widecombe in the Moor, with Hamel

WALKING ON DARTMOOR

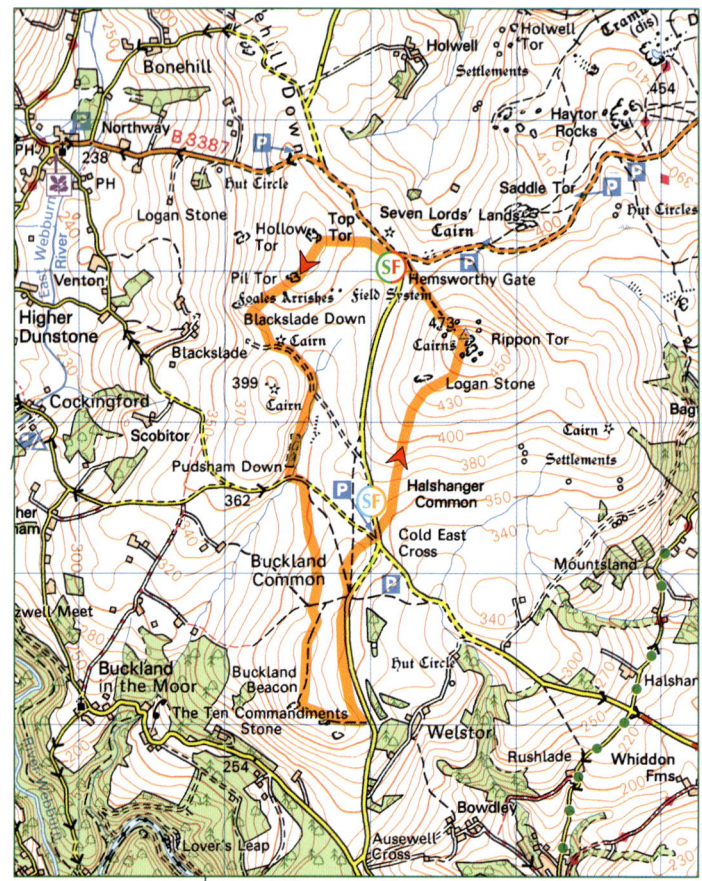

Down beyond (north-west), Chinkwell Tor (north) and Rippon Tor (east).

Turn left (south-south-east) along a path to a junction with a stony track and turn left (if you are collecting tors, the path continues in the same direction up to Wittaburrow Tor and cairn). Follow the track downhill.

Buckland Beacon

Go through the gate and keep right, following a path southwards alongside the stone wall on the right and a stream over to the left (the track heads south-east across the stream). After 350 metres, keep ahead through the pine trees to join a minor road.

Turn left crossing the bridge over the stream (Ruddycleave Water) to a car park entrance on the left and fork right. Follow the path southwards up through the bracken of Buckland Common. On reaching a stone wall (left), bear right following the path alongside the wall on your left to reach **Buckland Beacon**.

Buckland Beacon (383m) is one of several 16th-century beacon locations in Dartmoor that were set up to warn of the arrival of the Spanish Armada in the English Channel (other locations include Western Beacon and Ugborough Beacon). From the summit there are extensive views: to the east is the Teign Estuary and coast; moving right (south) is the South Hams region, then the outline of Brent Hill and the tops of Brent Moor; to the west is Corndon Down; and looking north there is Hamel Down, then Chinkwell Tor, Top Tor and Rippon Tor slightly east of north. On the southern side of the tor is the **Ten Commandments Stone**; two large granite slabs on which the Ten Commandments were carved by W A Clement in 1928. The work was commissioned by William Whitely, one-time Lord of Buckland Manor, to celebrate Parliament's rejection of a new Book of Common Prayer. Nearer the summit there is also an inscription commemorating the King George V's Silver Jubilee in 1935.

The Ten Commandments Stone on Buckland Beacon

View towards Rippon Tor from Buckland Common

Turn left (east), cross the stile in the stone wall and continue to Westor Rock. Keep ahead down to a T-junction and turn left (north) along the level path over Welstor Common, later keeping to the right-hand fork. Pass through an old boundary work and keep ahead to a stone wall.

Cross the stone stile with a minor road and stand of trees over to the right and keep ahead parallel with the road for 50 metres, then bear diagonally left following a narrow path northwards to a path junction. Turn right, now with Rippon Tor ahead, pass a boundary stone and continue north-eastwards to a minor road with a car park opposite (alternative start – SX 740 742), just left of the Cold East Cross road junction.

Keep ahead through the car park, cross another minor road and go through a gate in the stone wall opposite. Continue in the same direction for 50 metres and then bear left (northwards), soon following a boundary on the left uphill. Go through a gate at the top left corner and follow the path north-north-east to the top of **Rippon Tor**.

Rippon Tor (473m), home to Bronze Age burial cairns and a trig point, has some extensive views: looking north is Hound Tor, and moving clockwise there is Saddle Tor and Haytor Rocks (north-east), the Teign Estuary and coast (east), Buckland Beacon (south), Brent Moor (south-west), then round to the mast at Princetown, then Hamel Down and Chinkwell Tor (north-north-west).

From the trig point turn left following a path north-westwards downhill, aiming for the road junction. Go through a gate in the wall, keep ahead to the road and turn left through a gate beside the cattle grid back to the Hemsworthy Gate junction and car park.

SOUTH-EAST

Heading south-east down the route of the former Zeal Tor Tramway (Walk 15)

WALKING ON DARTMOOR

WALK 11
The stepping stones walk

Start/finish	Dunnabridge Pound car park on B3357 (SX 642 746)
Distance	11.25km (7 miles)
Ascent	340m
Time	3½hrs
Terrain	Good paths and tracks; sections of lane walking; four river crossings via stepping stones only
Maps	OS Explorer OL28
Refreshments	The Forest Inn (01364 631211) at Hexworthy
Public transport	None
Note	Take great care when using the stepping stones; do not attempt the walk after heavy rainfall or if the rivers are in flood

From Dunnabridge Pound the walk heads over to Laughter Hole and the East Dart River for the first of four river crossings; if this is flooded it's time to abandon the walk. Once across it's off to Babeny before crossing the East Dart River again via another set of stepping stones. The route then passes Brimpts Farm and the hamlets of Huccaby and Hexworthy to arrive at Sherberton for the third set of stepping stones that leads across the River Swincombe. The final leg of the walk crosses the West Dart River on a lovely curve of stepping stones before heading back to the start.

Exit the car park and turn right alongside the B3357 for 350 metres using the verge to reach the **Dunnabridge Pound** on the left, just after a track junction.

> **Dunnabridge Pound**, a large circular, stone-walled enclosure, dates back to the Bronze Age and may have been a walled settlement; more recently it has been used as a livestock enclosure. Take a look inside the entrance to see the large seat known as the Judge's Chair.

WALK 11 – THE STEPPING STONES WALK

The Judge's Chair at Dunnabridge Pound

After 850 metres there are two fenced enclosures on the right (SX 653 751). These are old engine shafts of the 19th-century Brimpts North tin mine.

Follow the outside wall of the pound clockwise (wall on your right) and pass through a gate to a signed junction. Bear right, following the track (bridleway to Laughter Hole Farm) north-eastwards for 1.5km (1 mile) to Bellever Forest. ◀ Keep ahead through the gate to a Y-junction (Walk 30 also follows this section) and fork right (bridleway) down to a track junction with gate ahead at Laughter Hole Farm. Turn right and immediately fork right on a narrower bridleway (Sherrill via Babeny) through the trees. Pass a wall and turn left down alongside this. Keep ahead through a gate and over a footbridge (over to the left is Laughter Hole House) to the **East Dart River** at Laughter Hole.

Carefully cross the river via the stepping stones at Laughter Hole. Keep ahead for 25 metres and then fork right (east-south-east) up a bridleway, later following a wall on the right. Go through a gate and continue along the enclosed track as it meanders downhill towards **Babeny**.

Stepping stones at Laughter Hole

Babeny Farm is one of Dartmoor's 'Ancient Tenements'. These are the oldest surviving farms on Dartmoor that are clustered around the East and West Dart Rivers. Other 'Ancient Tenements', which all date from the 13th and 14th centuries, include Dunnabridge, Brimpts, Huccaby, and Hexworthy.

Follow the signed route down past the farm buildings and turn left down the tarred track to the bridge over the Walla Brook – a great place to have a rest. Continue for 100 metres and turn right at a bridleway marker. Cross a small clapper bridge and follow the stream downhill for 150 metres to a junction. Turn right over a clapper bridge and then go left, following the stream on your left down to the East Dart River.

With care, cross via the stepping stones and turn left, following the river downstream. Go through a gate and

> Visit the Tin Mine Display, created by the Dartmoor Tinworking Research Group, to learn about tin mining in the area.

follow the bridleway as it swings right. Go through a gate beside a ruined house, known locally as Dolly's Cot, and continue across the field. Keep ahead up the track, passing gates on the way. On nearing **Brimpts Farm**, go through a gate and follow the signed track as it swings right through a gate and then swings left through another gate in front of a house. Continue along the track past the buildings. ◄

Bear right along the concrete track to a junction at the top of the rise. Bear right off the main track following a track through the trees to the road (B3357). With care, cross over and turn right along the verge for 100 metres to a junction (Hexworthy Cross) and turn left towards Hexworthy. Follow the lane for 850 metres (½ mile) passing **St Raphael's Church** (left) in the hamlet of Huccaby to reach Hexworthy Bridge over the West Dart River. ◄

> The small but interesting St Raphael's Church was built in 1869 as a combined chapel and schoolroom, and the pews are the original school desks.

Immediately after crossing the bridge, go right over a stone step stile beside the gate and follow the path (Dartmoor Way) up through the field. Cross a stile and continue through the next field to the far-right corner. Cross the wall and continue through the field towards **Hexworthy**. Go through gates at the farm to join a track and bear right between two thatched cottages; to visit the Forest Inn turn left along the track (soon becomes a lane) for 275 metres, then retrace your steps.

Follow the track uphill, cross the tarred drive (house to your right) and shortly bear right along the lane. Pass a cattle grid and continue downhill (on the left is a tin mining gert), then continue along the lane as it swings right (north) and passes a house (Wydemeet).

> A short walk along the track to the left at the bottom of the hill takes you to the site of the **Gobbett Tin Mine** (1836–74) which includes the remains of a blowing house and mill; there is also the portal of a tunnel used by Paignton Unitary District Council (PUDC 1929).

After crossing the bridge, fork right through a gate and follow the bridleway. Cross the **River Swincombe** via the stepping stones and continue northwards (river on your left). Cross another larger set of stepping stones across the **West Dart River** beside some trees. Continue northwards for 400 metres, keeping the river on your left before bearing right away from the river up through fields. Then follow the bridleway alongside the wall on your left up to the road. Cross over and turn left back to Dunnabridge Pound (on the right) and then retrace the outward route back to the car park.

WALK 12
Dartmeet figure-of-eight

Start/finish	Dartmeet car park on B3357 (SX 672 732)
Distance	13.25km (8¼ miles)
Ascent	450m
Time	4hrs
Terrain	Hilly walk on mostly paths and tracks; short sections on lanes, steep descent from Yar Tor and two crossings of West Dart River via stepping stones
Maps	OS Explorer OL28
Refreshments	At the Chalet café at Dartmeet
Public transport	None
Note	The southern loop involves two river crossings via stepping stones; do not attempt after heavy rain or if the river is flooded

Head to Dartmeet for a figure-of-eight walk that offers views, river crossings via stepping stones and a tearoom. If required, the walk can easily be split into two shorter walks. The shorter southern loop meanders through farmland and moor, crossing the West Dart River via two sets of stepping stones and taking in a visit of Combestone Tor. After arriving back at Dartmeet the northern loop heads upstream alongside the East Dart River to Sherwell before heading up to the top of Corndon Tor. After passing a memorial cross the walk arrives at Yar Tor and then makes a steep descent back to Dartmeet.

WALKING ON DARTMOOR

WALK 12 – DARTMEET FIGURE-OF-EIGHT

Aptly named **Dartmeet** is where the East Dart and West Dart rivers meet to form the River Dart. Just upstream of the bridge are the remains of the old medieval clapper bridge; the present road bridge was built in 1792.

South loop

Exit the car park at Dartmeet and turn right up the road (B3357), crossing the bridge over the East Dart River. At the right-hand bend, fork left and follow the path between the buildings. Go through the gate and turn left down to the West Dart River. Carefully cross via the stepping stones and keep ahead through the trees. Continue alongside the left-hand boundary through two fields to a track with buildings to the left at **Combestone**. Keep ahead along the track for 375 metres to a signed junction before a gate and cattle grid. ▶

If you do not wish to visit Combestone Tor you can turn right (west) here along the signed bridleway to continue the main walk.

Stepping stones across the West Dart River

Keep ahead past the cattle grid and follow the track. Immediately after crossing the leat (Holne Moor Leat) turn left alongside it for 50 metres, then turn right up to **Combestone Tor** (crossing the disused Wheal Emma leat on the way). After admiring the views, head to the car park (SX 670 718) and turn right, parallel to the road for 125 metres. Then turn right down the track, cross the cattle grid and immediately turn left (west).

> **Combestone Tor** (350m) has views across the wooded Dart Valley with Yar Tor and Corndon Tor (both visited on the northern loop) to the north-north-east; to the north-north-west is Bellever Tor.

Follow the bridleway downhill, pass through a wall gap and keep ahead. Shortly before the next wall turn right, keeping the wall on your left. At the river, bear left across the O Brook and then carefully cross the West Dart River via the large stepping stones at Week Ford.

Bear right and then left (northwards) up away from the river. Go through a gate and bear half-right along the track. Go through a gate just before the farm buildings at **Huccaby**, turn left for 20 metres to a track junction and turn right. After 15 metres fork right, go through a gate (footpath and Dartmoor Way High Moor Link) and keep ahead (east-north-east) through the field (marker posts). Turn right through a gate at the corner, follow the wall on the right, cross a stile and continue down the enclosed route to gates at the end. Turn left through the first gate and head down across the field to a gate beside the lower house. Go through and continue between buildings, retracing your steps before turning right down the road (B3357) to **Dartmeet**, then turn left into the car park (the Dartmoor Way High Moor Link goes straight on).

North loop
Head to the back of the car park and take the signed path to the right of the entrance to Badgers Holt. Go through the gate and keep ahead through the trees, passing below and left of a house. At the end of the wall on your left

WALK 12 – DARTMEET FIGURE-OF-EIGHT

continue northwards, keeping the East Dart River on your left for 1.4km (slightly under a mile) to a stream (Walla Brook). Turn right alongside this, heading upstream. Ignore a junction and clapper bridge on the left (this is used by Walk 11) and continue uphill, soon crossing a small clapper bridge.

Turn right up the lane, heading away from Babeney for 600 metres to **Sherwell**, passing Rogues Roost (left), then Sherwell Farm (right). Just before the stone building on the left, turn hard left along a track (path). Follow the track slightly west of north for 500 metres. Do not go through the gate ahead but bear right following the wall on your left for a while and then continue to a minor road beside a track junction. Turn hard right (south) and follow a path up the ridge of Corndon Down. After 1.6km (1 mile) pass two large Bronze Age burial cairns and continue up to **Corndon Tor** passing a third cairn.

Corndon Tor (434m), the highest point on the walk, offers a great view: to the south is Sharp Tor; moving right is Ryder's Hill (south-south-west); Yar Tor (next stop on the walk) is to the west; Bellever Tor and Laughter Tor are west-north-west; to the

The Cave-Penney memorial cross

north-west is Sittaford Tor, with Hangingstone Hill and Whitehorse Hill beyond; then moving right again are Hamel Down (north-north-east), Chinkwell Tor (north-east) and Haytor Rocks (east-north-east).

Bear half-right downhill, passing a **memorial cross** to a minor road. ◄ Cross over and follow the path westwards up to **Yar Tor**.

> The Cave-Penney Cross was erected in memory of Lieutenant Evelyn Cave-Penney who was killed in action in Palestine in 1918.

Yar Tor (416m) like its slightly higher neighbour offers another great view, but this time it includes Corndon Tor (east). The remains of a prehistoric cairn have been modified to form a stone shelter.

After admiring the views from the summit take the narrow path heading south-west down the steep slope towards **Dartmeet**. At a junction at the base of the hill, with a stone wall ahead, turn left and retrace the outward route back to the car park.

WALK 13
Dart Valley via Bench Tor and Sharp Tor

Start/finish	New Bridge car park (SX 711 709)
Distance	18km (11¼ miles)
Ascent	670m
Time	5½ hrs
Terrain	A long walk on mostly paths and tracks with some sections of lane, woodland and open moor; one steep ascent and a river crossing using stepping stones (alternative given)
Maps	OS Explorer OL28
Refreshments	At the Chalet café at Dartmeet
Public transport	None
Note	Do not use the West Dart stepping stones if the river is in flood; alternative route described

WALK 13 – DART VALLEY VIA BENCH TOR AND SHARP TOR

From New Bridge the route follows the wooded River Dart valley upstream. After a quick detour to the tranquil waters of Sharrah Pool it's a rather steep climb out of the valley before heading to Bench Tor for a view over the wooded valley. The route then continues to Dartmeet via stepping stones if the West Dart River is not in flood. After passing the Coffin Stone it's off to Sharp Tor and then Mel Tor for more views over the wooded valley and beyond. After following Dr Blackall's Drive for a while, the route heads back down to New Bridge.

Exit the main car park and turn right over the 15th-century **New Bridge** crossing the River Dart, then turn right again at the lay-by. Cross the footbridge and go through the gate. Follow the signed path (Two Moors Way and Dartmoor Way High Moor Link) southwards through the wood, with the River Dart on the right. After 600 metres fork right at the split to continue along the valley path through Holne Woods for a further 2.5km (1½ miles), later crossing a stream with a small waterfall on the left (SX 698 708). Cross the stile at the stone wall and turn left (south-west). ▶

> To visit the picturesque Sharrah Pool (SX 697 716) keep ahead along the path as it zigzags down to the river, then retrace your steps and turn right just before the stile.

Tranquil Sharrah Pool on the River Dart

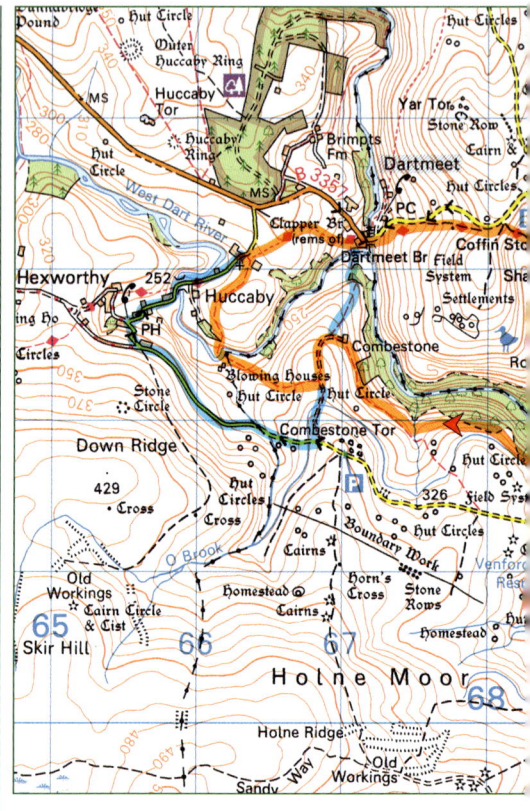

Follow the rather indistinct path steeply uphill, keeping the wall on your left (the way is quite steep here and requires care). On leaving the trees, keep ahead to a gate on the left and then bear right keeping the wall on your left. As the boundary falls away, keep ahead along the ridge to the summit of **Bench Tor**.

Bench Tor (312m) consists of several outcrops along the ridge. Views include the wooded Dart Valley, Yar Tor and Sharp Tor (north); the mast near

Walk 13 – Dart Valley via Bench Tor and Sharp Tor

Princetown (west-north-west); and Ryder's Hill (south-west) beyond Venford Reservoir.

Turn around and head back along the ridge before bearing right, heading south-west towards the reservoir. On joining the minor road turn right and follow it over the dam at **Venford Reservoir**. ▶ Once across, turn right following the boundary on your right (car park on the left). Keep ahead, following the path as it contours to the left and round the hill. Keep to the path through the

The reservoir, which was built to provide drinking water for Paignton, was completed in 1907.

trees, later dropping slightly to cross a clapper bridge over a stream, and continue along the path (north-west). Keep ahead with a wall on the left. Go through a gate and keep ahead through the narrow field, then go through another gate and continue between walls to Combestone Farm. Bear left up past the farmhouse (right) to a signed junction, where the surfaced track turns left; there are three choices from here depending on river conditions.

Alternative route via the Dartmeet stepping stones (only after drier weather)

Turn right (north-north-east) following the bridleway down the right-hand boundary through two fields. Continue northwards through the trees, keeping right (straight on) at a split to reach the West Dart River. Carefully cross via the stepping stones, keep ahead to a signed junction and turn right through the gate. Head past the buildings and turn right down the road (B3357) to **Dartmeet** (reduces walk by 2km/1¼ miles and minus 80m ascent).

Main route via Week Ford Stepping Stones

To continue via Week Ford Stepping Stones turn left (south-south-west) along the track for 375 metres to a signed junction before a gate and cattle grid. ◄ Turn right and follow the bridleway downhill, passing through a wall gap. Keep ahead and shortly before the next wall turn right, keeping the wall on your left. At the river, bear left across the O Brook and then carefully cross the West Dart River via the large stepping stones at Week Ford. Bear right and then left (northwards) up away from the river. Go through a gate and bear half-right along the track. Go through a gate just before the farm buildings, turn left for 20 metres to a track junction, then turn right. ◄ After 15 metres fork right, go through a gate (footpath and Dartmoor Way) and keep ahead (east-north-east) through the field (marker posts). Turn right through the gate at the corner of the field then follow the wall on the right, crossing a stile and continuing down

The route straight ahead along the track is the alternative route via Hexworthy Bridge (see later).

The route via Hexworthy Bridge joins here and turns left.

the enclosed route to gates at the end. Turn left through the first gate and head down across the field to a gate beside the lower house. Go through the gate and continue between buildings before turning right down the road (B3357) to the River Dart and **Dartmeet**.

> Aptly named **Dartmeet** is where the East Dart and West Dart meet to form the River Dart. Just upstream of the bridge are the remains of the old medieval clapper bridge; the present road bridge was built in 1792. Just to the north café and car park.

Alternative route via Hexworthy Bridge (no stepping stones)
Keep ahead up the track and then turn right along the lane to a junction. Turn right down to the Forest Inn on your left and keep right down the lane. Cross Hexworthy Bridge and continue up past St Raphael's Church (see Walk 11) to reach Huccaby Farm. Turn right up the track to a junction with farm buildings ahead and go left to enter a field; now continue along the Week Ford route (see sidebar above) (adds 1.6km/1 mile and 30m ascent).

Main route (continuing from Dartmeet)
Keep ahead along the main road (B3357) past the cattle grid and then follow a path (Dartmoor Way–High Moor Link) on the right uphill, keeping parallel with the road. ▶ On reaching the car park at the top of the rise, turn right (east-south-east) downhill, aiming for **Sharp Tor**. Cross the boggy stream and continue up to the summit.

> **Sharp Tor** (380m), the highest point on the walk, offers a great view south over the wooded Dart Valley to Bench Tor; moving right is Venford Reservoir, then Ryder's Hill, the mast near Princetown (west), Yar Tor (north), then the dome of Hamel Down; to the east is the area around Haytor, Rippon Tor and Buckland Beacon.

On the way, pass a large stone split lengthways into two pieces. This is the Coffin Stone (SX 6774 7331), where the pallbearers would rest their coffins on route to Widecombe in the Moor.

Following the Dartmoor Way High Moor Link towards Sharp Tor

Head east down to the minor road and turn left for 250 metres, then fork right to continue alongside the wall on the right. Follow the enclosed track as it curves right to reach the open moor. Fork right, still following a wall on your right, and proceed to **Mel Tor**.

The summit rock of **Mel Tor** (346m), which offers similar views to those from Sharp Tor, has several small rock basins formed by localised weathering. Apparently, flaming cartwheels were rolled down to the river from here on Midsummer's Eve.

The drive was constructed in the late 19th century for Dr Blackall, owner of Spitchwick Manor, so that he could drive his horse and carriage along while enjoying the views.

Turn left (south-east) downhill to rejoin the track at a corner and keep ahead, following Dr Blackall's Drive (Dartmoor Way and Two Moors Way) for 1.5km (1 mile), keeping right at a split just before Aish Tor. ◄ As the track curves left and starts descending, fork right (south) on a narrow path down through the gorse. On approaching a wall, bear right, keeping the boundary on the left, and continue to a junction with a wide, level track. Turn left along this track for 800 metres to join a minor road and turn right back to the car park.

WALK 14
Ryder's Hill and Snowdon

Start/finish	Holne village hall (SX 706 695); on-street parking available, or park at village hall
Distance	13.25km (8¼ miles)
Ascent	490m
Time	4hrs
Terrain	Paths, tracks and lanes; the high-level open moor section over Ryder's Hill has indistinct paths, can be rather wet underfoot and requires good navigation in low visibility
Maps	OS Explorer OL28
Refreshments	Church House Inn (01364 631160) and Community Shop and Tearoom (01364 631188) in Holne; the Tradesmans Arms (01364 631206) in Scorriton
Public transport	None

From Holne the route follows a lane to Michelcombe and then continues along the Sandy Way up Holne Ridge before turning south-west to the top of Ryder's Hill – the highest top in southern Dartmoor. From here it's a wander over the open moor to Snowdon and then on to Pupers Hill. Here the route turns east and soon follows the Two Moors Way all the way back to Holne passing through Scorriton on the way.

At the village hall stand looking at the church and turn right past the Church House Inn (left) to a staggered crossroads. Turn left for 25 metres, then turn left again, passing behind the pub, and follow the track as it swings right to its end. Turn left through the gate and follow the path through the churchyard. Leave through a gate on the right, head south-west across the field and then along the enclosed path to a road junction. Go straight on (west-south-west) along the lane for 900 metres to **Michelcombe**. Immediately after crossing the bridge, turn right and then keep ahead (west) up the track (bridleway) for 900 metres.

HOLNE

The village of Holne huddles round the Church of St Mary the Virgin, which dates from the 13th century. Head inside to see the magnificent early-16th-century carved pulpit and rood screen painted with images of saints; in the churchyard is a yew tree that is reputedly over 1000 years old. The village is also home to the Church House Inn and a community-run shop and tearoom.

Part of the painted rood screen inside the Church of St Mary the Virgin, Holne

Go through a gate at the top on to the open moor where the route splits. Keep ahead (west-north-west), soon crossing the clapper bridge over the disused Wheal Emma Leat, and continue uphill for 800 metres, following the Sandy Way to a junction near some **Bronze Age burial cairns** (low grassy mounds).

Turn left (west) for 350 metres and then head slightly north of west (half-right) up Holne Ridge, passing some boundary stones and a lone hawthorn tree, with **old mine workings** on the right. As the ground levels out, bear left

Summit of Ryder's Hill with a trig point and two boundary stones

(south-west), cross a gert (old mine working) and continue to cross two more gerts, 30 metres apart. Here the way splits; fork left (straight on) heading south-west for 800 metres (½ mile) to the top of **Ryder's Hill**.

Ryder's Hill, at 515m, is the highest top in southern Dartmoor, although it is a fairly featureless dome, crowned with the remains of a burial cairn, a trig point and two boundary stones. The smaller boundary stone is inscribed with an 'H' for Holne, while the taller stone, known as Petre's Bound Stone, is inscribed with a 'B' for Buckfastleigh. The high vantage point offers good views: looking south is Eastern White Barrow, then moving right is the conical-shaped hill at Red Lake (south-west), then the mast near Princetown (west-north-west); swinging round to the north-north-east is Hamel Down, then Haytor Rocks (north-east); to the south-east is Snowdon (next stop on the walk).

From Ryder's Hill there are a number of routes radiating out; take the one heading slightly east of south-east over fairly level, but rather wet, ground passing to the left of Wellabrook Girt (old tin workings) to the cairn on the summit of **Snowdon**.

Snowdon (495m) offers a good view similar to that from Ryder's Hill. On the summit are the remains of some Bronze Age burial cairns arranged in a north–south alignment, with the largest one being the most southerly.

Looking back (north-westwards) from Pupers Hill to Snowdon and Ryder's Hill

Like on Ryder's Hill, there are a number of paths visible from here; take the one southwards past the cairns and then head south-south-east to **Pupers Hill** (467m), passing the small tor of Outer Pupers to reach the cairn on the summit. ▶ From the cairn turn left (east) to reach the rocks at Inner Pupers. Continue eastwards down the grassy path towards **Lud Gate** for 475 metres, admiring the views ahead towards the coast at Teignmouth. At the cross-junction (SX 680 673) turn left (north-north-east), following the Two Moors Way down to the valley. Cross the footbridge over the River Mardle at Chalk Ford and bear right. The walk now follows the Two Moors Way back to Holne.

Go through a gate and follow the enclosed track before going through another gate. Now continue down the track for 1.7km (1 mile) to a junction in **Scorriton**. ▶ Turn right and, at the next junction, beside the small War Memorial and seats on the right, turn left down the lane for 400 metres to a T-junction. Turn left (Holne direction) along the lane, crossing the bridge over the Holy Brook to a right-hand bend and fork left (straight on) up the track. On reaching a lane, keep ahead (right) to a junction and fork right back to the village hall passing the shop and tearoom on the way.

Pupers Hill consists of three outcrops: Outer Pupers, Pupers Rock and Inner Pupers. From here there is a good view north-westwards back to Snowdon and Ryder's Hill.

Forty metres to the left is the Tradesmans Arms pub.

WALK 15
River Avon and Eastern White Barrow

Start/finish	Shipley Bridge car park (SX 680 628)
Distance	12km (7½ miles)
Ascent	315m
Time	3½hrs
Terrain	Paths and tracks; some sections over the high moor can be wet and are rather indistinct, requiring careful navigation in low visibility
Maps	OS Explorer OL28 (Dartmoor)
Refreshments	Occasional catering van at the car park; other options available off route at South Brent
Public transport	None

The walk follows the Dartmoor Way up alongside the River Avon to the Avon Dam Reservoir before heading along the Abbot's Way, still following the River Avon. After passing the Huntingdon Cross the route continues along the Two Moors Way for a while before crossing a picturesque clapper bridge. The river is now left behind to arrive at Crossways, where a detour can be made to Red Lake. The route continues to Western White Barrow and Petre's Cross, before crossing the open moorland to the distinctive outline of Eastern White Barrow. The final leg follows the course of the Zeal Tramway back down towards Shipley Bridge.

From the back of the car park at Shipley Bridge follow the path northwards past the toilets and then bear left (straight on) along the access road towards the Avon Dam Reservoir, with the River Avon on the right. ◄ At the junction beside a large boulder known as the **Hunters' Stone** (memorial to former Masters of the Dartmoor Foxhounds), keep ahead alongside the River Avon; the river (also known as the River Aune) rises in mires near Ryder's Hill and flows south for 41km (25 miles) to the coast at Bigbury-on-Sea.

On the west side of the car park are the remains of a 19th-century works where naphtha was extracted from peat, the building was later used in the clay industry.

WALK 15 – RIVER AVON AND EASTERN WHITE BARROW

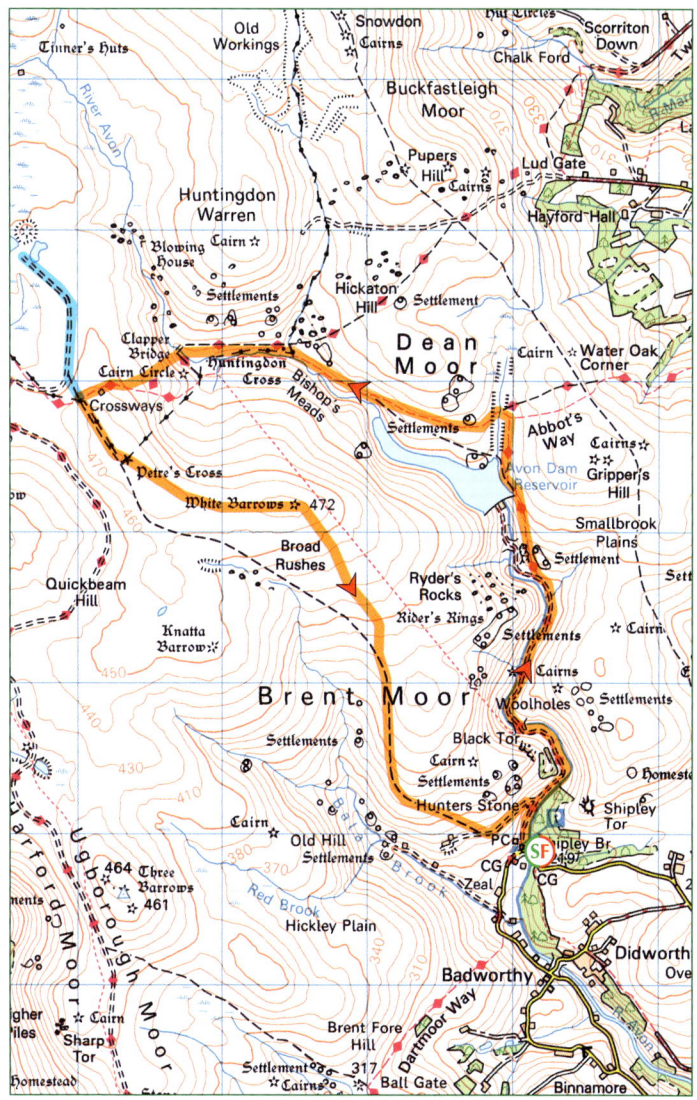

The Avon Dam Reservoir

Constructed in 1957, the reservoir provides water for the South Hams and Torbay regions.

The Abbot's Way (37km/23 miles) runs across Dartmoor's remote moorland, from Buckfast Abbey in the east to the ruins of Tavistock Abbey in the west.

Later pass a gate and then the ruins (left) of the former Brent Moor Manor. Keep to the access road as it crosses a bridge and continues with the river on the left for 1.2km (¾ mile) to a junction. Fork right and follow the stony track up to the dam. ◄

Keep ahead on a path with the reservoir on the left for a while and then continue with Brockhill Stream on the left (this area can be wet) to a junction with the Abbot's Way. ◄ Turn left across the stream (no bridge) and follow the good bridleway south-west and then west, soon with views ahead along the valley. Leave the reservoir behind and continue along the valley. Cross a clapper bridge over the Western Wella Brook to reach the **Huntingdon Cross** beside a stone wall. The Two Moors Way joins from the right.

> **Huntingdon Cross** is believed to have been erected as a waymarker for the Abbot's Way (see sidebar). However, in the 16th century Sir William Petre used the cross – along with three others, including Petre's Cross at Western White Barrow (visited later in the walk), one on Three Barrows (virtually destroyed) and one at Buckland Ford (which has disappeared) – to mark the boundary of his Brent Manor, which he bought following the dissolution of Buckfast Abbey.

WALK 15 – RIVER AVON AND EASTERN WHITE BARROW

Looking back across the clapper bridge over the River Avon – a great place for a rest

Continue past the wall, still following the river valley (can be a bit wet) to reach a picturesque clapper bridge – a great place for a break. Turn left across the clapper bridge, crossing the River Avon, and head west-southwest straight uphill. Later the route levels out a bit and then bears right along a defined path, heading westwards and keeping a small building over to the left to reach a Two Moors Way marker stone (SX 650 659). Keep ahead for 50 metres to a junction at Crossways, then turn left.

Detour to Red Lake

At Crossways turn right for 150 metres to join a track and bear right (straight on) to the small conical hill beside Red Lake; retrace steps back to Crossways and go straight on to rejoin the main route (2.3km/1½ miles return).

Red Lake China Clay Works operated between 1910 and 1932, and the remains of the site includes water-filled pits, a conical shaped spoil heap and

103

various ruins. The clay was transported in water along pipes to settling tanks near Crossways, before being sent via pipe down to the drying sheds at Bittaford.

Main route
Continue south-south-east up the path, keeping some spoil heaps on the left. ◀ At a split junction (SX 652 655), fork half-left on a path to the stone cairn and **Petre's Cross**.

Over to the right are the remains of settling tanks used for china clay extracted from Red Lake.

> **Petre's Cross** is another of the four crosses that were used by Sir William Petre (see earlier). The badly damaged cross sits among the remains of Western White Barrow, a Bronze Age cairn (burial mound).

From here the route continues south-eastwards and later east, passing some earthworks (tin workings) and following an indistinct, and at times rather wet, path aiming for the large cairn of Eastern White Barrow, marked as **White Barrows** on the map. ◀

For an easier alternative from Petre's Cross, retrace your steps and turn left to follow the old tramway route down to the Avon Filtration Station, missing out Eastern White Barrow.

> **White Barrows** is actually formed of two barrows: Eastern and Western (the latter was visited at Petre's Cross). Eastern White Barrow (where you are now) is a distinctive Bronze Age burial cairn consisting of a large circular stony mound, 26 metres in diameter with a secondary (more recent) cylindrical cairn situated on top (the combined effect makes it look a bit like a submarine). The cairn offers good views, including of East Devon and South Hams.

Looking eastwards (away from the path you used to approach the cairn), there are two paths. Take the right-hand one heading south-south-east downhill; soon you will see the old tramway which is the onwards route. Follow the vague path for 900 metres (½ mile) and then turn right (south) across the moor (no path) to join the old tramway and turn left. The walk now follows the course of the old tramway down to the Avon Filtration Station,

WALK 16 – OLD TRAMWAYS AND THREE BARROWS

later with a view of Brent Hill and a patchwork of hedge-lined fields ahead.

> The horse-drawn **Zeal Tor Tramway** was built around 1850 to transport peat cut from Red Lake Mire down to the naphtha works at Shipley Bridge; the tramway was later used by the Brent Moor Clay Company.

Turn left along the access track down to the junction passed earlier beside the Hunters' Stone and turn right, retracing the outward route back to the car park.

WALK 16
Old tramways and Three Barrows

Start/finish	Shipley Bridge car park (SX 680 628)
Distance	15.75km (9¾ miles)
Ascent	365m
Time	4½hrs
Terrain	Long walk on paths and tracks; the section between Three Barrows and Ball Gate is rather indistinct; some high-level open moor sections require navigation in low visibility
Maps	OS Explorer OL28 (Dartmoor)
Refreshments	Occasional catering van at the car park; other options available off route at South Brent
Public transport	None

From Shipley Bridge the walk follows the course of the former Zeal Tor Tramway up over Brent Moor, soon passing Petre's Cross and joining up with the Two Moors Way. The route then follows the path of an old tramway southwards over Quickbeam Hill, with distant views of the coast and Plymouth, before a quick trip up to the top of Three Barrows for a better view. The final leg heads over Wacka Tor and Brent Fore Hill before heading down to Ball Gate and following the Dartmoor Way back to Shipley Bridge.

Walking on Dartmoor

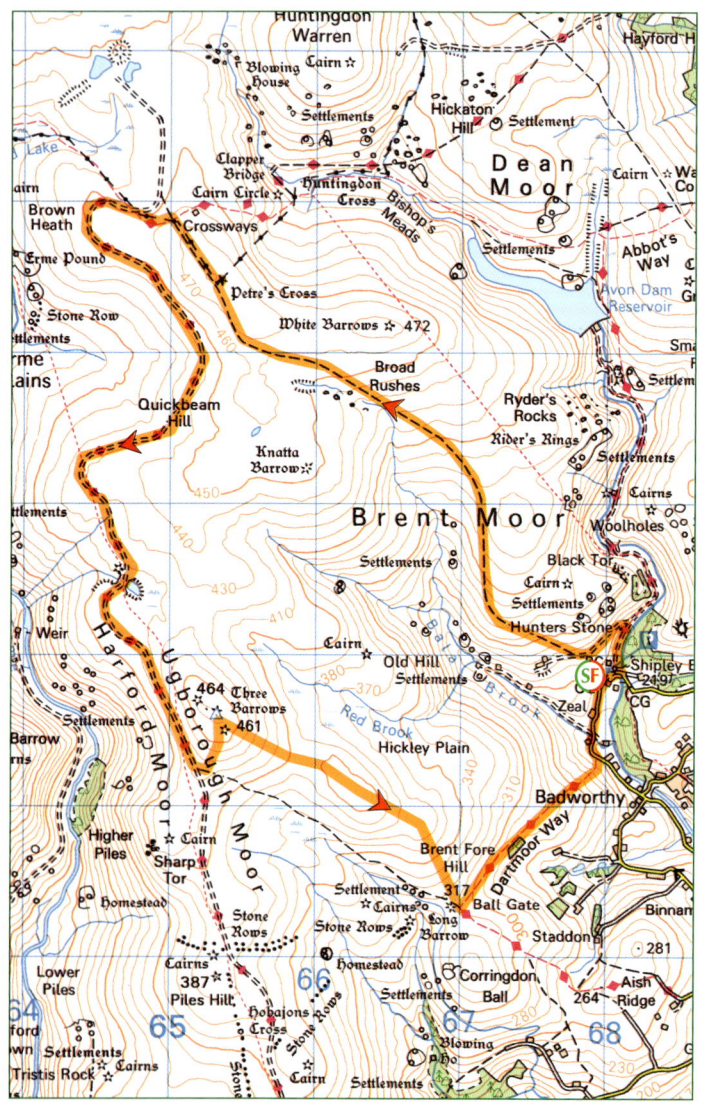

WALK 16 – OLD TRAMWAYS AND THREE BARROWS

From the back of the car park at Shipley Bridge follow the path northwards past the toilets and then bear left (straight on) along the access road towards the Avon Dam Reservoir, with the River Avon on the right. ▶ At a junction, beside a large boulder – the **Hunters' Stone** (a memorial to former Masters of the Dartmoor Foxhounds) – turn hard left and follow the access road uphill.

Some 50 metres before the entrance to the Avon Filtration Station (private) fork half-right (west-north-west) following a boundary wall several metres over to the left (in the gorse bushes). At the wall corner, keep ahead following the course of the former Zeal Tor Tramway as it soon swings north up the western side of Brent Moor.

> The horse-drawn **Zeal Tor Tramway** was built around 1850 to transport peat cut from Red Lake Mire down to the naphtha works at Shipley Bridge; the tramway was later used by the Brent More Clay Company.

Later the route swings north-west and continues to climb. Pass a stone '2 mile' marker (SX 6609 6487) on the right, with Petre's Pit (site of an early clay works) and a stream over on the left. The old tramway route levels out and swings right (crossing a ditch line or reave), heading north-north-west and passing just left of a boundary stone; Plymouth can be seen to the south-west beyond the rolling moors. Soon the route passes to the left of a cairn and **Petre's Cross** (Walk 15 also visits this point).

> Take a short detour to the right to visit **Petre's Cross**, one of four crosses that Sir William Petre had erected to mark the boundary of the Brent Manor that he bought following the dissolution of Buckfast Abbey. The badly damaged cross sits among the remains of Western White Barrow, a Bronze Age cairn (burial mound).

Continue north-north-west, aiming just to the right of the remains of old settling tanks used for china clay

---

On the west side of the car park are the remains of a 19th-century works where naphtha was extracted from peat. The building was later used in the clay industry.

The route straight on leads to Red Lake – see Walk 15 for details.

extracted from Red Lake, to a junction with the Two Moors Way at Crossways. ◀ Turn left (west) for 250 metres and then bear left (straight on) along the track; the route now follows the Two Moors Way along the fairly level track for 5.6km (3½ miles) round the side of **Quickbeam Hill**. After 4km (2½ miles) pass a large pond (Left Lake pond) on the left with a spoil heap on the right and cross the old bridge (SX 647 634).

> The track was the route of the 13km- (8 mile-) long **Red Lake Tramway**, a narrow gauge, steam-driven railway, built to transport supplies and workers between Bittaford and the clay works at Red Lake. The pond and spoil heap were the site of Left Lake China Clay Works, which operated between 1850 and 1858, and which was re-opened in 1922 for several years by the Red Lake China Works company. On Dartmoor a 'lake' is a short stream or brook.

Keep along the track for a further 1.6km (1 mile), passing below and right of Three Barrows to a faint path junction at a slight saddle (SX 651 622). Fork left (south-east) for 100 metres to a cross-path junction and turn left following the path up to the trig point on **Three Barrows** (461m).

> **Three Barrows** (464m), as the name suggests, is crowned by three Bronze Age cairns, or stone burial mounds, one of which is the largest on Dartmoor (roughly 40 metres in diameter and 2.5 metres high). The high vantage point offers a great view including Ugborough Beacon to the south and the coast at Plymouth to the south-west.

Stand at the trig point facing south-south-east (large cairn behind you) looking at the smaller cairn, and you will see three paths (the right-hand one was the route used on the way up). Ignore the middle one and take the left-hand path heading east-south-east downhill, passing

just left of the cairn. Then continue along the broad ridge to the outcrops of Wacka Tor (408m), passing an unfinished millstone beside the path on the way (SX 6607 6223). Keep ahead to Brent Fore Hill and then bear half-right (south-south-east) picking a suitable route down past boulders to **Ball Gate**.

The view looking south-east from Three Barrows – Wacka Tor (left) and Ugborough Beacon (right)

The rather large gateposts at **Ball Gate**, which look slightly out of place, are from the former Brent Manor. Some 70 metres west of Ball Gate are several large stones (SX 669 613); these are the remains of a Neolithic long barrow (burial mound), sometimes known as Corringdon Ball chambered tomb.

Do not go through the gate but turn left, now following the Dartmoor Way (bridleway) north-eastwards over the open moor, soon with a stone wall and Merrifield Plantation on the right; the route now follows the Dartmoor Way back to the start. Keep ahead between stone walls and then straight on to cross a stream (signpost), and after 60 metres go through a gate. Follow the stony, tree-shaded bridleway (Diamond Lane) downhill. Go through a gate and turn left along the lane, passing a house (Bala Brook) and later a farmhouse (Zeal), then head back to the car park.

WALK 17
Butterdon Hill, Ugborough Beacon and Sharp Tor

Start/finish	Ivybridge Railway Station (SX 647 565); parking at station or on-street parking along Coles Lane near Stowford Bridge
Distance	16.5km (10¼ miles) or 12km (7¾ miles)
Ascent	450m or 360m
Time	5hrs or 3½hrs
Terrain	A long walk over hilly, high-level open moor on tracks and paths; some paths are rather indistinct; good navigation required in low visibility
Maps	OS Explorer OL28
Refreshments	None on walk; several choices in Ivybridge
Public transport	Trains to Ivybridge Station; good bus links to Plymouth and Totnes

From Ivybridge the walk follows the Two Moors Ways and Dartmoor Way out on to the open moor before heading up Western Beacon, the first of several of Dartmoor's most southerly hills that are visited on the walk, which, incidentally, all offer great views. The route then heads over Butterdon Hill and Ugborough Beacon to arrive at Spurrell's Cross before continuing to Sharp Tor. The walk then heads south following part of an ancient stone row before visiting Hangershell Rock and following an old tramway for a while before heading back to the start. A shorter walk missing out Sharp Tor is also described.

From the top (north) end of the station car park stand facing the railway station and turn left along the tarred path/cycleway. Then continue along Coles Lane (pavement) for

Walk 17 – Butterdon Hill, Ugborough Beacon and Sharp Tor

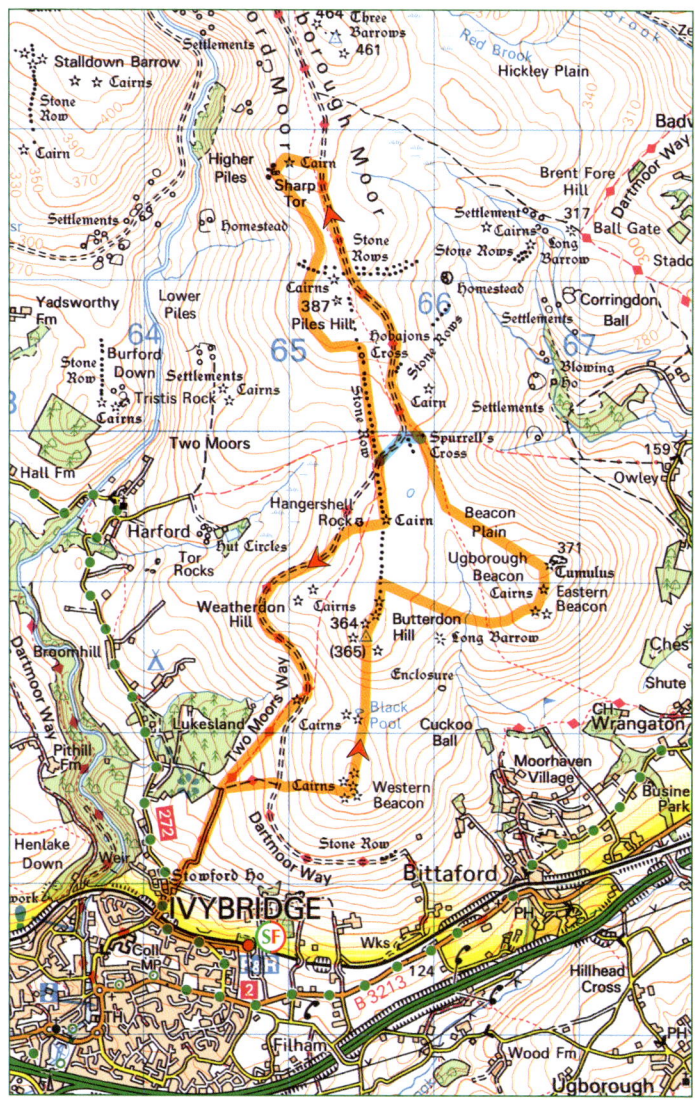

> From the summit of Dartmoor's most southerly top there are good views over the South Hams to the sea.

400 metres, passing the bus stop. Turn right at the junction (signed to Harford/Lukesland), cross Stowford Bridge over the railway and continue up the lane for 250 metres.

On reaching Stowford Farm (left), turn right along the enclosed track (bridleway) following the Two Moors Way and Dartmoor Way uphill. Go through the gate on to the open moor to a Y-junction. Take the right-hand fork heading eastwards up to the top of **Western Beacon** (334m), keeping ahead at a crossing track (route of the tramway to Redlake) on the way. ◀

Head northwards following a line of boundary stones to a col at **Black Pool**. Then keep ahead up to the trig point on **Butterdon Hill**, passing the Longstone – a taller than average boundary stone – on the way.

> On the summit of **Butterdon Hill** (365m) there are two large Bronze Age cairns and a few smaller ones; this also marks one end of the Butterdon Hill Stone Row (see later). Views include Penn Beacon, with Plymouth in the distance (west), Brent Moor and Three Barrows (north), and southwards to the coast.

From the trig point continue northwards along the line of stones for 350 metres to a cross junction (SX 656 590). Turn right following a rather indistinct path past a small pond, heading east-south-east down to Lud Brook (stream). Cross over and follow the path eastwards up the slope, passing just left of a cairn, and follow the path as it curves left (north) to the top of **Ugborough Beacon**.

> From the summit of **Ugborough Beacon** (371m) there are great views south over South Hams to the coast, then – moving clockwise – there are views of Western Beacon (south-west), Butterdon Hill (west), Stalldown Barrow (north-west) and Sharp Tor; Three Barrows and Brent Moor are to the north, while the distinctive outline of Brent Hill is to the east.

Head west-north-west slightly downhill across Beacon Plain to a junction with a good path and turn right, later

Looking north-east from Ugborough Beacon

passing just left of a cairn to reach a cross-junction with a bridleway at **Spurrell's Cross**. ▶ The cross-junction marks the point where you have to decide whether to opt for the shorter walk or continue with the longer walk. For the shorter walk turn left to a junction with a track and turn left along this for 250 metres. Then turn left (south) to rejoin the main walk following a stone row southwards; see the sidebar later in the route instructions.

To continue on the longer walk, head diagonally left (north-west) from Spurrell's Cross to a track and bear right (straight on) along this for 2km (1¼ miles), passing Glasscombe Ball (right) and Piles Hill (left). Once level with a cairn over to your left, turn left across the grass and continue past the cairn to **Sharp Tor**.

> The outcrop of **Sharp Tor** (414m) is a great place to sit for a while, looking west across the River Erme valley, with its ancient oak woodland (Piles Copse), past the domed outline of Stalldown Barrow to Plymouth Sound.

The weather-beaten wayside cross on the old monastic route between Buckfast Abbey and Plympton Priory is the only example on Dartmoor of a cross with spurred limbs, a design favoured in the 14th century.

Spurrell's Cross

The path follows the course of an old underground china clay transportation pipe and there are several metal-covered inspection hatches beside the path.

Facing west on the top of the rocks, turn left (south-south-east) downhill; you should be able to see the onward route. Soon follow a fairly level path as it contours round the west side of Piles Hill. ◄ Having passed Piles Hill the path curves to the left and reaches a **stone row** at right-angles to the path. Turn right following the stones, soon passing **Hobajons Cross**. Keep ahead at a cross-junction and cross straight over the stony track. The shorter route rejoins along the track from the left and turns left (south).

Butterdon Hill Stone Row is the second longest stone row on Dartmoor. The single line of fairly small stones, partly hidden in the vegetation, stretches for 2km (1¼ miles) between Butterdon Hill and Piles Hill and dates from the late Neolithic/early Bronze Age. **Hobajons Cross** is a small standing stone with a Greek-style cross carved on its western side.

Continue southwards up beside the stone row to a cairn and turn right to the small, but picturesque, tor of **Hangershell Rock**. Head diagonally left down to the track and bear left, following the track for 1.5km (1 mile) to a junction and a Two Moors Way marker stone (SX 651

582). Fork right (south-west) following the Two Moors Way down to a gate passed earlier in the walk and retrace the outward route back to the start.

> The track was originally the route of the 8-mile-long narrow gauge tramway – known locally as the **'Puffing Billy'** – built in 1911 to transport supplies and workers between Bittaford and the china clay works at Red Lake (see Walk 15).

WALK 18
Erme Valley and Stalldown Barrow

Start/finish	Ivybridge (SX 635 566); limited on-street parking along Station Road
Alt start/finish	Ivybridge Railway Station (SX 647 565)
Distance	17.75km (11 miles) or 21km (13 miles)
Ascent	460m or 500m
Time	5hrs or 6hrs
Terrain	Long walk on paths, tracks and lanes; high moor section over Stalldown and option to Stall Moor has indistinct paths that can be wet and that require good navigation in low visibility
Maps	OS Explorer OL28
Refreshments	Selection in Ivybridge
Public transport	Trains to Ivybridge Station (off route); good bus links to Plymouth and Paignton

From Ivybridge the walk heads north along the Erme valley passing Bronze Age settlements and Piles Copse which sits just across the River Erme. At Downing's House there is the option to continue to the stone circle and stone row on Stall Moor. Both routes then head up Stalldown Barrow, home to an impressive stone row, Hilson's House and a great view. The route then heads south over Hanger Down and Henlake Down on the way back to Ivybridge. An option to start from Ivybridge Railway Station is also described.

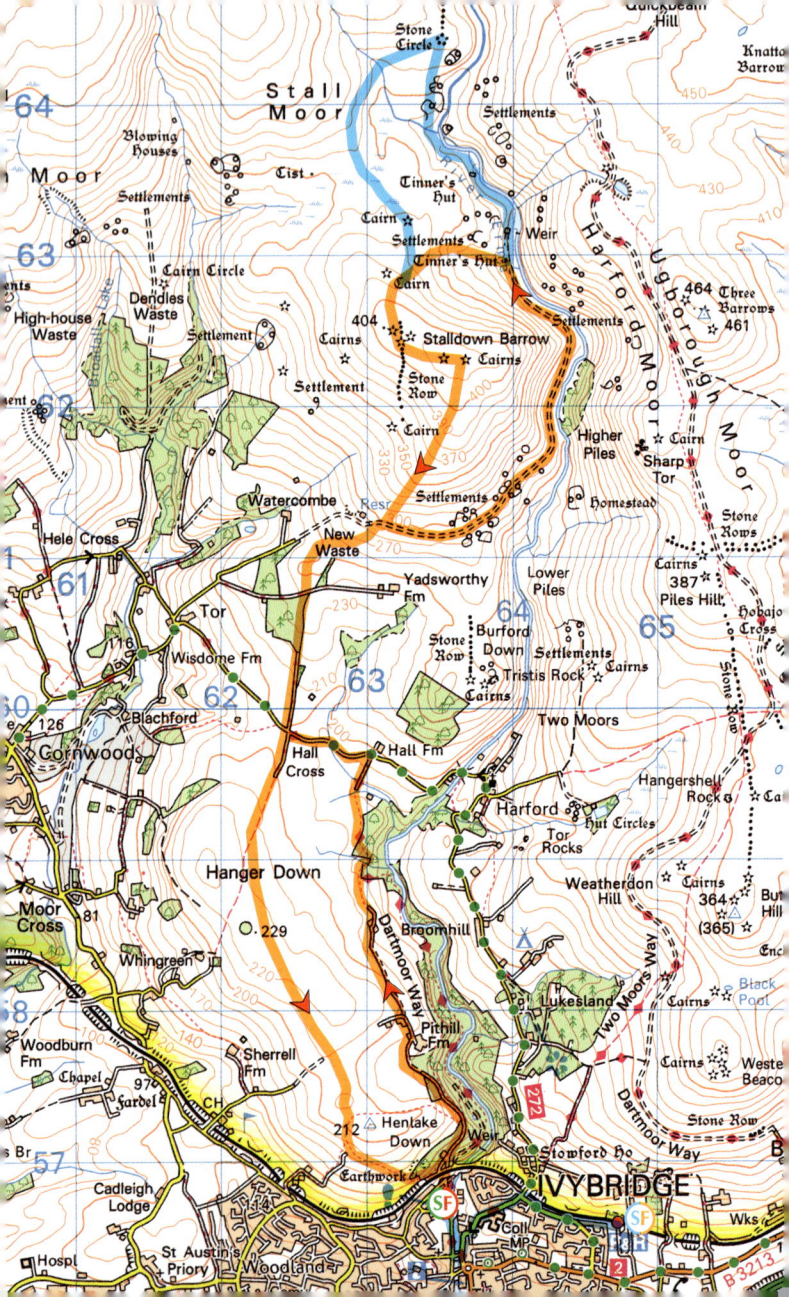

WALK 18 – ERME VALLEY AND STALLDOWN BARROW

To start from railway station
Exit the railway station (car park ahead) and turn right (west) along the combined foot and cycle path. Continue along Coles Lane to a junction on the right and turn left down Harford Road for 650 metres to a junction. Turn right over the bridge and then immediately turn right along Station Road. Adds 1.6km (1 mile) each way.

Main route
Head north along Station Road and pass under the viaduct. ▶ Continue up the lane (signed Hall Farm via Wilkey's Moor) for 1.2km (¾ mile) ignoring all side paths. Bear left to pass **Pithill Farm** and continue along the track passing some barns and going through several farm gates. Keep ahead through the field to the far-left corner; on the way views to the right include Butterdon Hill and Western Beacon. Go through the right-hand gate and follow the enclosed track down past a house and through more gates. Keep ahead across the field to a path junction and go through a gate; the Dartmoor Way joins from the right. Continue through the trees, bear left and go through a gate. Keep left and go through another gate into a field. Turn right along the field edge and continue through the next field heading diagonally right down to the corner of a stone wall; over to the right is King's Barn.

Follow the enclosed track to a lane opposite **Hall Farm** and turn left. Follow the lane westwards for 650 metres to a crossing track at **Hall Cross**. Turn right along the track (the Dartmoor Way goes straight on) and later keep ahead along the bridleway to a junction with a track; Yadsworthy Farm (private) is away to the right. Turn left along the track for 50 metres, then turn right through a gate onto the open access land of **New Waste**. Head north, then north-east and later east to pass to the right of the reservoir/water treatment works boundary; spot the clapper bridge near the boundary corner. Continue across open ground to the far-right corner and leave over a stile beside a gate in the stone wall. Keep ahead up to a track and turn right along this, later passing a large circular Bronze Age enclosure over on your right. ▶

The impressive viaduct was built in 1894. Beside it are the granite piers of Isambard Kingdom Brunel's original viaduct, which was built in 1848.

Up to the left is Stalldown Barrow, whilst ahead is Sharp Tor and Piles Hill on the opposite side of the River Erme.

Following the track up the Erme valley with Piles Copse on the opposite bank of the River Erme

Keep ahead along the track for 2km following the River Erme upstream. On the way there is a great view of Piles Copse on the opposite bank of the River Erme; Piles Copse is one of Dartmoor's three ancient oak woods – the others are Black-a-Tor Copse (Walk 36) and Wistman's Wood (Walk 26). Continue until you reach a stream (Downing's Brook) at **Downing's House** (marked 'tinner's hut' on the map). ◀ Here you have to decide whether or not to follow the extension to 'The Dancers' stone circle.

Extension to Stall Moor Stone Circle and Stone Row

Continue along the track to the weir and then follow a vague path along the valley, later crossing a stream and then crossing Bledge Brook. Continue northwards on a vague path through the long grass up to the **stone circle**. Turn left (west-south-west) picking a route through the grass (there is a vague path) and cross Bledge Brook at a ford (SX 631 642). Bear left on a path following a ditch on the right. Keep curving left, eventually heading south-south-east over flat ground, picking the best route past wet areas to reach a burial cairn. Now head south to rejoin the main route up **Stalldown Barrow** (see sidebar below).

Twenty metres to the left, on the north side of the stream, is a great example of a tinner's beehive hut – known as Downing's House – where the miners stored their tools.

The **stone circle** on Stall Moor, known as 'The Dancers', consists of 26 stones encircling the remains of a burial cairn. This marks the southern end of a late Neolithic stone row, said to be the longest in Britain, which heads north for 3.4km to a cairn on Green Hill. You can, if you want, follow the stone row northwards for 1.2km (¾ mile) to the point where it crosses the River Erme and then retrace your steps.

Main route

To continue the main walk, turn left (west) just after crossing Downing's Brook, following a vague path uphill as it slowly curves left, eventually heading south up to the stone row on Stalldown Barrow. ▶

The extension from The Dancer's Stone Circle rejoins from the right on the way (SX 632 628).

Stalldown Barrow (415m) has a number of interesting features, including several Bronze Age cairns and an impressive late Neolithic/early Bronze Age stone row with a north–south alignment running for 500 metres over the brow of the hill; the tallest stones are known as the 'Cornwood Maidens' and, from a distance, they look like walkers. To the east is Hillson's House; legend has it that an abandoned baby was found up here by a local farmer, the baby was named Hillson (son of the hill), and years later he built the small stone structure known as Hillson's House on the summit cairn. Views from here include the coast to the south; moving right are Plymouth Sound (south-west), Penn Beacon (west), Green Hill (north), Three Barrows (east) and Butterdon Hill (south-east).

Follow the stone row to the cairn circle and turn left (east) to a cairn and Hillson's House. ▶ From the cairn follow a path southwards downhill, later bearing slightly right (south-west) towards the water treatment works and reservoir, passing through the clitter on the way. Turn right along the track used earlier in the walk and shortly go left to the stile beside a gate in the wall. Retrace the

A great place to sit and admire the views.

Stalldown Stone Row

outward route diagonally right across New Waste. Pass the corner of the treatment works and continue south-west and then south across open ground to leave through a gate in the wall.

Turn left along the track towards Yadsworthy Farm for 50 metres, then turn right (south) along the enclosed bridleway and keep ahead to a lane at **Hall Cross**. Cross straight over the lane and continue along the enclosed track. Go through a gate and follow the bridleway slightly west of south for 350 metres before forking half-left (south) over Hanger Down passing to the left of Hanger Down Clump (copse). Keep to the right of a pond and head south-south-east along the side of the hill. Pass just left of a fenced reservoir; keep ahead as the boundaries close in. Go through a gate and follow the enclosed path to another gate. Follow the wide path down the right-hand side of **Henlake Down** as it curves left and continues down to a path junction. Go through the gate and follow the enclosed path downhill, passing under a small bridge to join the lane used earlier and turn right back to the start.

SOUTH-WEST

The impressive Hingston Hill or Down Tor cairn circle and stone row (Walk 22)

WALK 19
River Plym and Dewerstone Rock

Start/finish	Shaugh Bridge car park (SX 533 636)
Alt start/finish	Cadover Bridge car park (SX 554 645)
Distance	6.75km (4¼ miles)
Ascent	220m
Time	2hrs
Terrain	Lower-level paths, track and lanes; woodland and open moor
Maps	OS Explorer OL28 (Dartmoor)
Refreshments	The White Thorn pub (01752 839245) at Shaugh Prior (detour)
Public transport	Bus links from Plymouth to Shaugh Bridge

A half-day walk from Shaugh Bridge that meanders up through Dewerstone Wood before heading over Wigford Down to Cadover Bridge, passing an ancient cross on the way. After crossing the River Plym, the route follows part of the Dartmoor Way along the lovely wooded valley back to Shaugh Prior, with a view of the Dewerstone Rock on the way. A detour to Shaugh Prior, home to the White Thorn Inn, is also described.

Head to the far end of the car park with the old china clay buildings on your right, pass the National Trust map and information board, and head over the footbridge across the River Plym. ◄

> The river rises at Plym Head, south of Princetown, and is joined by the River Meavy just after the footbridge, before continuing southwards to Plymouth.

In the **car park** are the remains of china clay drying sheds or kilns, built between 1870 and 1895, but closed in 1952. The china clay, which was suspended in water, flowed along a pipe from the Wigford Down–Shaugh Lake clay pits (near Cadover Bridge) down to Shaugh Bridge, where it was dried for onward transportation (you'll see the pipe and some inspection chambers on the return

WALK 19 – RIVER PLYM AND DEWERSTONE ROCK

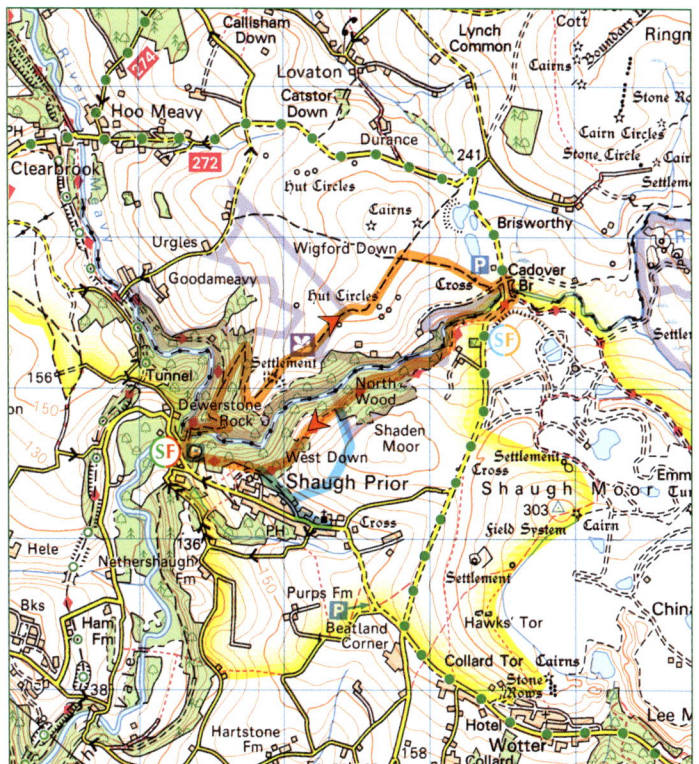

route). Up behind the drying sheds there are settling tanks (these are passed on the return route). The area just north of the footbridge was the site of a 19th-century brickworks and a Ferro-ceramic mine.

Keep right after the footbridge to follow the wide granite boulder path eastwards up through Dewerstone Wood. Follow this path as it swings sharp left and continues to rise. After 25 metres ignore a narrow path off to the right and keep ahead along the level track (originally a tramway for transporting granite from the nearby

WALKING ON DARTMOOR

The first part of the walk follows a stony path up through Dewerstone Wood

This was a cable-operated inclined tramway used to transport granite. The bolt holes are still visible in some of the granite sleepers, and at the top there is part of the old winding structure.

quarries) as it soon curves right past a large granite outcrop, and then continue for 250 metres to a Y-junction.

Fork right (north-north-east) up the straight track. ◄ Turn sharp right (south) and continue along the upper tramway track; look out for the large block of dressed granite abandoned beside the track. Continue past an old quarry and soon bear left (east) up to the outcrops on Dewerstone Hill (227m).

From the summit head north-eastwards (trees over to the right), then continue with a wall over on the right and the summit of **Wigford Down** over to the left (there are several parallel paths heading roughly in the same direction). Later, keep to the wall as it swings right (east-south-east) down to a **stone cross**. Cadover Cross – also

WALK 19 – RIVER PLYM AND DEWERSTONE ROCK

known as 'the Cross on Wigford Down' – was originally a marker for monks travelling between Plympton Priory and Tavistock Abbey; parts of the cross date from the 13th century, although it has since been repaired.

Keep ahead to a track, turn left to join a road and then turn right. Cross **Cadover Bridge** over the River Plym and keep right at the junction to enter a car park on the right (there is sometimes an ice cream van here). Continue through the car park to the western corner and follow the path through a gate; the walk now follows the Dartmoor Way back to Shaugh Bridge. Keep to the upper of several paths through the trees with the river to the right (this area is a great place for a sit or a lunch stop). ▶

Cross a stream and continue up a rise, now following the path higher above the river through North Wood (National Trust) to a stile, then cross over into West Wood (National Trust). Here there is the option of a pub visit in Shaugh Prior, or you can choose to continue with the walk. To continue the walk, keep ahead through open woodland, with views across the valley to the Dewerstone Rock, a rocky crag on the tree-covered slope which has inspired poets, artists and rock climbers. At this point, the path still follows the disused pipe, then passes some old tanks to reach a path junction near a house. ▶

Shaugh Prior detour

Having crossed the stile turn left (south) up past some trees and moss-covered boulders with a wall over to the left. Then bear right, keeping the boundary on your left; on the way up there is a view north-west of the Dewerstone Rock. Follow the narrow path downhill (with views of Plymouth ahead) to a gate and turn sharp left through it. Follow the path alongside the fence and go down some steps. Turn left along the track to the road and turn left again; the pub is on the right and the **church** is ahead on the left. Retrace your steps back down the road, turn right just after the village hall entrance and head back along the track used earlier. Near the end of the track go right up the steps and continue through the gate. Bear left through the trees to rejoin the main route and turn left (adds 1.2km/¾ mile).

The path follows the course of a pipe, which you can see in places, that conveyed china clay slurry from the Wigford Down–Shaugh Lake clay pits down to Shaugh Bridge.

The pub detour rejoins here from the left.

Shaugh Prior is home to the White Thorn Inn and a 15th-century church with an unusual dedication to St Edward, King and Martyr. Fourteen-year-old Edward succeeded his father Edgar as King of England in AD975. However, his reign was short-lived, and he was murdered in AD978; he was succeeded by his half-brother, Ethelred the Unready. At the east end of the village, 250 metres on from the pub, beside a road junction, there is a well-preserved medieval wayside cross.

Main route

To continue the walk, head towards a gate but do not go through it. Stay to the right of the fence and follow the path signed to Shaugh Bridge. Continue down through the trees to a fence, go through the gate and continue down past some disused settling tanks (part of the china clay works). Just before reaching the road ahead (with a house – Endomoor – opposite) bear right on a track past some ruins and go down the steps back the car park (alternatively turn right down the road back to the car park).

WALK 20

Drizzlecombe and Gutter Tor

Start/finish	Ringmoor Down (SX 558 666); parking area near Ringmoor Cottage
Alt start/finish	Gutter Tor car park (SX 578 672)
Distance	12km (7½ miles)
Ascent	300m
Time	3½hrs
Terrain	Paths and tracks over medium-level open moor, stream crossings; some sections require navigation in low visibility
Maps	OS Explorer OL28
Refreshments	None on route; The Royal Oak (01822 851924) at Meavy (2.5km off route)
Public transport	None

WALK 20 – DRIZZLECOMBE AND GUTTER TOR

This walk, to the east of Yelverton, visits a number of important Bronze Age sites including stone circles and rows. The walk also passes the atmospheric Ditsworthy Warren House – used in Steven Spielberg's film *War Horse* – and the ruins of Eylesbarrow Tin Mine, from where a short detour visits Eylesbarrow. For those seeking rocky tors and views, the walk visits Legis Tor, Higher Hartor Tor and Gutter Tor, all offering great views including Plymouth Sound and Bodmin Moor. If required, the walk can easily be split into two shorter walks by using the track between Ditsworthy and Gutter Tor car park.

Exit the car park beside Ringmoor Cottage and immediately double-back up the track, then cross a stile beside a gate (footpath sign). The route immediately splits; take the right-hand fork (the left-hand one is the return route). Follow the grassy track south and ignore all crossing routes as the track starts curving left following the contour of the hill, with Brisworthy Plantation over to the right. Continue round the slope, getting closer to a boundary on the right, then head east to the **stone circle**, with Legis Tor beyond.

Brisworthy Stone Circle

Bronze Age **Brisworthy Stone Circle** now consists of 24 stones, although originally there may have been over 40. The Ringmoor Cairn Circle is the remains of a burial cairn and the adjacent stone row, which also dates from the Bronze Age, is 350 metres long.

Turn left (north-north-west) slightly uphill to **Ringmoor cairn circle and stone row**. Now turn right and follow the grassy route east down to Legis Lake (stream). Cross the stream and keep ahead, soon following a boundary on the right for 300 metres, passing the remains of a farmstead on the way. Turn right through a gate and follow the path south to **Legis Tor** (310m). ◄

After admiring the views, turn around to face north and take the middle path diagonally right (north-east),

> The slope below the tor, which heads down to the River Plym, once formed part of a large rabbit warren.

leaving through another gate in the boundary wall. Here the path splits; take the middle route in the same direction (north-east) to a path junction beside a fence and gate on the right. Go through the gate and head diagonally left, heading east-north-east and then east, passing a wet area, to reach Ditsworthy Warren House (private). ▶

> A track to the north heads to Gutter Tor car park which can be used to shorten the walk if required.

> **Ditsworthy Warren House** dates from the 18th century and was inhabited by the keeper of Ditsworthy Warren, which was used to farm rabbits until it was abandoned in the 1940s. Film buffs might recognise the house, as it was used in Steven Spielberg's film *War Horse* (2010), complete with a temporary thatched roof.

Pass just to the left of the building and follow the track east and then north-east, with the River Plym some distance over to the right. Cross a stream and continue to the impressively large standing stone at the start of the first **stone row** at Drizzlecombe.

> **Drizzlecombe** consists of a number of impressive Bronze Age relics, including three stone rows, which include two very large standing stones and a large 22-metre-diameter burial cairn, known as the Giant's Basin. Further up there are more stone cairns and the remains of ancient enclosed settlements and hut circles.

Continue up beside the stones, passing the Giant's Basin (over to the right). Pass the impressive 4.2 metre-high standing stone, known as the 'Bone Stone', and follow the next stone row uphill, and then keep ahead to reach Higher Hartor Tor (415m). ▶ Head diagonally left (just east of north) on a grassy route to a stony track and turn left to a track junction surrounded by the **ruins of an old mine** on Eylesbarrow; the onward route keeps left down the track, or you can take a detour to the summit of Eylesbarrow.

> Views include Plymouth Sound, Cornwall, Sheeps Tor (west), Sharpitor and the distinctive outline of Brent Tor and its church (north-west).

Looking south-west from the ruins of Eylesbarrow Tin Mine with Gutter Tor in the distance on the left

The extensive remains of **Eylesbarrow Tin Mine** date from the early 19th century, although the area has been worked for tin for much longer. The site included two water-powered lifting wheels, a smelting house and at least 25 vertical shafts and several adits (horizontal shafts), which were cut to reach the tin lodes.

Extension to Eylesbarrow Hill

Turn sharp right up the track for 500 metres and then turn left across the grass, passing some old tin workings, to reach the two Bronze Age cairns on the summit of **Eylesbarrow** (454m). Also on the summit is a boundary stone with a flattened iron spike looking like a cobra's head. This is inscribed with "FB 1807" and "WB" and was used to mark the boundary between the Dartmoor Forest and the old manor of Walkhampton (sadly, this is a replica made in 2015). Views from up here include Plymouth Sound (south-west) and views west over Cornwall to Bodmin Moor, including the chimney on Kit Hill, the mast on Caradon Hill and distinctive Brent

Tor and its church; much nearer are Sheeps Tor, Leather Tor and Sharpitor, with the large mast near Princetown to the north. To return to the main route, retrace your steps to the junction and keep ahead (adds 1.5km/1 mile and 30m ascent).

Main route
To continue the main walk, follow the stony track south-westwards downhill for 2km (1¼ miles), keeping right at the split. Near the bottom, pass a stand of trees surrounding a building (Gutter Tor Refuge bunkhouse) on the left to reach a car park (SX 578 672 – alternative start). Turn left up a grassy path to a crossing track and keep ahead with a fence on right to reach the summit of **Gutter Tor**. ▶

The track to the left is from Ditsworthy.

> **Gutter Tor** (345m) consists of two main rock outcrops; atop the south-western tor is a good example of a rock basin with a drainage channel caused by localised weathering. The views from here are similar to those from Eylesbarrow Hill.

Go between the two rock outcrops and head diagonally right to the fence. Cross the stile and continue in the same direction to the trig point, which is maintained by the Dartmoor Search and Rescue Team. From here there are two clear routes across Ringmoor Down; take the right-hand one heading west, staying just left of ridgeline, ignoring all crossing routes and later aiming for the left edge of a small wood. Continue downhill, keeping the boundary and trees on the right, before crossing the stile back to the car park.

WALK 21
Burrator Reservoir, Meavy and Sheeps Tor

Start/finish	Burrator Reservoir Norsworthy Bridge car park (SX 569 693)
Distance	13.25km (8¼ miles) or 7.5km (4¾ miles)
Ascent	400m or 230m
Time	4hrs or 2¼hrs
Terrain	Decent paths and tracks, some lane walking, lower-level moor, fields and woodland
Maps	OS Explorer OL28
Refreshments	The Royal Oak (01822 851924) at Meavy
Public transport	Buses from Yelverton call at Meavy

From Norsworthy Bridge the walk heads west, skirting past Burrator Reservoir before crossing the dam. After following a disused railway the route heads down to picturesque Meavy with its village green, pub and church. From here it's off to Sheepstor via lanes and tracks passing the Marchant's Cross on the way. The next stop is Sheeps Tor for a great view, before heading back via Deancombe. A shorter walk missing out Meavy is also described.

From the car park turn left (south) along the road, following it as it swings right then passes Burrator Arboretum and Nature Reserve car park on the left. Follow the road for 250 metres and turn left along a track (bridleway), keeping right at a split. Go through a gate to a junction and turn right (bridleway to Sheepstor Village) as it contours round and below Sheeps Tor. Continue between the walls and follow the bridleway as it curves left (south), soon following a wall and trees on your right. Follow the bridleway as it swings right, go through a gate leaving the open moor and continue down to a road; here there is a choice to make.

Shorter route

Turn left along the road, keeping left at the junction to reach a junction beside the stone cross in **Sheepstor**, and keep ahead; the longer route joins from the right (see sidebar later).

Main route

Turn right along the road for 150 metres to the right-hand bend and turn left. Go through a gate and follow the track, with **Burrator Reservoir** on the right.

> **Burrator Reservoir**, completed in 1898, was built to supply water to Plymouth and has two dams: the larger Burrator Dam (over which the road travels)

and a smaller earth bank dam known as Sheepstor Dam.

Keep to the track as it swings right across the small dam, then fork right along a narrower tree-shaded path for 300 metres, keeping the reservoir on your right and a road over to the left. Turn left up the steps, go through a gate and turn right along the road across the dam to a junction. Turn right following the road for 275 metres to a small waterfall – actually an outflow from the Devonport Leat – and turn sharp left up the track (cycle path). After 275 metres turn right up some steps to another track (former railway) and turn left (southwards). ◄

> *This was site of the Burrator and Sheepstor Halt on the former branch line that ran between Yelverton and Princetown from 1883 to 1956.*

At the Y-junction, fork right along the level track (dismantled railway) for 750 metres as it curves right (west). Just before the trees ahead, turn left down a footpath. Cross the road and continue downhill, crossing a leat via a bridge. ◄ Go through a gate to a road and turn left then immediately right down the lane. At the junction in **Meavy** turn left, with the village green on the right. Continue to another junction and turn left.

> *This is the late 16th-century Drake's Leat (or Plymouth Leat), built to supply water to Plymouth.*

> The village green in **Meavy** is overlooked by an ancient oak tree (claimed to be around 900 years old), the village cross and the 500-year-old Royal Oak pub. Behind the pub stands the 15th-century St Peter's Church. There are a number of interesting roof bosses inside the Drake Chapel – named after Sir Francis Drake (1647–1718), a distant relative of Sir Francis Drake of Spanish Armada fame.

Follow the road eastwards to a junction. Turn right (Cadover direction) and, as the road swings left, go straight on to cross the River Meavy via the stepping stones (alternatively follow the road as it makes a loop over a bridge). Follow the road up to a junction beside the **Marchant's Cross**. ◄

> *The Marchant's Cross, a large 13th-century wayside cross, marks the junction of what, in medieval times, were important monastic routes.*

Turn left along the lane for 550 metres towards Yeo Farm. On reaching the entrance to **Yeo House** (left), turn right on a footpath, crossing two stiles and a footbridge.

WALK 21 – BURRATOR RESERVOIR, MEAVY AND SHEEPS TOR

Follow the left-hand fence (stream on the right) as it curves left to a stile. Follow the enclosed path to another stile, then continue up the track. Shortly before a field gate, fork left along a narrower enclosed route. Turn left up a ladder stile beside a tree and then follow the path north and east through Burrator Wood. Turn right through a boundary work, then left along the enclosed path, crossing a stile on the way. At the end go over a stone step stile and follow the left-hand field edge to the corner.

Go through a gate, keep ahead for a few metres and then head diagonally left down across the field towards a house. Leave through the gate and turn right along the track to a lane. Turn left to a T-junction in Sheepstor opposite a **medieval wayside cross** and turn right. ▶

The shorter walk rejoins from the left.

Sheepstor is home to the 15th-century St Leonard's Church. Go inside to see the fine early-20th-century wooden rood screen (sadly a copy of the original that was removed in 1861) and the carved oak bench-ends. In the churchyard are the tombs of three members of the Brooke family, who, between

Medieval wayside cross and St Leonard's Church at Sheepstor

them, ruled as Rajahs of Sarawak from 1841 until 1946; James Brooke was granted Sarawak (now part of Malaysia) and the title Rajah by the Sultan of Brunei in 1841. To visit the church take the path to the right behind the cross and go through the lych gate.

Follow the road as it soon swings left; on the left is the carved stone canopy of St Leonard's Well, although this is not the original location of the Holy Well. Follow the road as it swings right and continue to a junction. Turn left up the lane for 600 metres to a small parking area on the left, just before the trees on the right. Turn left, following the path northwards up past boulders towards **Sheeps Tor**, keeping right of the rocky outcrop (often used by climbers), and then bear left to the summit.

Sheeps Tor (369m) offers a great view: to the west is Burrator Reservoir, to the north is Leather Tor and Sharpitor, north-east there is Down Tor with the tall mast near Princetown in the distance, east is Eylesbarrow and south-east is Gutter Tor.

Looking west to Burrator Reservoir – from Sheeps Tor

From the top (with the reservoir behind you) head east down the slope towards the trees. Bear right alongside the stone wall, keeping the wall and trees on your left. Cross a stream and bear left before following a fence on the left. Go through a gate and follow the bridleway downhill. Cross the clapper bridge over the Narrator Brook and keep ahead to a junction. ▶ Turn left along the track for 1.2km (¾ mile) back to the start, passing the ruins of Middleworth Farm (left), which was abandoned in the early 20th century with the opening of the Burrator Reservoir.

> Just to the right along the track known as Deancombe Lane are the ruins of Deancombe Farm, first mentioned in 1381.

WALK 22

Down Tor, Nun's Cross and Fox Tor

Start/finish	Burrator Reservoir Norsworthy Bridge car park (SX 569 693)
Distance	15.25km (9½ miles) or 9.25km (5¾ miles)
Ascent	370m or 235m
Time	4½hrs or 2¾hrs
Terrain	Long walk on paths and tracks; sections across open high-level moor, especially Nun's Cross and Fox Tor area, require good navigation in low visibility and can be rather wet
Maps	OS Explorer OL28
Refreshments	None on the walk; The Burrator Inn (01822 600250) at Dousland and The Royal Oak (01822 851924) at Meavy – both off route
Public transport	None

From Norsworthy Bridge the walk heads east up to the top of Down Tor for a great view. Then it's off past a Bronze Age cairn circle and stone row to arrive at Nun's Cross – most likely Dartmoor's best-known cross. From here the route heads out to Fox Tor and visits Childe's Tomb with views over the infamous Foxtor Mires; for a shorter walk you can miss out this section. Next stop is Crazy Well Pool passing a couple of medieval crosses on the way before heading back down to Norsworthy Bridge.

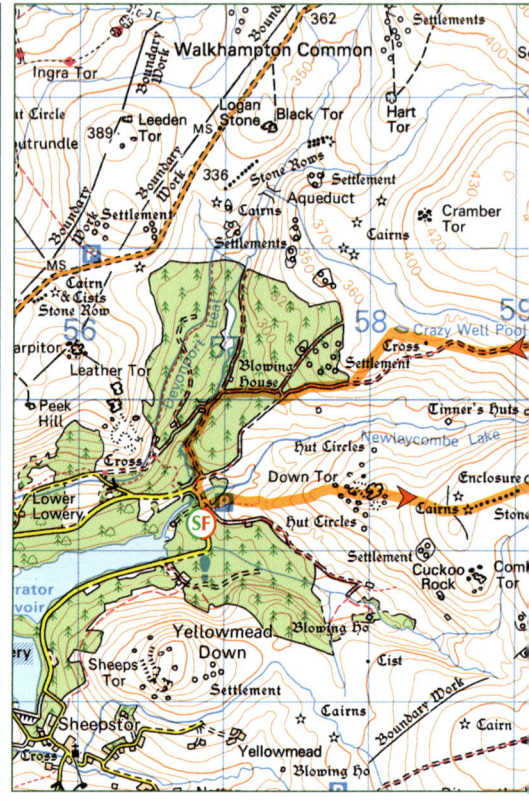

Take the track from the back of the car park heading south-east for a few metres and turn left through a gap in the boundary. Follow the path westwards up through several small fields passing through gaps in the old boundaries and continue up to the summit of **Down Tor**. Keep ahead past the outcrops and head east-south-east over open ground with a stone wall over to the right. Continue over a slight rise to reach a **cairn circle and stone row**.

WALK 22 – DOWN TOR, NUN'S CROSS AND FOX TOR

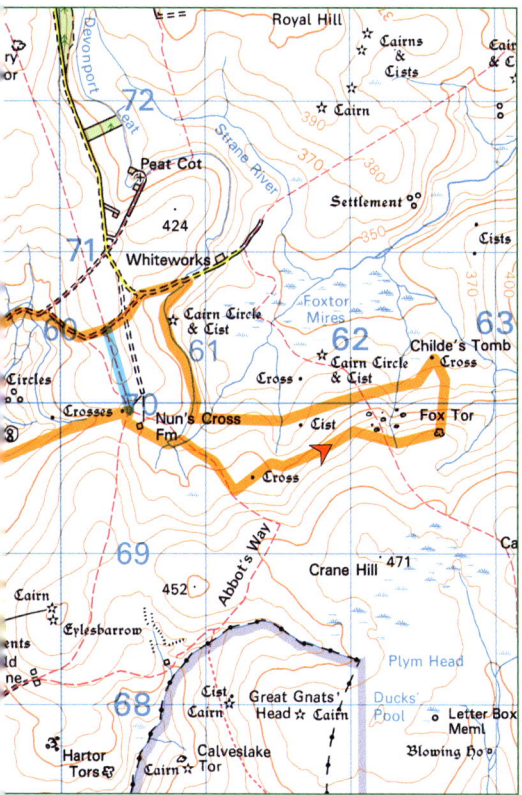

Down Tor (366m) offers some great views. Starting west and moving clockwise are Burrator Reservoir (west), Leather Tor and Sharpitor (north-west), then Norsworthy Plantation; to the east are the rounded summits near Nun's Cross, then Gutter Tor (south) and Sheeps Tor (south-west). Down Tor's impressive Bronze Age stone row – known as either Hingston Hill or Down Tor Stone Row – runs for about 350 metres and consists of over 150 stones. At the

The impressive Hingston Hill or Down Tor cairn circle and stone row

western end is a Bronze Age stone cairn circle and burial mound.

Head east-north-east alongside the stone row, passing a **Bronze Age burial cairn**; over to the left are the remains of a large circular stone enclosure. Continue in the same direction over the moor, aiming for the head of a slight valley. Pass to the right of a stone wall surrounding the Devonport Leat (see Walk 23 for information) in a dip where it emerges from a tunnel, and pass to the right of a ruined building and tree. Keep ahead past the old tin mine workings to a track beside a **stone cross** near Nun's Cross Farm and turn right (south). ◄

For the shorter walk missing out Fox Tor, turn left (north) up the track for 550 metres to a cross-junction and turn left to rejoin the main walk (if taking this route, continue reading from the second last paragraph of the route instructions).

The **cross**, known as Siward's or Nun's Cross, is one of the oldest crosses on Dartmoor and was first mentioned in 1240. The cross stands on the old monastic route between Buckfast Abbey and Tavistock Abbey. Nun's Cross Farm was built in 1870 by John Hooper and his wife who had leased the land from the Duchy of Cornwall. The farm was abandoned in the 1950s, although it is now used by a local school as a rustic bunkhouse.

WALK 22 – DOWN TOR, NUN'S CROSS AND FOX TOR

Follow the track southwards for 100 metres and just after the boundary on the left, turn left towards Nun's Cross Farm. Keep the boundary and building on your left. Cross a footbridge and continue, with the Devonport Leat on the left, to a junction with a bridleway beside a bridge. Turn right (south-east) up the bridleway for 550 metres to an old boundary bank; turn left (north-east) along this, soon passing a stone inscribed with a cross. At a path junction, turn right slightly uphill to Little Fox Tor and continue up to **Fox Tor**. Turn left (north) down the clitter slope, pass through a gateway in the wall and bear diagonally left to **Childe's Tomb**.

Fox Tor (438m) has views to the north-west over the infamous Foxtor Mires, said to have been the inspiration for the fictional Grimpen Mire in Sir Arthur Conan Doyle's Sherlock Holmes novel *The Hound of the Baskervilles*; Nun's Cross Farm is said to have inspired Merripit House. **Childe's Tomb** (reconstructed in the late 19th century) consists of a cross and granite pedestal base built over an ancient cist. A legend about the tomb talks of Childe the Hunter who perished at this spot after becoming lost in a snowstorm while out hunting.

Crazywell Cross on the way to Crazy Well Pool

Turn left and head back to the wall, then bear right alongside this for 1.6km (1 mile), crossing two streams before heading up to the Devonport Leat. ◄ Turn right alongside the leat to a minor road. Turn left along this for 325 metres and fork left at the marker-post following a bridleway slightly uphill. Keep ahead at a cross junction to reach another track junction and keep ahead again. The shortcut joins from the left.

At a gate in the wall on the left, a path diagonally right heads down to an old wayside cross (275 metres each way). This is known as Goldsmith's Cross, named after Lt Goldsmith who found the remains of the damaged cross here in 1903.

Follow the track as it curves right and then fork left to a junction with the Devonport Leat at Older Bridge. Keep ahead along the track; after 700 metres there is a stone cross some 50 metres over to the left. The medieval cross, known as Newleycombe Cross, is another of the crosses marking the ancient route between the abbeys at Tavistock and Buckfast. Continue along the track for a further 650 metres to a point where the track curves left and heads more steeply downhill, then fork right (straight on). Follow the level path slightly north of west, passing a stone cross on the way, to reach **Crazy Well Pool**. ◄

To miss out Crazy Well Pool just follow the main track downhill.

Crazy Well Pool, once thought to be bottomless, is actually the result of tin mining in the area. The nearby cross is another wayside marker on the monastic route between Tavistock and Buckfast. From here there is a good view ahead of Sharpitor, Leather Tor and Burrator Reservoir, with Sheeps Tor to the south-west.

Keep ahead (water on the right) to the western edge of the pool and bear left (south-south-west) down a path to rejoin the track and turn right. ◄ Follow the track westwards, with a plantation on the right, and turn right at the first track junction, then left at the next. Continue downhill, keeping ahead as a track joins from the right, and at the next junction beside Leather Tor Bridge keep left down the track with the river on your right. ◄ On reaching a T-junction turn right to the minor road at a bend and turn left back to the car park.

Anyone missing out Crazy Well Pool rejoins here.

A stile on the right (SX 5678 6959) gives access to the River Meavy and the ruins of a blowing house where tin ore was crushed and smelted.

WALK 23

Leeden Tor, Sharpitor and Leather Tor

Start/finish	Car park on B3212 below Leeden Hill (SX 560 708)
Distance	9.25km (5¾ miles)
Ascent	280m
Time	2¾hrs
Terrain	Short walk mostly on paths and tracks over open moor and through woodland alongside a leat; open moor sections may require navigation in bad visibility
Maps	OS Explorer OL28
Refreshments	None on walk; nearby at Princetown
Public transport	Buses between Tavistock and Yelverton stop at the car park

A fairly easy figure-of-eight walk visiting a number of tors offering some great views. The northern loop visits Leeden Tor and Ingra Tor, while the southern loop visits Sharpitor and Leather Tor, which stand high above Burrator Reservoir. The return route follows part of the lovely Devonport Leat through plantations before heading back to the start.

Northern loop

From the more westerly of the two adjacent car parks, stand with the B3212 and Sharpitor behind you and head north-north-east up a grassy path to a slight summit, passing a number of stone hut circles. Then head north to **Leeden Tor**. Continue to the most northerly outcrop and turn half-left (west-north-west) on a path down to **Ingra Tor**, keeping to the left side of the outcrop to avoid the former granite quarry which has some steep drops; take extra care in low visibility.

> **Leeden Tor** (389m) offers a great view. Starting in the west and moving clockwise is Cornwall, then Brent Tor and its church (north-west); nearer are Cox Tor, Merrivale Quarry and Great Staple Tor;

WALKING ON DARTMOOR

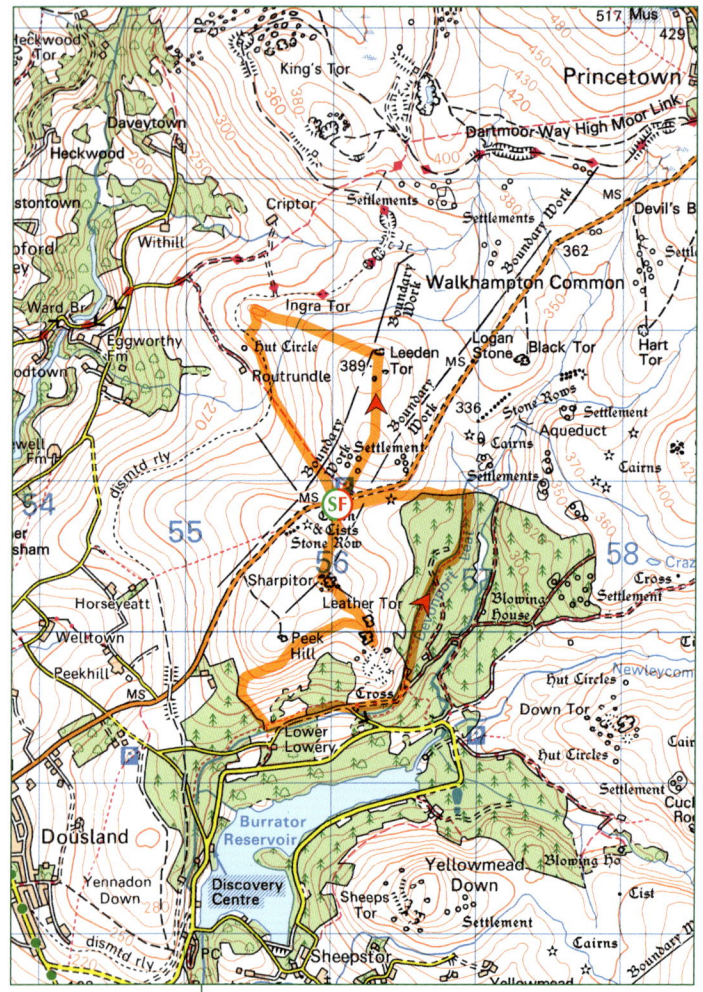

continuing round are Swelltor Quarry, Great Mis Tor and the mast near Princetown (north-east); to the south-east is Eylesbarrow, then Sharpitor

WALK 23 – LEEDEN TOR, SHARPITOR AND LEATHER TOR

(south), then round to the sea at Plymouth. Ingra Tor (339m) offers a similar view, with views to the north-west across the Walkham Valley to Sampford Spiney and Cornwall beyond.

On reaching Ingra Tor turn left (south-west) down to a track (former railway) and turn left for 400 metres. Shortly after the end of the left-hand fence, fork left (south-south-east) up a grassy route for 800 metres to arrive back at the car park.

The track was once part of **Princetown Railway** which ran from Princetown to Yelverton where it connected to the line between Plymouth and Tavistock; the line, which opened in 1883, closed in 1956. This superseded an earlier horse-drawn tramway – the Plymouth and Dartmoor Tramway – built for Sir Thomas Tyrwhitt to transport granite, which opened in 1823 and followed a similar route.

Southern loop
From the more westerly of the two car parks, cross over the B3212 and follow the grassy path slightly west of

Dartmoor ponies on Peek Hill

south up to the summit of **Sharpitor**. Bear left (south-east) following the line of the tor, and then continue straight on to **Leather Tor**.

> Views from **Sharpitor** (406m) include Leather Tor (south-east), Burrator Reservoir, Cornwall (west) and Leeden Tor (north). The rather dramatic, steep-sided Leather Tor (370m) gives a view back to Sharpitor and a better view over Burrator Reservoir.

After exploring the summit rocks – which are a bit exposed in places so care is required – head back to the start of the tor and turn left following the grassy path contouring round the hill, keeping left and below the summit of **Peek Hill** (400m). ◄ Continue passing just right of a rock outcrop and head towards the trees.

It's worth a short detour to the top of Peek Hill for another great view of Burrator Reservoir.

On reaching the plantation turn left, keeping the trees and a wall on the right down to a four-way junction with a footbridge ahead. Do not cross the footbridge but turn left (signed footpath to Cross Gate), soon passing through an oak wood. After passing through a boundary, bear right to a minor road and go left (straight on) along the road, heading east-north-east with Devonport Leat on the right for 400 metres.

> The 43km (27 mile) **Devonport Leat** was constructed between 1795 and 1802 to supply water to Plymouth Docks (later known as Devonport). The leat starts at a weir on the West Dart River (SX 608 779) to the north of Wistman's Wood and was supplemented with water from the Cowsic and the Blackbrook rivers. The leat now ends at Burrator Reservoir.

Just before the road curves right to cross the leat at Cross Gate, fork left (straight on) along a track keeping the leat on your right, passing some seats and a **stone cross**. At the split, fork right across the leat and immediately turn left following the path alongside the leat (now on your left) for 200 metres to a junction with a track. Keep ahead along the track (leat on left). Go through the gate and continue alongside the leat through Stanlake Plantation, always keeping the water on the left for 1.2km (¾ mile), ignoring all other routes, passing several stone footbridges, a memorial seat and crossing a stile on the way.

Leave the plantation through a gate and turn left to cross the leat. Head west keeping the stone wall a few metres to the left as it's a bit wet next to the wall. As the wall turns left go straight on following a vague track towards the B3212. Shortly before the road, fork left and continue parallel to the road before turning right across the road back to the car park.

WALK 24
Devonport Leat and Black Tor

Start/finish	Princetown National Park Visitor Centre (SX 590 734); adjacent car park
Distance	12.5km (7¾ miles)
Ascent	245m
Time	3½hrs
Terrain	Paths and tracks over open moor and alongside Devonport Leat; River Meavy crossing may be difficult after heavy rain
Maps	OS Explorer OL28
Refreshments	Several choices in Princetown
Public transport	Good bus connections from Princetown to Yelverton and Tavistock

From Princetown the walk heads to South Hessary Tor before continuing to Siward's or Nun's Cross, probably Dartmoor's best-known ancient cross. From here the route follows the Devonport Leat until it cascades down to cross a small aqueduct. Then it's off to Black Tor before passing a double stone row and cairn circle on the way to Hart Tor. From here it's a fairly easy walk back to Princetown.

PRINCETOWN

Princetown owes its existence to Thomas Tyrwhitt who had a vision of creating a settlement on the high moor. By the end of the 18th century he had established Tor Royal Farm, then in 1809 he came up with the idea of building a prison to house French, and later American, prisoners of war; HMP Dartmoor is still in use today. The Church of St Michael was built in the early 19th century, as was the former Duchy Hotel (now the Dartmoor Visitor Centre). It was here that Sir Arthur Conan Doyle stayed when he started writing his famous Sherlock Holmes story *The Hound of the Baskervilles*. Princetown is also home to England's highest brewery and a newly-built whisky distillery.

From the visitor centre in Princetown head over to the roundabout (junction of the B3357 and the B3212) and take the lane opposite, just left of the late 18th-century Plume of Feathers pub; to the left is the Fox Tor Café. Keep ahead along the track, go through the gate and follow the gravel path (bridleway) for 1.2km (¾ mile) to **South Hessary Tor**.

> **South Hessary Tor** (454m) is the highest point on the walk, with views including North Hessary Tor, with its large mast, to the north-west; to the south-west is Hart Tor, with Leeden Tor beyond; and to the left of this are Sharpitor and Leather Tor. On the summit is a small cobra-shaped metal boundary marker; there is another of these markers on Eylesbarrow (Walk 20).

Keep ahead along the gravel path for 2.5km (1½ miles) to a wayside cross near **Nun's Cross Farm** (see Walk 22 for information), passing some boundary stones on the way. ◀

The boundary stones, inscribed 'PCWW 1917', were erected by the Plymouth Corporation Water Works to mark the catchment area for the Burrator Reservoir.

Turn right and follow the path west-south-west past mine workings to reach a stone wall above the Devonport Leat (see Walk 23 for information) as it exits a tunnel, with a ruined building and a tree on the right. Keep to the right of the leat, pass a cross, and then continue alongside

WALK 24 – DEVONPORT LEAT AND BLACK TOR

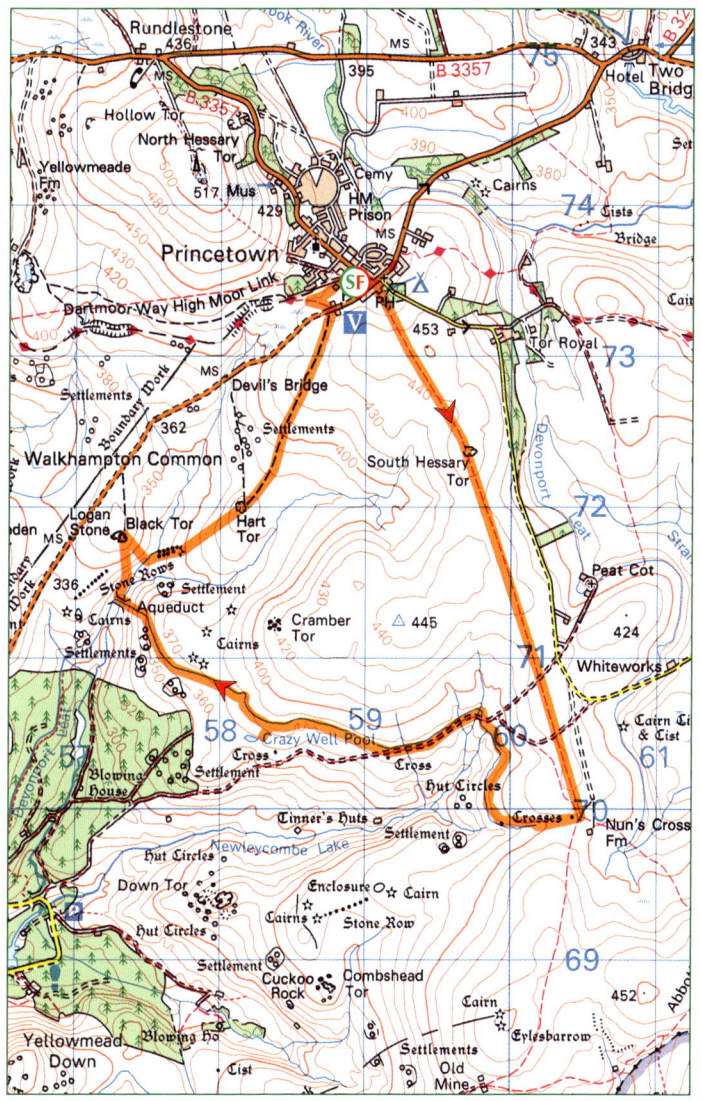

149

The Devonport Leat emerging from the tunnel – the walk stays on the right

The memorial cross, known as Hutchinson's Cross, was erected in 1968.

There is a path down either side of the leat, both of which may be boggy.

the leat on your left. ◀ On reaching a gravel track and bridge over the leat (Older Bridge) turn left across the leat then immediately turn right; the walk continues along the leat, which is now on your right, for 3.1km (2 miles). After 1.6km (1 mile) at a clapper bridge over the leat (SX 583 705) you can make a short 100-metre detour down to the left to visit **Crazy Well Pool** (see Walk 22) before returning to the leat and turning left.

The leat continues to descend as it curves round Raddick Hill. Cross over via one of the two stone slab footbridges and follow the leat as it cascades down a steep section. ◀ Continue over the aqueduct using the wooden walkway on the right-hand side of the leat, crossing over the River Meavy. Keep ahead to where the leat swings left and turn right on a path beside an old wall on your left. Dogleg left-right through the wall and continue to an old boundary, then fork left up to **Black Tor**.

From **Black Tor** (376m) there is a view south along the River Meavy towards Burrator Reservoir,

The small waterfall on the River Meavy below Black Tor – a great place for a rest

including Sharpitor and Leather Tor to the right and Sheeps Tor to the left. To the north is North Hessary Tor, crowned by the large mast, while slightly north of east is Hart Tor with South Hessary Tor beyond. Black Tor's northern outcrop has a large logan stone.

Turn right (south-east) down towards the River Meavy, aiming for a tree, to reach the small, but picturesque, Black Tor Waterfall (SX 5749 7165) beside the ruins of two blowing houses – a great place for a rest. ▶ Cross the River Meavy via the metal plank footbridge (care required after heavy rainfall) and turn left upstream (ruin on your right) to a track; to the left is a ford and another metal plank bridge that can be used to cross the river. Bear right to the **Hart Tor double stone row**. ▶

Continue alongside the stone row past the cairn circle and keep ahead up to **Hart Tor** (397m). From the tor there are several paths, take the wide grassy path heading north-north-east uphill, aiming just to the right of a plantation. On reaching the B3212 on the western edge

The water-powered tin smelting mills were where tin ore was crushed and smelted to extract the tin.

The stone row consists of 90 stones with a Bronze Age burial cairn circle at the eastern (upper) end.

151

of **Princetown**, cross the road and bear left along a gravel track (bridleway) to a junction. Turn right along the path with a fence on your left. Continue through a gate to join a lane near the Dartmoor Brewery and bear right past the fire station (right) to the car park on the right, with the visitor centre beyond. ◄

> Left along the B3357 is the Old Police Station Café and the Prince of Wales pub.

WALK 25
Great Mis Tor and Lich Way

Start/finish	Princetown National Park Visitor Centre (SX 590 734); parking nearby
Distance	21.25km (13¼ miles)
Ascent	540m
Time	6¼hrs
Terrain	Long walk over remote high-level moor requiring good navigation in low visibility; river and stream crossings may be impassable after heavy rainfall; paths indistinct at times and can be rather wet
Maps	OS Explorer OL28
Refreshments	Several choices in Princetown
Public transport	Good bus connections to Princetown from Exeter and Tavistock
Note	Part of the walk is within the Merrivale Range – check that it is open before walking; do not attempt river crossings after heavy rainfall

A fairly long roller-coaster walk with sections of remote moorland, river crossings, ancient sites and some lovely views. After leaving Princetown the first stop is North Hessary Tor with its rather large mast which can be seen from much of Dartmoor. Then it's off down past Rundlestone Tor before heading up to Great Mis Tor visiting Little Mis Tor on the way. After enjoying the views the route heads over Greena Ball and then down to cross the River Walkham before visiting the stone circle and standing stone on Langstone Moor. The walk then heads east along part of the Lich Way (often spelt Lych), fording a couple of streams before passing Lydford Tor to arrive at Beardown Tors. The final leg heads through fields back to Princetown.

WALK 25 – GREAT MIS TOR AND LICH WAY

From the visitor centre in Princetown (see Walk 24 for information) head west past the car park and, just before the fire station, fork right on a signed path through the trees. Cross over the Dartmoor Brewery access road, keep ahead along the lane and go through the gate on to the open moor. Now follow the path up alongside the right-hand boundary to **North Hessary Tor**.

North Hessary Tor (517m), which affords some great views, is home to a 196m-high mast that was built in 1955; the mast, which can be seen from much of Dartmoor, is an easily identifiable landmark in fine weather.

Continue north-north-west alongside the wall on the right, then keep ahead along the track for a while before forking left to Rundlestone Tor (500 metres to the west is Hollow Tor); ahead you can see Great Mis Tor. Continue

The Mistor Pan rock basin on Great Mis Tor

WALKING ON DARTMOOR

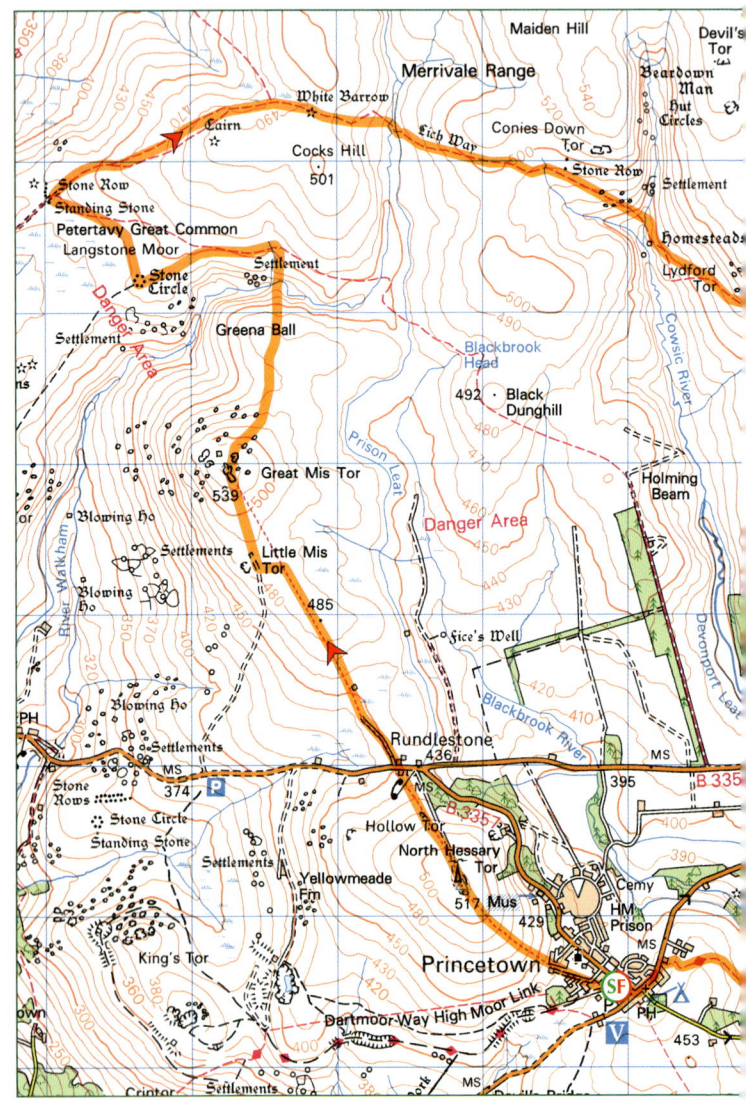

WALK 25 – GREAT MIS TOR AND LICH WAY

north-north-west down to a wall, cross the ladder stile and keep ahead through the fields to the B3357 at Rundlestone. Cross over and follow the enclosed track opposite, passing through a gate. After the left-hand wall turns left, keep ahead alongside the right-hand boundary for 800 metres before forking left to **Little Mis Tor** (482m). Turn right up to the top of **Great Mis Tor**; if the red flag is flying you must not proceed with the walk beyond this point.

Great Mis Tor (539m), a fairly large tor with a number of outcrops, offers great views: looking southeast is the mast passed earlier; moving clockwise are Leather Tor and Sharpitor, with Plymouth Sound in the distance; to the west are views across Cornwall, and just west of north are Great Links Tor and Fur Tor (north-north-east), then Higher White Tor, Beardown Tor (east) and, in the distance, Hamel Down. On the main outcrop, just north of the flagpole, is a fine example of a rock basin known as the Mistor Pan.

Head down past a military hut to enter the Merrivale Range and continue northwards over the flat summit of Greena Ball, keeping west (left) of the wet marshy ground of Mistor Marsh. Then descend to the River Walkham at Dead Lake Foot and, with care, cross via the boulders (that act like stepping stones) at SX 5660 2819, about 40 metres right of where the stream joins; if flooded, either abandon the walk or try crossing upstream just north of a ford at SX 573 782, or alternatively continue east and turn left along Prison Leat rejoining the walk near Sandy Ford. Once across the river head uphill for 250 metres with Dead Lake (stream) on your left to a bridleway and turn left. Ford the stream and continue westwards to a split (SX 5620 7840), fork left following an indistinct path first west and then west-south-west to a **stone circle**. Turn right (north) on a vague path as it curves left (anti-clockwise) – keeping to the right of Langstone Mire which should be avoided – to the **standing stone** with White Tor beyond.

> Langstone Moor has a number of late Neolithic and Bronze Age sites. The **stone circle**, sadly damaged during the Second World War, now has only 10 stones in situ. Some 200 metres to the south of the stone circle are the remains of a complex hut settlement comprising 35 hut circles, while to the north the 3m-high **standing stone**, or menhir, forms the southern end of an indistinct single stone row.

Turn sharp right (east-north-east) on a track (bridleway), soon following a wall on your left gently uphill. Where the wall turns left, keep ahead (east) along the bridleway to **White Barrow** on your right with Cocks Hill (501m) further south; the walk is now following the Lich Way.

> The **Lich Way**, which ran between Bellever and Lydford, was used by residents of the small farmsteads in the surrounding area so that they could bury their dead at Lydford parish church; the word 'lich' or 'lych' has its origins in Old English, meaning 'body'. White Barrow is a grass-covered Bronze Age burial cairn.

Continue downhill and, with care, cross the River Walkham at a ford (Sandy Ford); you may need to look upstream for a suitable crossing point. Then cross a stone

WALK 25 – GREAT MIS TOR AND LICH WAY

clapper bridge over the old Prison Leat and head over Conies Down. ▶ Continue downhill and, with care, cross the Cowsic River at Broad Hole (Traveller's Ford) before following the path up to a wall (200 metres downstream of the ford there are stepping stones across the Cowsic River (SX 5915 7840); further downstream at Holming Beam there is a footbridge (SX 594 770)). Go through the gate and follow the left-hand path south-eastwards uphill and pass just south of Lydford Tor (505m). (The tor is worth a quick detour for the views of the Beardown Tors.) Then bear half-right (south-eastwards) towards **Beardown Tors**.

The leat was built to supply water to the prison at Princetown. To the left of the path at SX 5857 7899 there are the indistinct remains of a double stone row.

Beardown Tors consists of three granite stacks: a northern one (507m), an eastern one with a military flagpole (511m) and a western one with military huts (512m) – see Walk 26 for more details.

Pass just right of the outcrop with the flagpole and continue southwards over flat, wet ground. Go through a gate and head down Beardown Hill. Continue along the track, passing between the plantations. Go through a gate and continue to a bridge over the Devonport

Take in a visit of Lydford Tor for a view of the three outcrops of the Beardown Tors

> The leat, which starts on the West Dart River to the north of Wistman's Wood, was constructed to supply water to Plymouth Docks (later known as Devonport).

Leat. ◄ Keep ahead and, just before **Beardown Farm**, turn right to a gate and stile. Follow the track as it soon swings left to a junction and turn right. Immediately after crossing the bridge over the Cowsic River turn right alongside the fence on the right. At the corner turn left, still following a fence on your right, then keep ahead through a gate to the B3357. To the left is Two Bridges (see Walk 26).

Turn right for 250 metres, crossing the leat and, at the slight bend, turn left across the road. Go through a gate and follow the signed bridleway across the field to a wall beside some trees. Go through the gate and across the field, soon crossing the leat again. Leave through a gate, cross over the road and go through the gate opposite. Continue through the trees and through another gate.

Bear half-left across the field, go through a gate and continue to a gateway in the far-right corner. Follow the bridleway and cross the footbridge over the Blackbrook River. Bear right to the wall, then bear right again following the wall on your left, heading west with the river on your right. Cross a footbridge, turn left through a gate and follow the path up towards a house (Batchelor's Hall). Go through a gate, bear right up the track and go through another gate. Keep ahead to a junction and turn right uphill. Cross a bridge over the Devonport Leat for a final time and go through a gate. Follow the track up alongside the left-hand boundary towards Princetown, go through a gate and continue along the track as it swings right and left. ◄ Go through a gate and turn left along the B3212, later passing the Fox Tor Café to the roundabout beside the **visitor centre** and the Plume of Feathers pub. Turn right (B3357) and then fork left back to the car park.

> There is a good view of the austere granite buildings of HMP Dartmoor, originally built in the early 19th century to house French prisoners of war.

WALK 26

Longaford Tor, Rough Tor and Beardown Tors

Start/finish	Two Bridges car park on B3357 (SX 609 750)
Distance	13.25km (8¼ miles) or 14.25km (9 mile)
Ascent	340m or 350m
Time	4hrs or 4¼hrs
Terrain	Tracks and paths; high, open moor sections with indistinct paths can be wet and require navigation in low visibility; stream crossing may be difficult after rainfall
Maps	OS Explorer OL28
Refreshments	Two Bridges Hotel (01822 892300) at Two Bridges
Public transport	Buses between Newton Abbot and Tavistock stop at Two Bridges
Note	The extension to Devil's Tor lies within the Merrivale Firing Range – check before walking this part

From Two Bridges the route heads north towards Wistman's Wood before continuing along a broad ridge passing Littaford Tor, Longaford Tor and Higher White Tor. A wet section then leads to the ruins of Brown's House before crossing the infant East Dart River to arrive at Rough Tor. From here you can either take an extension into the firing range to visit Devil's Tor and the Beardown Man or head down past Crow Tor. Both routes then head to Beardown Tors before following the tranquil Devonport Leat for a while on the way back to Two Bridges.

TWO BRIDGES

Two Bridges, home to the late 18th-century Two Bridges Hotel, is probably named after the two 18th-century bridges that were built here over the West Dart and Cowsic rivers. These were later replaced with a single bridge downstream; however, in the 1930s another bridge was built just upstream, so Two Bridges still lives up to its name.

From the car park follow the track northwards through the gate heading away from the road. Pass a house and

WALKING ON DARTMOOR

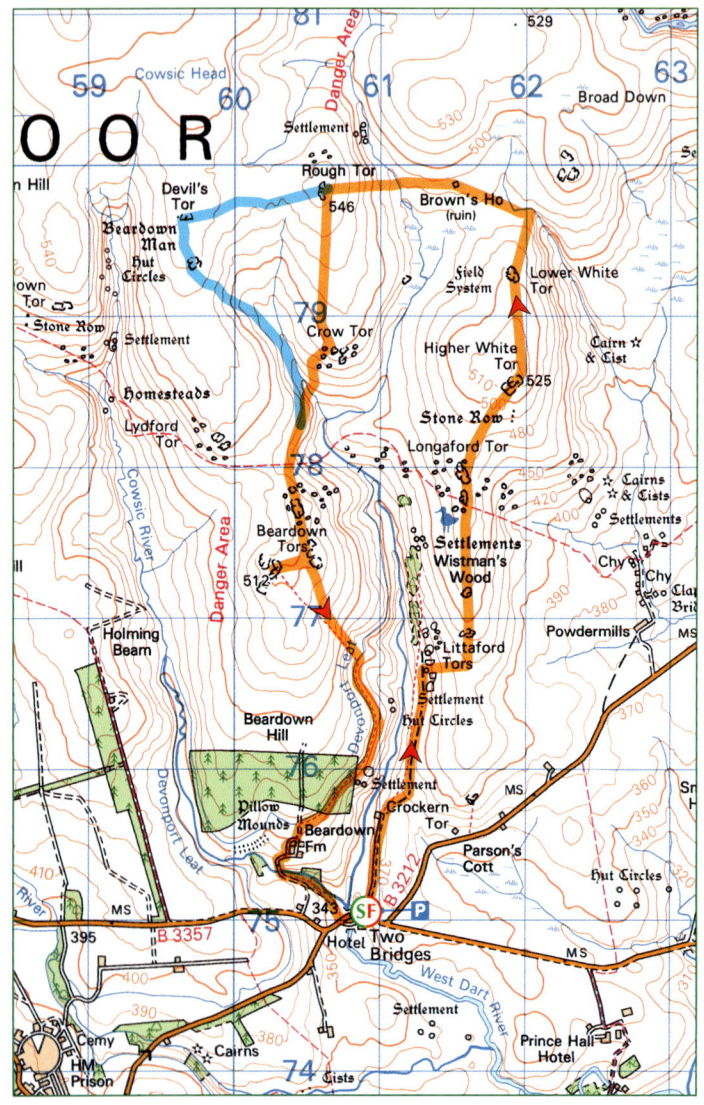

WALK 26 – LONGAFORD TOR, ROUGH TOR AND BEARDOWN TORS

Heading north along the West Dart Valley towards Wistman's Wood

follow the track as it bears right, then swing left and go through a wall gap. ▶ Keep ahead (northwards) up the valley for 850m (½ mile) and cross a stile at the wall; 300 metres ahead is Wistman's Wood. However, after crossing the stile the walk turns right (east) up beside the wall to the corner and then turns left (north) to **Littaford Tors** (466m).

Up to the right is Crocken Tor, which was the meeting place of the Stannary Parliament between the 14th and 18th centuries.

> **Wistman's Wood** National Nature Reserve, which is tucked along the west-facing slope of the West Dart Valley, is one of only three high-level ancient oak woods in Dartmoor, the others being Black-a-Tor Copse (Walk 36) and Piles Wood (Walk 18). This is a rare and fragile environment where moss-covered pendunculate oak trees grow among large boulders clothed in moss and lichen.

Continue along the broad ridge to the pyramid-shaped **Longaford Tor** (507m). ◄ From the northern outcrop bear half-right (north-north-east) up to **Higher White Tor** (525m) – from here there is a good view south along the ridge – and continue northwards to **Lower White Tor** (507m). Continue slightly east of north down towards the corner of a stone wall in a slight dip with a stream. Do not cross the stream but turn left (west-north-west) on a vague path to arrive at **Brown's House**. This area can be a bit wet so you'll need to pick the best route. ◄

Views include Beardown Tors (west), the mast near Princetown (south-west), Bellever Tor (south-east), and Higher White Tor and Rough Tor (north).

If you head directly towards Brown's House make sure to keep east (right) of Rowter Marsh.

> **Brown's House**, now little more than a ruin, was built by Dr Brown in 1812. However, he failed to get permission from the Duchy of Cornwall, who responded by setting a rent that he could not afford; this in turn led to the house being abandoned in 1830.

Continue westwards on a decent path slightly downhill and cross the infant West Dart River (this may cause problems after heavy rainfall). Once across, continue westwards up the path to **Rough Tor**, the highest point on the walk (546m). ◄ From here you have a choice of continuing the walk or taking the extension to Devil's Tor (assuming the firing range is open). To continue with the main walk (which stays outside the firing range) head south downhill following a path alongside the military range poles. Later, fork left to **Crow Tor** (494m) before heading back to the path alongside the poles. ◄ Follow the path across the stream at Foxholes, head uphill and bear left. Cross a ladder stile at the wall and continue southwards up to **Beardown Tors**.

A military flagpole and huts mark the edge of the Merrivale Firing Range.

Crow Tor offers a nice view south along the West Dart valley.

> **Beardown Tors** consists of three granite stacks: a northern one (507m), an eastern one with a military flagpole (511m) and a western one with military huts (512m). All three offer great views which include Great Mis Tor (west) and the mast near Princetown (south-west); to the south are the South Moor tops, to the east is Littaford, Longaford and Higher White tors, and to the north are Rough Tor and Devil's Tor.

WALK 26 – LONGAFORD TOR, ROUGH TOR AND BEARDOWN TORS

The Two Bridges Hotel

Devil's Tor extension

From Rough Tor head slightly south of west into the Merrivale Firing Range on a vague path over fairly level ground, picking the best route to reach **Devil's Tor** (549m) with Beardown Man just to the west. ▶ Head south for 350 metres and, after passing an outcrop, bear half-left (south-east) down the grassy slope to reach a path coming in from the left. Bear right along this following the valley, with the stream over to the left. Shortly after drawing level with Crow Tor the path bears right as it contours round to a ladder stile at the wall and then heads south to **Beardown Tors**. To visit Crow Tor, head east across the stream once you are level with outcrop and continue up to the tor, then follow the main route.

The impressive Beardown Man is a 4000-year-old standing stone (or menhir). At a height of 3.5m, it is the second tallest standing stone on Dartmoor.

Main route

Looking south from the eastern outcrop with the flagpole, take the left-hand of two paths heading south-south-east

The late 18th-century Devonport Leat, which starts at a weir on the West Dart River just to the north of Wistman's Wood, was built to supply water to Devonport Dockyard.

down to a stone wall. Go through the gate and bear left down the grassy slope. Cross the footbridge over the leat and turn right (southwards) alongside it. ◄ Keep ahead at another bridge and shortly cross a stile to follow the leat through the plantation. Leave over another stile and continue to a track, passing another stile. Turn left down the track towards **Beardown Farm**.

On nearing the buildings, turn right over a stile beside the gate and follow the track west then south to a track junction and turn right. Continue down the track as it swings left and then crosses a bridge over the Cowsic River. Immediately after the bridge fork left at the footpath sign and follow a path through the trees. Cross a stile and continue through the beech wood to leave via another stile. Follow the fence on the left, then go up some steps and over a footbridge. Follow the left-hand fence down to a stile and continue between the stone walls, crossing a stile on the way. Turn left alongside the road (B3357) back to the car park on the left. The Two Bridges Hotel is beside the older 19th-century bridge.

WALK 27

Foggintor, King's Tor and Merrivale

Start/finish	Four Winds car park on B3357 near Merrivale (SX 560 749)
Distance	13km (8 miles)
Ascent	300m
Time	3¾hrs
Terrain	A medium-level walk on paths and good tracks; some lane walking and sections alongside the B3357
Maps	OS Explorer OL28
Refreshments	Dartmoor Inn (07495 218911) at Merrivale – short detour
Public transport	Buses from Tavistock, Newton Abbot and Yelverton stop at the Dartmoor Inn (Merrivale) on the B3357

Walk 27 – Foggintor, King's Tor and Merrivale

From Four Winds the route heads out past Yellowmead Farm to visit Foggintor Quarry, before following the course of the former Princetown Railway. After a quick visit up King's Tor, the walk rejoins the track and passes Swelltor Quarry heading towards Ingra Tor. Then it's off northwards along the Walkham Valley heading towards Merrivale, where a short pub detour can be made. The final section passes the impressive Merrivale prehistoric sites before heading back at Four Winds.

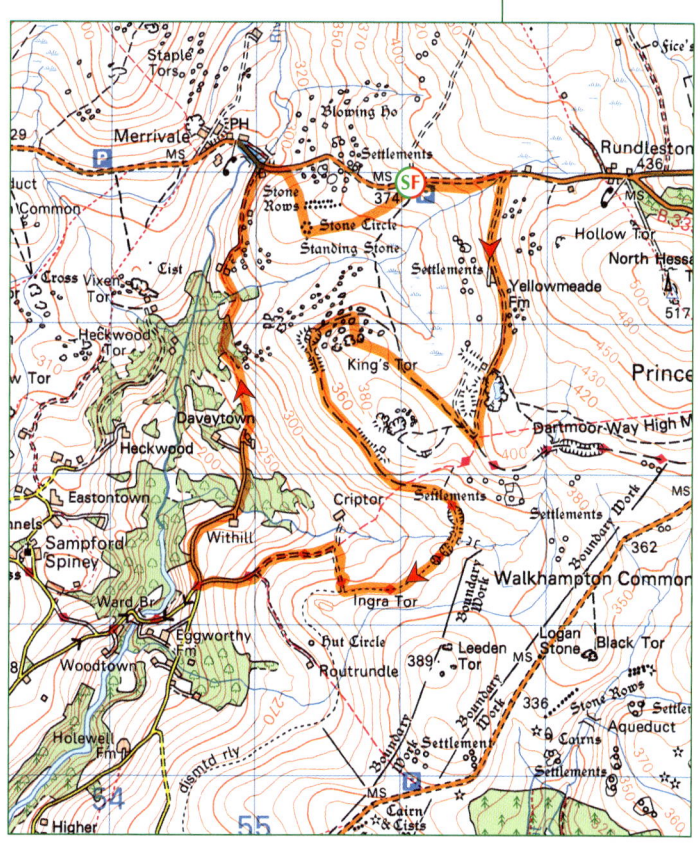

WALKING ON DARTMOOR

King's Tor

The water-filled quarry, which is worth a visit, is off to the left.

At Four Winds car park stand facing the road and turn right (east) across the open moor, keeping parallel to the B3357 to reach the entrance track for **Yellowmead Farm**. Turn right along this track and keep left at the split to reach the ruined buildings and massive granite spoil heaps of Foggintor Quarry. ◂

Foggintor Quarry (formerly known as the Royal Oak Quarry), which provided granite for Nelson's Column in London as well as the prison in Princetown, opened in 1820 and closed in the early 20th century. The car park where the walk started was originally the site of Foggintor School, which was built for the children of quarry workers. However, as work at the quarry started to decline, the school closed and became a private residence known as Four Winds. The house was demolished in 1964, although the stone walls that surrounded the play areas and garden still stand among the trees.

Keep ahead along the track to a track junction and turn sharp right (north-west), aiming towards King's Tor (not the track between the earth banks) and ignoring a crossing route. After 700 metres, as the track starts to curve to the right, fork left on a path up to **King's Tor**.

The track was once part of **Princetown Railway**, which ran from Princetown to Yelverton, where it connected to the line between Plymouth and Tavistock; the branch line, which opened in 1883, closed in 1956. This superseded an earlier horse-drawn tramway – the Plymouth and Dartmoor Tramway – which followed a similar route. The tramway, which opened in 1823, was built for Sir Thomas Tyrwhitt to transport locally quarried granite. **King's Tor** (388m) offers a great view west over the Walkham Valley to Pew Tor and Vixen Tor, with Cornwall beyond; views to the north-west include Cox Tor and Staple Tors above Merrivale Quarry; continuing clockwise, views include Great Mis Tor (north), the mast at Princetown (east) and south past Ingra Tor to Sharpitor.

Head northwards down from the tor, picking a route through the clitter to rejoin the track, then turn left. Continue along the track it as it curves left and heads through a cutting, then over a bridge, heading south-east passing below and right of the disused Swelltor Quarries.

Shortly after crossing the bridge, an old siding forks left up to **Swelltor Quarries**; 250 metres along the siding are twelve abandoned granite corbels that were cut in 1903 (SX 5561 7340). The corbels were surplus to requirements for the widening of London Bridge; the bridge was sold to an American in 1968 and shipped over to Lake Havasu, Arizona.

The Merrivale standing stone

To visit Ingra Tor (339m) bear left off the track up past the former quarry to the tor, then retrace your steps.

Follow the track as it makes a large sweeping curve to the right, passing over a bridge and then under another. Continue for a further 750 metres (½ mile) towards **Ingra Tor** (and quarry) and turn right through a gate, following the Dartmoor Way High Moor Link. ◄ Continue down the grassy track (ahead is a Criptor farm with King's Tor beyond) to a junction and turn left along the track, still following the Dartmoor Way.

Bear right at the next track junction and follow the lane down to a cross-junction (Criptor Cross). Turn right (Daveytown ¾) and follow the lane past Withill Farm (right). Cross a bridge then continue uphill past the entrance to Park Town (left). As the lane curves right to **Daveytown**, go straight on along the track (bridleway).

Follow the walled and tree-lined stony track through four gates heading uphill, then keep ahead towards Hucken Tor. Go through a gate and continue along the track through the oak wood and then cross the bridge over the picturesque Pila Brook as it tumbles down over moss-covered boulders – a great place to rest a while.

Keep ahead and shortly go through a gate to pass Longash Farmhouse and continue through two more gates. Follow the track northwards for 750 metres (½ mile) towards Merrivale, with a view of Great Staple Tor above the disused Merrivale Quarry.

Go through a gate and past a house (Hillside) to the road (B3357), then turn right. ▶ Follow the verge uphill and, at the end of the stone wall, turn right (south-south-east) up over the open moor to reach the western end of the **stone rows**. After exploring the stone rows continue in a similar direction to visit the **stone circle and standing stone**. On reaching the standing stone turn left (east-north-east) and head towards the trees and car park at Four Winds, passing the remains of the hut circles on the way.

> Dartmoor has a number of wonderful prehistoric sites and **Merrivale** is close to the top of the list. The two double stone rows run roughly east–west, separated by a stream. The southern one, which is also the longer at 260 metres (the northern one is 180 metres long), includes the remains of a cairn circle in the middle. Some 50 metres to the south-east of the cairn circle is a cist (a box-shaped burial chamber formed from large flat stones) with a split cover stone. Some 125 metres to the south of the western end of the stone rows is a stone circle, and beyond this is a tall standing stone, or menhir. The area also has a number of Bronze Age hut circles, including some between the stone rows and the B3357 road.

To visit the Dartmoor Inn, cross over the road and turn left down to the pub on the right, then retrace your steps (200 metres each way).

WALK 28
Cox Tor, Great Staple Tor and Pew Tor

Start/finish	Pork Hill car park on B3357 (SX 530 751)
Distance	9km (5¾ miles)
Ascent	280m
Time	2¾hrs
Terrain	Mostly on paths and open moor; higher parts may require navigation in low visibility
Maps	OS Explorer OL28 (Dartmoor)
Refreshments	Ice cream van at Pork Hill car park; Dartmoor Inn (07495 218911) at Merrivale – short detour
Public transport	Buses from Tavistock, Newton Abbot and Yelverton stop at the Dartmoor Inn (Merrivale) on the B3357

A fairly easy half-day walk visiting several tors, a historic leat and an ancient cross. After leaving the car park the first stop is Cox Tor, then it's on to Roos Tor before heading south to Great Staple Tor, the highest point on the walk. We then drop down to Merrivale, where you can make a short detour to the Dartmoor Inn. The route continues south-westwards passing Heckwood Tor to arrive at Pew Tor. From here the walk heads north over Feather Tor to arrive at the picturesque Windy Post Cross, standing beside the Grimstone and Sortridge leat. The final leg heads over Barn Hill back to the car park.

From the car park head north across the B3357 and keep ahead up the stone-strewn slope to the trig point on **Cox Tor**.

> **Cox Tor** (442m) offers the first great view of the walk: to the west are Cornwall and Bodmin Moor; moving clockwise and much nearer is the distinctive outline of Brent Tor and its church (north-west); to the north-north-east is White Tor and the high

WALK 28 – COX TOR, GREAT STAPLE TOR AND PEW TOR

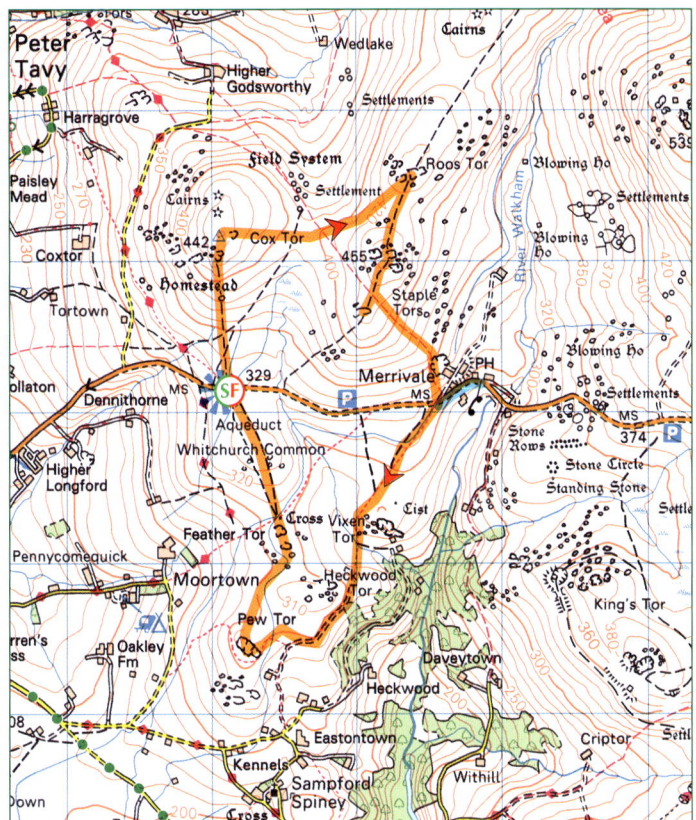

tops above Okehampton; to the east beyond Roos Tor and Great Staple Tor is Great Mis Tor; then there is the mast near Princetown, and finally there is King's Tor and Pew Tor in the south with the coast beyond.

After admiring the views, turn right (east) down to the slight saddle and pass the pond (this is often dry, especially in the summer). Bear half-left (east-north-east),

171

Walking on Dartmoor

> Although there is a warning flagpole, Roos Tor lies outside of the Merrivale firing range boundary, views from the top are similar to those from Cox Tor.

curving left up to the top of **Roos Tor** (454m) with its military range flagpole. ◄ Turn around and follow a path south-south-west down through the clitter to a slight saddle and then up to the top of Great Staple Tor – marked as **Staple Tors** on the map.

> **Staple Tors** consists of Great Staple Tor (455m), Middle Staple Tor (431m) and Little Staple Tor (the latter is much nearer the road and off route). Great Staple Tor, the highest point on the walk, consists of several large granite outcrops offering some great views that are similar to the views from Cox Tor.

> Before that, to visit Middle Staple Tor, keep ahead to the outcrop and then return to the junction and turn right.

Continue south-south-west towards Middle Staple Tor (431m) to reach a cross junction with a bridleway where the walk turns left. ◄ Follow the bridleway south-eastwards downhill to reach the fence above Merrivale Quarry. Turn right, heading south with the quarry on your left, down to the B3357 beside the old quarry access track.

> **Merrivale Quarry** (originally known as Tor Quarry) was operational from 1876 until 1997. Granite from Merrivale was used in the construction of a number of grand buildings in London, as well as for the Falklands War Memorial at Port Stanley.

Cross straight over the B3357 and follow the waymarked footpath opposite. For a pub visit after crossing the road, turn left down the verge to the pub on the left across the road, then – following your pub visit – retrace your steps and turn left along the waymarked footpath (400 metres each way). Continue south-west along the path with the Grimstone and Sortridge Leat on your left; further to the left is a stone wall.

> The **Grimstone and Sortridge Leat** starts from Grimstone Head Weir on the River Walkham to the north of Merrivale. At the Bullseye Stone beside Windy Post Cross (see later) the leat splits. The main part heads for the medieval manor houses of

Windy Post (or Beckamoor) Cross beside the Grimstone and Sortridge Leat

Grimstone and Sortridge (with branches to several farms on the way), while the branch that passes through the Bullseye Stone heads south past Pew Tor.

Soon cross over the leat and keep ahead, still with the wall over to the left and then go straight on to a path junction beside some large boulders, with a wall and **Vixen Tor** over to the left. ▶ Continue southwards, keeping the wall on your left. Cross a stream and continue uphill with the wall still over to the left. Keep ahead along the stony path/track as it passes to the left of **Heckwood Tor** and swings right, now heading west. As the track swings left towards Pewtor Cottage, leave the track and go straight on (west) up the grassy slope to the top of **Pew Tor**, crossing the leat (see earlier) on the way.

Note that Vixen Tor is on private land – there is no public access.

Pew Tor (318m) consists of several granite stacks and offers some great views. To the west is Cornwall and Bodmin Moor; north-west is the distinctive outline of Brent Tor and its church; to the north are Cox

Tor and Great Staple Tor; north-east is Great Mis Tor; to the east is a view across the Walkham Valley to King's Tor with the mast at Princetown beyond; and to the south-east is Sharpitor.

From here, head north-north-east across fairly level ground to reach Feather Tor (313m), crossing the leat again. Continue northwards to meet the Grimstone and Sortridge Leat again (see earlier) at the point where it splits, beside a **stone cross**.

The **cross**, known as Windy Post Cross (or Beckamoor Cross), is a well-preserved wayside cross dating from the late medieval period, which may be a replacement for an earlier cross. Spot the Bullseye Stone where the leat splits; the stone, which has a circular hole through it, is placed across the leat channel so that only a limited amount of water is diverted from the main channel; if required, this can easily be closed off.

Either step over the leat, or head to the right (north-east) for 75 metres to cross via the footbridge and double-back to the split. Once across, head north-north-west over **Whitchurch Common** (Barn Hill, 336m) back to the car park.

NORTH-WEST

Heading through Tavy Cleave beside the River Tavy (Walk 34)

WALK 29
Peter Tavy and White Tor

Start/finish	Smeardon Down car park near Peter Tavy (SX 521 779)
Distance	11.5km (7¼ miles)
Ascent	380m
Time	3½hrs
Terrain	Decent paths, tracks and lanes, fields and a number of stiles; higher open moor sections may require navigation in low visibility
Maps	OS Explorer OL28
Refreshments	Peter Tavy Inn (01822 810348) at Peter Tavy
Public transport	Buses between Tavistock and Okehampton stop at Mary Tavy – off route (see text for information about alternative start/finish points)

From the car park the route follows the Colly Brook down to Peter Tavy, home to St Peter's Church and the Peter Tavy Inn. Then it's off past St Mary's Church at Mary Tavy before heading through fields to the hamlet of Horndon. After following an old mining leat for a while, the route crosses the River Tavy and heads on to the open moor for a great view from White Tor. The final section heads past Stephen's Grave back to the car park.

From the car park, turn right down the lane for 350 metres and, as the wall curves left, bear left over the grass and go through a gate. Follow the enclosed bridleway down past a building, then go through a gate to a four-way junction and turn right (bridleway to Peter Tavy). ◄

Continue down towards **Peter Tavy**. Keep ahead along the lane past some houses, bear left over the bridge and then immediately turn right down a path, with the Colly Brook on the right. Continue past the Methodist Chapel and bear right to a T-junction. Turn right to a split-junction and keep left along the lane to the Peter Tavy Inn; the middle fork leads to St Peter's Church.

◄ Before that, keep ahead for a short distance to a footbridge and a nice view of the Colly Brook tumbling over the rocks, then return and turn left.

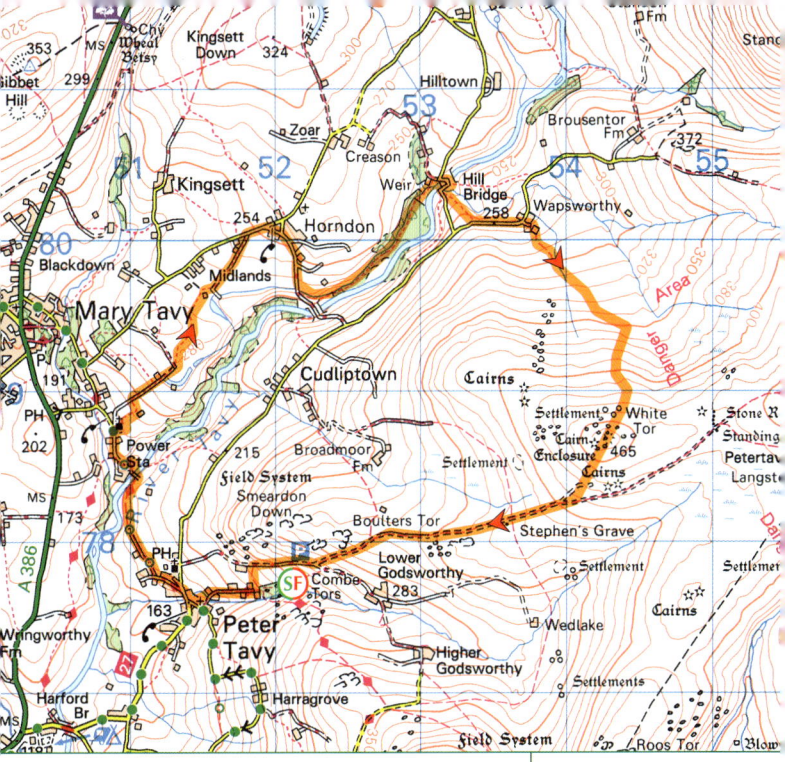

Peter Tavy is home to the 14th- and 15th-century St Peter's Church and the Peter Tavy Inn. The inn is housed in a 15th-century building, although the first record of it being an inn dates from the early 1800s.

Follow the track for 40 metres to a junction and turn right along the track (bridleway and Dartmoor Way). Go through a gate and keep ahead alongside the right-hand wall to a junction. Turn left over the footbridge, crossing the River Tavy. Bear right through a gate and follow the track uphill. Pass the entrance to the hydroelectric power station and follow the lane for 150 metres. Turn right through a gate at **St Mary's Church**; anyone using the bus joins the route here having alighted in Mary Tavy

(War Memorial) and followed Bal Lane south-eastwards, keeping ahead at two road junctions (1.2km/¾ mile each way).

> Located away from the village centre, **St Mary's Church**, like its near neighbour, dates from the 14th and 15th centuries. The area around Mary Tavy was home to the Wheal Friendship Mine, once one of the world's largest copper mines.

The 19th-century building and chimney, part of the Wheal Friendship Mine, was where miners' wet clothes (from working underground) would be dried before the next shift.

Follow the signed path through the churchyard passing to the right of the church. Turn left at the marker post to the opposite side of the churchyard, then turn right and leave over a stone stile in the corner. Follow the left-hand field edge, go through a gate and turn left along the field edge to another gate. Turn right along the enclosed path and cross a stile into the next field where the path splits. Keep right along the field edge, passing just right of an old chimney. ◄ Keep ahead through a gate into the next field where the path splits and take the right-hand fork heading diagonally left (north) across the field.

Cross the ladder stile, follow the right-hand field edge and cross the stone stile into the next field. Head diagonally left, go through the gate entrance then through a small gate and follow the enclosed path. Go through two gates, passing a small barn, then follow the hedge-lined track as it swings right. Where the track starts curving left, turn right over a ladder stile. Head east across the field, then go over another stile. Turn left along the track to a lane and turn right towards **Horndon**.

Fork right at the junction, then keep right at two more junctions following the lane to its end (house on the left). Keep ahead down the track for 150 metres to a footpath sign and turn left over the stile into the field. Follow the path along the right-hand side of a leat for 1.2km (¾ mile), crossing two stiles and passing two gates on the way, later passing through Creason Wood (Woodland Trust). ◄

Hill Bridge leat was built to take water from the River Tavy to power a water wheel at the Wheal Friendship Mine.

Cross a metal bridge which marks the start of the leat, with the River Tavy and fish ladder on the right. Follow

The walk follows the path alongside the Hill Bridge Leat for a while

the path to the left, go through a gate (or use the metal ladder) and turn right across **Hill Bridge**. Continue along the lane and, just before the left-hand bend, turn left at a footpath sign and cross the stone stile. Head south-east up through the field, passing into the next field, and leave via a stone stile at the top right corner, then turn left along the lane for 350 metres. ▶

> Alternatively keep along the lane up to a T-junction and turn left.

Turn right along a track signposted to Higher Wapsworthy and bear right past the buildings. Go through a gate and continue south-eastwards through the field, soon with stone walls on either side. Then go through a gate on to the open moor. Cross the footbridge and continue south-eastwards with a stone wall over on the left for 600 metres, aiming for a gate in the far wall near a warning post for the Merrivale Firing Range. Do not go through the gate, but turn right uphill, keeping the wall on your left. Follow the wall as it curves left for 25 metres, then turn right (south-south-west) up the boulder strewn slope to **White Tor**. ▶

> There is a military flagpole on the summit, but White Tor lies outside of the Merrivale Firing Range.

White Tor (465m), site of a late-Neolithic settlement, offers a great view: to the north are Great

Following the bridleway towards Smeardon Down

Links Tor and Hare Tor; continuing clockwise are Standon Hill (north-east), Cocks Hill (east), Great Mis Tor (south-east) and the mast near Princetown; to the south are Roos Tor and Cox Tor; to the west are Cornwall and Bodmin Moor; and slightly north of west and much nearer is the distinctive outline of Brent Tor and its church.

The small granite post, simply inscribed with a letter 'S', is reputedly the grave of George Stephens, who took his own life over the love of a woman.

Head south-south-west, meandering past boulders, and then keep ahead to a junction with a stony track (bridleway). Bear right to a 4-way bridleway junction beside **Stephen's Grave**. ◄ Go straight on (westwards) along the track, through a gate and continue between stone walls. Keep ahead down the track to a lane and turn right back to the car park.

WALK 30
Postbridge and Bellever Tor

Start/finish	Postbridge National Park Visitor Centre beside B3212 (SX 649 788); car park adjacent
Distance	11.75km (7¼ miles) or 10.5km (6½ miles)
Ascent	365m or 310m
Time	3½hrs or 3hrs
Terrain	Decent paths and tracks, woodland and medium-level open moor; option via stepping stones may be impassable after heavy rainfall and has two steep sections
Maps	OS Explorer OL28
Refreshments	Village shop and East Dart Inn (01822 880213) at Postbridge
Public transport	Postbridge has bus links to Tavistock, Newton Abbot and Yelverton
Note	Do not attempt the Laughter Hole stepping stones if the river is in flood

From the Postbridge visitor centre the route heads up through Bellever Forest passing several ancient sites to arrive at Bellever Tor. After admiring the view it's off to Laughter Tor and its large standing stone. There is then a choice: for the adventurous, you can head across the East Dart River via stepping stones before passing through Bellever; if you don't fancy the stepping stones, or if the river is in flood, take the easier route through the forest to Bellever. The final leg heads through woods and open moor back to the car park, visiting a well-known and much-photographed clapper bridge on the way.

Go to the end of the car park with the visitor centre on the right and exit via the path. Turn left to the B3212, cross over and take the lane opposite signposted for Bellever. Just after the cattle grid, fork right along the entrance track of the Bellever Forest car park (alternative start) and keep left, following a track uphill to a Y-junction.

Fork right and, after 120 metres, fork left up a narrow path through the trees to a clearing and the remains of a Bronze Age settlement at Kraps Ring. Skirt round the right-hand side, then continue southwards over Lakehead Hill, passing a small stone row at the summit and then a couple of **cairn circles**, one housing a cist. ◀ Continue down to a crossing bridleway, turn left and, shortly before the trees, turn right on to a wide path. Pass an old wall and continue west of south up to **Bellever Tor**.

One hundred and fifty metres to the left from the stone row on the top of Lakehead Hill is a short stone row, a large cist and the remains of a cairn circle (SX 645 776).

Bellever Tor (443m), which consists of a number of fairly large granite outcrops and a trig point, offers a great panoramic view. Just south of west is the mast near Princetown, and – moving clockwise – Beardown Tors, Higher White Tor, Rough Tor and Cut Hill, with Sittaford Tor to the north; continuing round is the broad outline of Hamel Down (north-east), then Haytor (east), Rippon Tor and round to Ryder's Hill in the south.

East Dart River at Bellever Bridge looking south

WALK 30 – POSTBRIDGE AND BELLEVER TOR

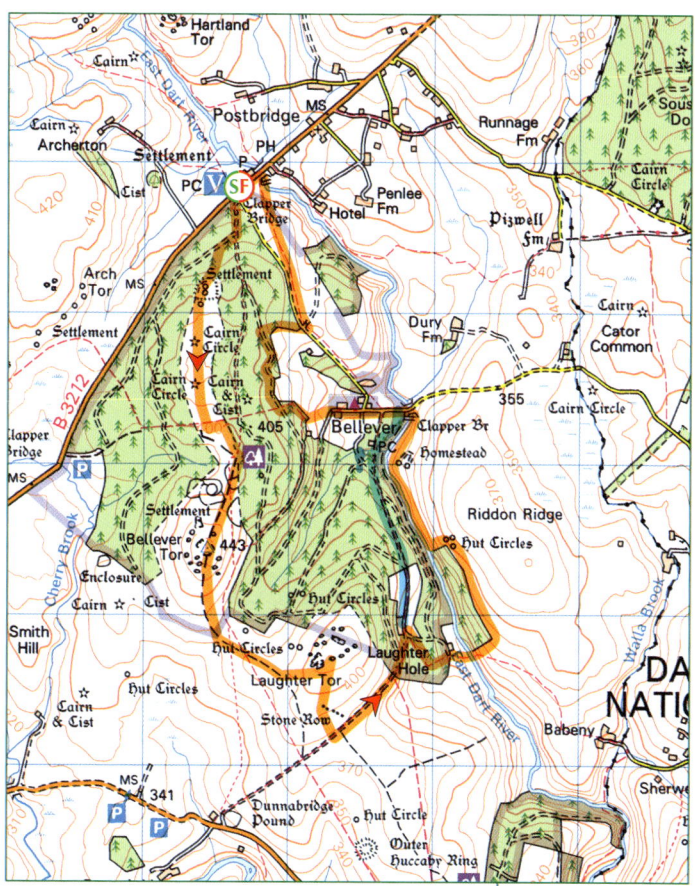

Head south down from the tor, go through a gate at the junction of walls and keep ahead with the wall on the right. ▶ After 25 metres fork left heading away from the wall for 450 metres to a split junction (SX 6494 7560). Fork left up to the top of **Laughter Tor** (427m), passing to the left of a stone walled sheep pound or enclosure. Turn around and head south downhill, passing just left of

If the gate is locked, head over the stile on the right and quickly go left through another gate, then turn right alongside the wall.

Despite having a fairly unassuming summit, Laughter Tor does offer a view similar to that from Bellever Tor. The 2.4m-high standing stone, or menhir, dates from the late Neolithic/early Bronze Age.

the walled enclosure to a path junction beside a standing stone. ◀

Head slightly east of south through an old gate entrance in the stone wall, then shortly fork left to join a track (bridleway). Turn left along this (Walk 11 also follows this track) and go through a gate to enter Bellever Forest. At the split, fork right (bridleway) down to a track junction just before a gate and farm buildings at Laughter Hole Farm. Here there is a choice to be made, you can either opt for the stepping stones route or the easier forest route.

Longer route via Laughter Hole Stepping Stones

At the junction, with the gate and farm buildings ahead, turn sharp right (south-east), then immediately fork right on a narrow bridleway (Sherrill via Babeny) through the trees. Pass a wall, turn left alongside this and continue down to the East Dart River. Cross via the stepping stones at **Laughter Hole** – if flooded, do not attempt to cross but instead retrace your steps and use the easier forest route. Once across the river, follow the wall steeply up to the corner. Turn left and continue alongside the wall to another corner. Turn left to follow the wall steeply down to the river. Turn right, following the river upstream to a ruined medieval clapper bridge. Join the lane and turn left (west) towards **Bellever**, crossing over the river.

Easier forest route (no stepping stones)

Keep ahead through the gate, passing the old farm buildings, and continue along the track between the fields (part of a Devon Wildlife Trust reserve – see later). Go through a gate back into the wood and keep right (straight on) at the junction. Shortly after a track joins from the right, fork right at a split. Then fork right again to continue alongside the East Dart River (river on the right) to the remains of a medieval clapper bridge. Join the lane and turn left (west) towards **Bellever**.

WALK 30 – POSTBRIDGE AND BELLEVER TOR

Both routes

Continue along the lane, passing the entrance to the car park (toilet facilities) on the left to a junction. Keep ahead (west), following the lane past the youth hostel (right), and continue along the track. Go through the gate, continue up to and through another gate to enter the forest, then turn right (bridleway). Where the track swings left, a gate straight ahead gives access to Devon Wildlife Trust's Bellever Moor and Meadow Reserve. ▶

Continue up the track to a junction and turn right for 600 metres to another junction. Turn right down the track (signed River and Forest Trail), soon following a wall on the right. Go through the gate and cross the lane to a track opposite (if you opted to walk through the Devon Wildlife Trust reserve, you rejoin here). Turn left and follow the bridleway heading just west of north parallel to the lane down towards Postbridge.

Go through a small gate and head down to the East Dart River. Continue upstream to the picturesque, and

A signed route can be followed through the meadows to the minor road (see the map on the gate); then turn left to rejoin the walk at the track on the right (SX 651 779).

The impressive (and well-known) clapper bridge at Postbridge

> The first record of a bridge here was in the 14th century. To the right (east) along the B3212 is the East Dart Hotel.

rather popular, **clapper bridge** and then turn left along the path to the road. ◄ Head south-west along the pavement, turn right across the B3212 to the village shop (tearoom) and turn left back to the car park on the right.

WALK 31
Postbridge to Fur Tor

Start/finish	Postbridge National Park Visitor Centre on B3212 (SX 649 788); car park adjacent
Distance	19.25km (12 miles)
Ascent	480m
Time	5½hrs
Terrain	A long walk over remote, high-level moor with indistinct paths that can be very wet underfoot; very good navigation required in low visibility; river and stream crossings
Maps	OS Explorer OL28
Refreshments	Village shop and East Dart Inn (01822 880213) at Postbridge
Public transport	Postbridge has bus links to Tavistock, Newton Abbot and Yelverton
Note	Part of the route is in the Okehampton firing range – check it is open before walking; if the river at Kit Steps is flooded, do not attempt to cross – instead retrace the outward route back to the start

From Postbridge the route heads over Broad Down to visit a small but picturesque waterfall on the East Dart River before following the river upstream through Sandy Hole Pass. The river is then left behind as the route heads up to the summit of Cut Hill – Dartmoor's joint third highest summit – by way of the wonderfully-named North-West Passage Peat Pass. From Cut Hill it's a fairly level wander over to the impressive granite stacks of Fur Tor. After savouring this remote location, the route retraces itself before crossing the East Dart River at Kit Steps. It then heads to Sittaford Tor via Statts House before arriving at the Grey Wethers stone circles. From here it's a gentler walk back to Postbridge, visiting Hartland Tor on the way.

WALK 31 – POSTBRIDGE TO FUR TOR

Exit the car park beside the national park visitor centre and turn right along the gravel path (Drift Lane) for 600 metres. Go through a gate on to the open moor and start rising, later following a wall on your right. Dip down to cross Braddon Lake (stream) before continuing, keeping the wall on your right. Go through another gate and continue beside the wall for 250 metres, then fork left (north-north-west) up to a wall. Cross the stile and continue over Broad Down before descending slightly to the small **waterfall** (SX 627 810) on the East Dart River. ▶

Continue upstream following a narrow path, keeping the river over to your right and skirting round wet areas. Keep ahead through **Sandy Hole Pass**, staying close to the river. Then bear left away from the river to skirt round a wet area, crossing a stream and passing an outcrop, known as Broada Stones (SX 617 817). Keep ahead with the river over to the right for 500 metres to a junction near Kit Steps (SX 614 820) shortly before reaching Cut Hill

The East Dart River rises to the west of Whitehorse Hill and joins with the West Dart River at Dartmeet to form the River Dart. For a better view of the waterfall, cross the river just upstream and double back.

One of the memorial plaques marking the North-West Passage Peat Pass on Cut Hill

WALKING ON DARTMOOR

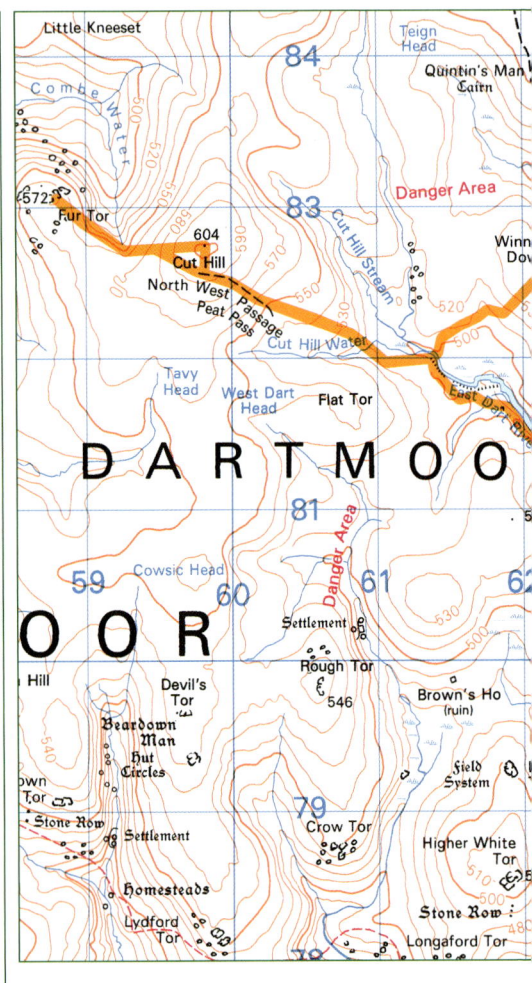

The return route from Fur Tor comes back to this point.

Water (stream); Kit Steps is where East Dart River tumbles past boulders forming a small picturesque cascade. ◄

Bear west for 325 metres, then start heading west-north-west and cross Cut Hill Water (stream) to reach a

WALK 31 – POSTBRIDGE TO FUR TOR

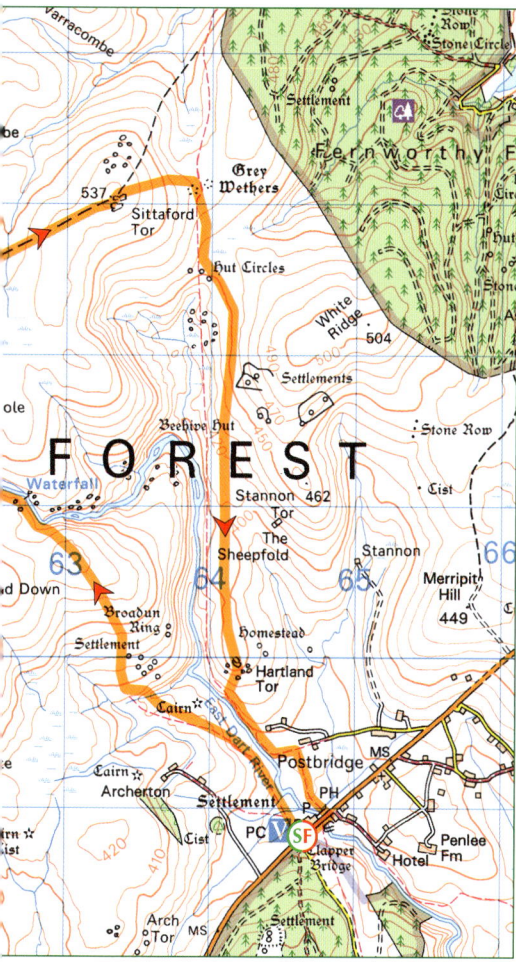

range marker pole; the route now enters the Okehampton Firing Range and skirts alongside – but does not enter – the Willsworthy Firing Range, which is on your left. Follow the path up alongside the range poles to reach the

> The North-West Passage Peat Pass is one of several peat passes on Dartmoor made by Frank Phillpotts. The one on Winney's Down (which is used later in the walk) is another of these passes; it was dug to provide a drier/easier route through the blanket bog.

lower marker stone of the **North-West Passage Peat Pass** (SX 6015 8243). ◄ Continue up the pass, still following the range poles to the upper peat pass marker stone (SX 5979 8255). Just after passing this, turn right (north) to the top of **Cut Hill**.

The flat-topped **Cut Hill**, the joint third highest top in Dartmoor at 604m, is crowned by an extensive, but partly eroded, blanket bog. Although it looks uninteresting there are several things to see, including a late Neolithic/early Bronze Age burial mound (SX 5981 8273), a recumbent stone carved with the word 'Jew' (SX 5991 8279) and a Neolithic stone row consisting of several large recumbent slabs of granite. Views include High Willhays (north-north-west), Hangingstone Hill and Whitehorse Hill (north-north-east), Sittaford Tor (east), Higher White Tor (south-south-east), Beardown Tors (south), Great Mis Tor (south-west), and Fur Tor (west).

From Cut Hill the onward route can be seen; head west slightly downhill, passing a range pole, and then follow a path west-north-west to **Fur Tor**.

Majestic **Fur Tor** (572m) consists of a great jumble of granite outcrops and is considered one of Dartmoor's most remote places – a great place to rest a while and enjoy the surroundings. From here

Looking north-west to Great Links Tor from Fur Tor

WALK 31 – POSTBRIDGE TO FUR TOR

there are some lovely views: to the south-west is Great Mis Tor; moving clockwise there is Tavy Cleave with Hare Tor and Sharp Tor beyond; to the north-west are views across the Amicombe Brook to Amicombe Hill and Great Links Tor; then finally High Willhays (north-north-west).

Now retrace the outward route, this time keeping to the right of the top of Cut Hill, and follow the path down the peat pass, then across Cut Hill Water to arrive back at the East Dart River. With care, cross just downstream of where Cut Hill Water joins the East Dart River using the boulders at the start of Kit Steps (SX 6137 8202). ▶ If the river is in flood after heavy rain, do not try and cross, but instead retrace the outward route back to Postbridge.

Once across, head north and then east-north-east (keeping to the north of Broad Marsh) to the lower marker stone (SX 6185 8228) for the peat pass on Winney's Down. Head north-east uphill to the upper marker stone (SX 6207 8250) and immediately turn right (east) to the ruins of **Statts House**. ▶ There are several paths here, take the one heading east-north-east directly towards **Sittaford Tor** (537m), dropping down to cross a stream on the way.

> For information on **Sittaford Tor**, see Walk 32. About 450 metres after crossing the stream and 50 metres to the right of the path are the remains of the Sittaford Stone Circle (SX 6302 8281). Only discovered in 2007, the stone circle – which consists of a number of recumbent stones 'hidden' among the grass – is the second largest on Dartmoor and dates from the late Neolithic/early Bronze Age period; nearby is a solitary standing stone.

On reaching Sittaford Tor, cross the stile just to the right of the rocks. Follow the path downhill, keeping the wall over to your left, to a junction. Turn right (south) and continue to the impressive **Grey Wethers Stone Circles** (see Walk 32). Continue southwards on a wide route for 400 metres to a junction, then fork left to follow a path

---

There is also another possible crossing point 300 metres upstream at SX 6118 8222.

The remains of a simple post-medieval peat cutter's shelter.

Hartland Tor looking south

along the left side of the valley, heading south for 1.3km (¾ mile) to a stone wall. ◄ Keep ahead across the stile and continue, passing an old wall to a slight split; fork left to the top of **Hartland Tor** (the right-hand fork passes to the right of the tor).

> Some 300 metres to the left is the stone-walled Sheepfold. The enclosure was originally built in the early 19th century for the manufacture of starch from potatoes, but it was later adapted as a sheepfold.

Although **Hartland Tor** (409m) is not as dramatic as some of Dartmoor's higher tors, it does offer a nice view; to the south is Bellever Tor, swinging right is Higher White Tor and Rough Tor (west), then slightly west of north is Sittaford Tor, then Fernworthy Forest (north-east).

From the tor bear half-right downhill and continue along the path down to a gate. Go through the gate and continue along the tree-shaded path, then go through another gate and follow the river. Go through a third gate and turn left along the field edge to the corner. Turn right to continue, with the field edge on your left. Pass through two sets of gates to reach the B3212. ◄ Turn right to cross the East Dart River, either following the road or crossing via the impressive **medieval clapper bridge**. Continue past the village shop/tearoom (right) back to the car park on the right.

> The East Dart Inn is to the left.

WALK 32

Fernworthy Reservoir, Grey Wethers and Watern Tor

Start/finish	Fernworthy Reservoir car park (SX 669 839)
Distance	17.25km (10¾ miles) or 10km (6¼ miles)
Ascent	480m or 280m
Time	5hrs or 3hrs
Terrain	Paths and tracks; easy sections through woodland; remote, high-level open moor sections require good navigation in low visibility
Maps	OS Explorer OL28
Refreshments	None on route; nearest at Chagford
Public transport	None
Note	Lies just outside the Okehampton firing range – do not stray west of the boundary markers if the range is closed

From Fernworthy Reservoir the walk heads up through Fernworthy Forest on to the open moor to visit the Grey Wethers stone circles; here the two routes go separate ways. The short walk heads back to the forest, while the longer walk heads out over the moor to impressive Watern Tor. From here, the longer route heads back to the forest, passing the ruins of Teignhead Farm. Both routes then descend through the forest, passing an ancient stone row and circle before following a path clockwise round the reservoir back to the start.

Head towards the car park entrance and bear right in front of the building (toilet and information boards) to a track. Turn right (north-west) along this for 250 metres with the reservoir over to the right. Bear left through a small gate and continue along the gravel path, following the reservoir path. Keep ahead through the trees, cross a footbridge and follow the path as it curves right then left, passing just left of a bird hide. Go through a gate, keep ahead to a lane and turn right along this for 400 metres. After crossing Sandeman Bridge, turn left onto a forestry track. Keep ahead (right) at the track junction through Fernworthy Forest.

WALKING ON DARTMOOR

Fernworthy Reservoir was built in 1942 to supply drinking water to the Torquay area. Fernworthy Forest, the largest plantation on Dartmoor, was originally planted in the 1920s to replenish timber supplies following the First World War.

The track later curves left and crosses a bridge over a stream before heading up to a track junction. Turn right, then fork right at the Y-junction heading downhill and cross a bridge over a stream. Continue up to a T-junction and turn left. Keep ahead as the track ends and cross a ladder stile over the stone wall. Immediately turn right up beside the boundary on the right (may be wet) to a path junction beside a gate on the right.

Turn left (west-south-west), keeping the wall on your right to a gate on the right. Here the short walk goes right through the gate and the long walk keeps ahead, but – before that – turn left for 150 metres to visit the **Grey Wethers**.

The Grey Wethers – two adjacent stone circles between Fernworthy Forest and Sittaford Tor

The **Grey Wethers** consists of an impressive pair of Bronze Age stone circles; the name 'wether' is an old word for sheep, and – from a distance – the stones are said to resemble a flock of sheep grazing.

Short walk variation

Once through the gate head north-north-east and, at the split, fork right (straight on) up towards the trees. Then bear left alongside the boundary to a gate on the right and go through this to rejoin the longer walk.

Main route

Continue west-south-west alongside the wall up to **Sittaford Tor** (537m). Cross the ladder stile over the stone wall just left of the tor and bear right. The walk now follows the wall on your right, which quickly swings right, heading north-west for 1.1km (¾ mile) crossing two streams in a slight valley (Little Varracombe); you may need to look upstream for a suitable crossing point – do not attempt if flooded.

Where the wall starts curving right, keep ahead north-westwards up to **Quintin's Man** (552m) where you can find the remains of a **Bronze Age burial cairn**, military huts and a flagpole. Turn right heading slightly east of north following a vague path close to the red and white marker poles that mark the eastern edge of the Okehampton range; do not stray to the west if the range is in use.

On the way, the path crosses a stream in a small valley – Great Varracombe – passing below and east of Whitehorse Hill. The route then continues along a broad ridge to reach a large stone **cairn** (remains of a Bronze Age burial mound). ◄ From the cairn, head north to **Watern Tor**.

The flat ground as it passes Walla Brook Head can be rather wet after periods of rain, especially in the winter.

> **Watern Tor** (536m), with its fascinating horizontal jointing, consists of several outcrops running northwards for 200 metres. The well-known Thirlstone – a gap between two of the outcrops – can be found at the northern end. Views from here include Hangingstone Hill (west), Wild Tor and Steeperton Tor (north-west), Cosdon Hill (north), Castle Drogo (north-east), Kestor (east), Easdon Hill (east-south-east) and Hamel Down (south-east).

At Watern Tor turn around to face south (with the outcrops behind you) and head half-left of the approach route, heading south-south-east to the corner of a stone wall. Cross the wall via the ladder stile and turn right (southwards) following the wall, which is on your right. On reaching a stile on the right, bear half-left on a path following an old boundary line south-south-east over Manga Hill towards a stand of trees. On nearing Manga Brook bear left and continue downhill, keeping the stream over to your right. Nearing the bottom of the valley, a path over a clapper bridge on the right gives access to the ruins of **Teignhead Farm**.

WALK 32 – FERNWORTHY RESERVOIR, GREY WETHERS AND WATERN TOR

The atmospheric ruins of **Teignhead Farm**, sheltering under a stand of trees, date from the late 18th century; the farm was abandoned in 1943. You can still see an old fireplace in the remains of the farmhouse, along with field walls and gateposts.

Keep ahead and cross the North Teign River via a picture-perfect clapper bridge dating from the early 1800s. Head uphill and go through a gate to enter Fernworthy Forest. ▶

Both routes now follow the track (bridleway) eastwards, uphill at first before descending and ignoring all crossing track junctions. Where the track levels out at a cross-junction, keep ahead for 100 metres and then detour left past two large boulders to visit the stone circle before returning back to the track and turning left.

Fernworthy stone circle, which consists of 27 stones, lies adjacent to three stone rows and some burial cairns, forming a 'ritual complex' dating from the late Neolithic/early Bronze Age.

Continue along the track, soon heading downhill, and leave through a gate. Immediately turn left through

The shorter walk joins from the right just before the gate.

Thornworthy cist on the shore of Fernworthy Reservoir

> The Thornworthy Cist (SX 6674 8434) – an oblong-shaped stone box with a lid – is the remains of a Bronze Age burial chamber.

another gate and follow the reservoir path in a clockwise direction, keeping ahead through a couple of gates. Continue along the path; passing through a wet area, as it curves to the right (east). After passing an inlet the path stays close to the water's edge to reach the dam; on the way lookout for the **Thornworthy Cist** on the left. ◄

Just past the dam, bear right through a gate and follow the zigzag path down to a footbridge. Cross the **South Teign River**, bear left uphill, then right along the track for a short distance before forking left up a path. Turn right along a tarred track to the dam. Go through the gate and continue alongside the water to a junction and turn left to the car park.

WALK 33
Fernworthy Reservoir, Scorhill and Kestor Rock

Start/finish	Fernworthy Reservoir car park (SX 669 839)
Distance	18.5km (11½ miles) or 15km (9¼ miles)
Ascent	515m or 445m
Time	5½hrs or 4½hrs
Terrain	A long walk on paths, tracks and lanes; open moor sections (Thornworthy Tor, Scorhill and Buttern Hill) require good navigation in low visibility; sections can be wet
Maps	OS Explorer OL28
Refreshments	Northmore Arms (01647 231181) at Wonson
Public transport	None

From Fernworthy Reservoir the walk heads up through Fernworthy Forest on to the open moor of Chagford Common. After passing a standing stone and stone rows on Shovel Down, the route crosses the North Teign River to reach the wonderful Scorhill Stone Circle. From here the longer route heads to Buttern Hill before following lanes to Wonson – home to the Northmore Arms pub – and then continues to Gidleigh; the shorter walk heads directly to Gidleigh. Both routes then visit Kestor Rock and Thornworthy Tor before heading back to Fernworthy Reservoir.

WALK 33 – FERNWORTHY RESERVOIR, SCORHILL AND KESTOR ROCK

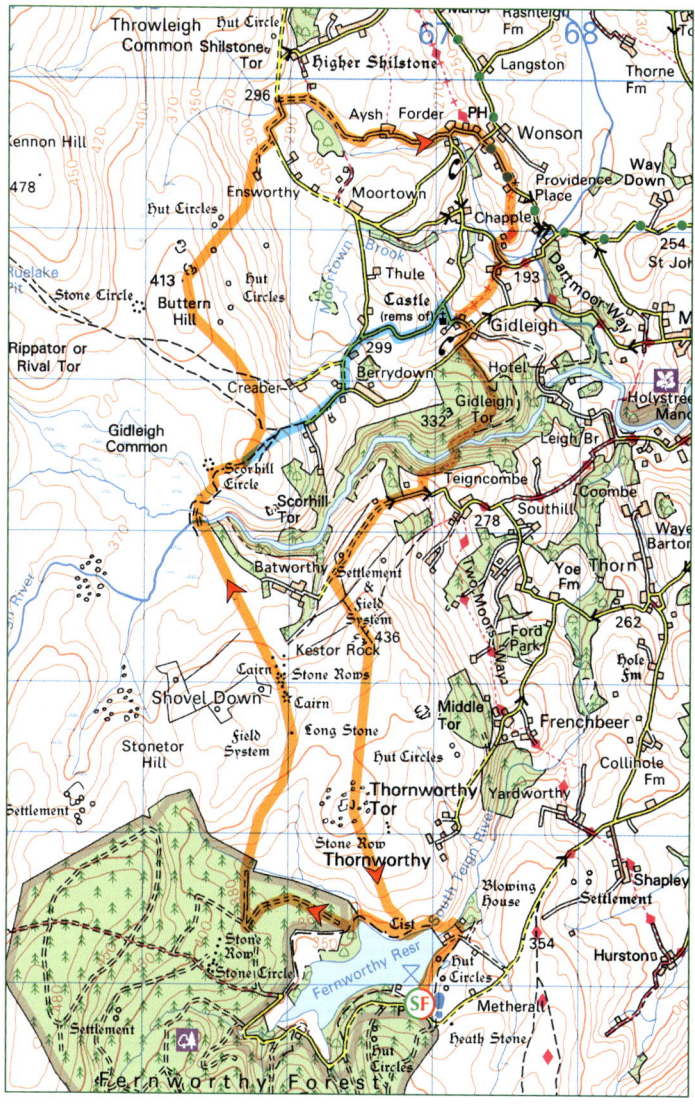

WALKING ON DARTMOOR

The reservoir was completed in 1942 to supply drinking water for the Torquay area.

From the north corner of the car park head towards Fernworthy Reservoir and turn right along the waterside path, keeping the water on your left. ◄ Go through a gate (dam on left) and keep ahead along the tarred track for 25 metres, then go left on a path down to the river. Cross the footbridge and follow the zigzag path up to the far side of the dam. Continue along the waterside path for 600 metres (water on left) passing a **cist** (right) on the way. ◄

The box-shaped Thornworthy Cist (SX 6674 8434) is the remains of a Bronze Age burial chamber.

Cross a footbridge and bear left through a gate to a track junction. Fork half-right through a large gate and follow the track west-north-west through the forest to a junction. Turn right, then immediately fork right (north) and follow the track through a gate to the open moor. Continue uphill north-north-east, later keeping left at a split to arrive at the **Long Stone**.

The **Long Stone**, the first of several Bronze Age relics to be found on Shovel Down, is Dartmoor's fourth tallest menhir (3.1m); more recently it was used as a boundary marker between Chagford Parish, Gidleigh Parish and the Duchy of Cornwall land. The other remains include several stones rows – including both double and single rows – and the Fourfold Cairn Circle.

Double stone row on Shovel Down

WALK 33 – FERNWORTHY RESERVOIR, SCORHILL AND KESTOR ROCK

There are two main paths from here; take the left one (straight on) heading north following a line of stones over the brow of the hill to reach a **double stone row** and continue alongside this. ▶ Continue along the path heading north-north-west, running parallel to and 175 metres west of the trees and wall. Cross the clapper bridge over the North Teign River. Keep ahead to cross a clapper bridge over the Walla Brook and head north-east. ▶ Cross a bridge over the Gidleigh Leat and head north to the **Scorhill Circle**.

> Atmospheric **Scorhill Circle**, which measures 27 metres in diameter, dates from the Bronze Age. The circle now consists of 23 upright and 11 recumbent stones, although there may have originally been more.

On reaching the stone circle turn right (east-north-east) up over the brow of the hill where there is a choice to be made.

Shorter walk variation
For the shorter walk keep ahead down between the walls, go through the gate (small parking area) and follow the lane downhill. Go left at the junction and keep right at the next three junctions to reach the church in **Gidleigh**. Follow the lane to a T-junction (Gidleigh Cross) and turn right to rejoin the longer walk.

Main route
Bear left (north) after the brow of the hill, keeping a stone wall on your right. Where this turns right head north-west up the slope, aiming for distant Cosdon Hill. As the ground levels out, continue for 200 metres northwards along the flat summit of **Buttern Hill** (413m) to the low granite outcrop. Turn half-right (north-east) downhill, passing rocks and bracken. Keep ahead with a wall on your left; later a wall comes in from the right. Continue down the track with a wall on the right and pass Buttern Farm to join a lane.

A double stone row heads towards Batworthy Corner from the remains of the Fourfold Cairn Circle (SX 6596 8603).

To visit the Tolmen Stone (a large boulder with a circular hole at SX 6550 8708) turn right alongside the Walla Brook for 125 metres. From here, turn left (north) uphill towards Scorhill Circle.

Kestor Rock and rock basin

Turn left to a junction (Ash Green Cross) and turn right along the lane for 1.4km (1 mile) passing through Ash (or Aysh) to a junction at Forder. Turn left, following the lane to a three-way junction (Barrow Way Cross) at **Wonson**. ◄

A hundred metres to the left is the Northmore Arms pub.

Keep ahead (turn left if coming up from the pub) along the lane for 350 metres to Providence Place. Pass the small Methodist Chapel (left) and turn right at a gate just after the house (right). Follow the walled track downhill, passing some buildings at Coombe and crossing a stream. Turn left along the lane to a junction just after the bridge and turn right up the track (byway). Keep left past the buildings and continue up to a lane in **Gidleigh**, then turn left (the shorter walk joins from the right). ◄

Just to the right (west) is the late 15th-century Holy Trinity Church; inside is a wonderful 16th-century rood screen. Beside the church (visible from the lane only) are the ruins of a fortified manor house (private).

Having turned left, continue to the junction (Gidleigh Cross) and turn right uphill for 125 metres. Turn left along the track, passing a gate to enter Gidleigh Wood and keep ahead for 300 metres to a Y-junction. Follow the signed path straight on between the two tracks. Head down through the trees, passing below the outcrops of **Gidleigh Tor**, and turn right along the track to a footpath sign. Turn left and cross the footbridge over the North Teign River.

Follow the path steeply uphill, crossing over a track on the way to another track at the top. Turn right and then left, following the track up past a gate. Turn right along the lane for 850 metres (½ mile), passing a cattle grid to reach the Round Pound on your right. ◄ Continue for

The circular enclosure – with the remains of a large, centrally placed hut – dates from the late Bronze and Iron Age.

150 metres and turn left (south-east) following a path up to **Kestor Rock**.

> **Kestor Rock** (436m) is a prominent granite stack with an impressive rock basin; views include the high tors near Okehampton (north-west), Cosdon Hill (north-north-west), Meldon Hill (east), Hamel Down (south-east) and Fernworthy Forest (south).

From the top, several paths radiate out; take the one heading south across level ground for 750 metres to a stile and wall (it can be wet near the wall), then keep ahead to **Thornworthy Tor**. ▶ Continue south-south-east, picking a suitable route across Thornworthy Down, heading down to a wall and fence junction at the right-hand end of a line of trees. Cross the stile beside the gate and follow the wall on your left. Where this turns left, keep ahead to the **reservoir** and turn left, retracing the outward route back to the car park.

The tor (424m) has an impressive perched boulder and views of Fernworthy Reservoir to the south.

WALK 34
Willsworthy, Tavy Cleave and Hare Tor

Start/finish	Willsworthy Range car park (unsigned) on east side of A386 (SX 517 834)
Distance	13km (8 miles) or 15km (9¼ miles)
Ascent	300m or 350m
Time	3¾hrs or 4¼hrs
Terrain	Decent paths and tracks on lower sections; Tavy Cleave is quite rocky in places beside the river; high-level moor sections (Hare Tor and Chat Tor) are remote and require good navigation in low visibility
Maps	OS Explorer OL28
Refreshments	None on route; nearest is Dartmoor Inn (see Walk 35)
Public transport	None (for nearest bus stop see Walk 35)
Note	The walk lies within the Willsworthy Firing Range – you must check before walking

The walk sets out through the Willsworthy Range, soon following Mine Leat. The scenery becomes more rugged as the route heads up through Tavy Cleave following the lovely River Tavy upstream as it tumbles and cascades over boulders. The shorter walk soon heads up to Hare Tor, while the longer route visits Chat Tor and Sharp Tor before heading to Hare Tor. Both routes continue to Ger Tor for a great view over the cleave before following an old wall downhill and skirting round White Hill back to the start.

From the car park follow the tarred access track heading away from the A386 for 800 metres, passing a couple of junctions. At the third junction (signed Troop Shelter), turn right (southwards) along the track to a stone-walled and grass-roofed building. Keep ahead to a path junction just before a footbridge and turn left (east-north-east), keeping Mine Leat on your right. ◄

> The leat, which is now followed to its source, was built to feed water from the River Tavy to mines located north of Mary Tavy, and later to the Wheal Jewell Reservoir.

> The **Willsworthy Range** dates from the early 20th century, when the War Department obtained the tract of land that once formed the Willsworthy Manor. The area was marked by 46 boundary stones, each inscribed with the letters 'WD' and a post number.

Follow the leat as it swings right, crossing Willsworthy Brook on the way. Continue along the track passing through two gates and bear right to a small bridge. (This area was the site of Reddaford Farm, first mentioned in the 14th century and abandoned in the early 20th century.) Cross over the leat and immediately turn left to follow a path alongside the leat (which is now on your left). ◄ As the leat swings left, passing below **Nat Tor**, the scenery becomes more rugged as the valley narrows, ahead on the left is Ger Tor (see later) and to the right is the steep slope of Standon Hill.

> After 700 metres, at a small bridge, a path to the right leads to the Lane End car park (SX 537 823), which can be used as an alternative start for a shorter walk.

On reaching a small building and weir at the leat take-off, cross the footbridge and continue along a vague path following the River Tavy on your right for 1.6km (1 mile) through picturesque Tavy Cleave, scrambling over boulders and rocks at times – the going can be a bit tough and

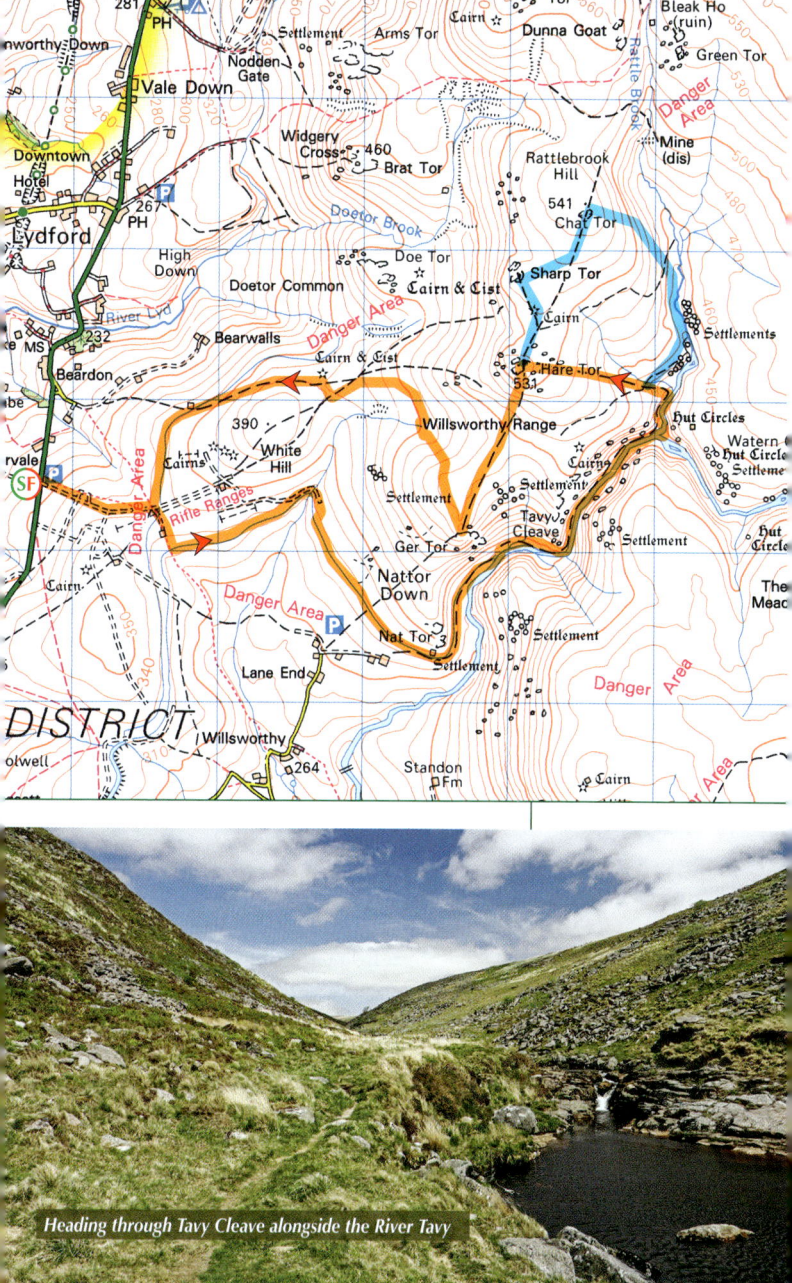

Heading through Tavy Cleave alongside the River Tavy

There is a small concrete PO (Post Office) marker post – used for the early military telecommunications network on Dartmoor – and a War Department boundary stone (WD 21) at Deadlake Foot (SX 561 840).

requires care. On reaching the confluence of the Rattle Brook and the River Tavy, bear left heading north, following the Rattle Brook on your right for 300 metres to Dead Lake (stream) at Deadlake Foot. ◄ Turn left up the slope with Dead Lake on your right for 250 metres to a path junction.

Here you have a choice of either continuing directly to Hare Tor or following the extension via Chat Tor and Sharp Tor. To continue directly to Hare Tor, keep ahead (west-north-west) as the stream bears off to the right, then follow the grassy path up to **Hare Tor**.

> **Hare Tor** (531m), crowned with a military flagpole, offers a great view. Looking north is Sharp Tor with Great Links Tor beyond, moving clockwise is the Dunna Goat Tors, Amicombe Hill and Kitty Tor (flagpole), while much nearer is Chat Tor. Further round is Great Kneeset (north-east) and Fur Tor just south of east. Continuing round are the mast and tors near Princetown (south-east), while to the south is Ger Tor, Standon Hill and White Tor. To the west is Cornwall, with Doe Tor and Brat Tor topped by the Widgery Cross to the north-west.

Extension via Chat Tor and Sharp Tor

Turn right (north-eastwards), contouring round the slope back towards the Rattle Brook, and head upstream, keeping the Rattle Brook on your right. Pass old tin mine workings (Kerbeam Mine) to reach the range poles, marking the boundary between the Willsworthy Range (left) and the Okehampton Range (right). Bear left (north-west) up Rattlebrook Hill, crossing a track and following the poles for 450 metres, then bear slightly left (west-north-west) up to **Chat Tor**. Turn left and follow a decent path south-south-west for 300 metres before bearing half-right (west-south-west) to **Sharp Tor**. From here follow a vague path south-south-east to a cairn and boundary stone (WD 19), then continue southwards up to **Hare Tor**.

> The small outcrop of **Chat Tor** (541m), with its distinctive horizontal jointing (similar to Watern Tor

Looking back from Hare Tor to Sharp Tor and Chat Tor

visited on Walk 32), forms the highest point on Rattlebrook Hill. Sharp Tor (519m) offers similar views to those from Hare Tor.

Main route

From Hare Tor head south-south-west downhill and then over level ground to **Ger Tor**. ▶

> **Ger Tor** (438m) has a great view from its granite outcrops down into the valley and along the River Tavy, which was followed earlier in the walk. To the south is White Tor and west is Cornwall.

Turn sharp right, heading north-north-west, to reach a stone wall and bear right, keeping the wall on your left. Continue downhill, pass through the wall for a while to skirt past a small reservoir, before following the wall/earth bank as it curves left. Go through a gate and immediately turn right, following the fence on your right to a track, with a gate on the right. Turn left along a track skirting round the north side of **White Hill**, admiring the views to the north, to a track junction beside a building on your right. Fork right across the stream and immediately fork

If you want, you can detour south-south-east to the Tavy Cleave Tors, which offer a good view along Tavy Cleave, before contouring round to Ger Tor.

left to follow a grassy route, with the stream on the left, soon curving left. Continue southwards to the tarred track used earlier and turn right, retracing the outward route back to the car park.

WALK 35
Great Links Tor and Widgery Cross

Start/finish	Car park east of A386/Lydford junction near Dartmoor Inn (SX 525 853), accessed through a gate
Distance	12.5km (7¾ miles) or 15.75km (9¾ miles)
Ascent	400m or 470m
Time	3¾hrs or 4¾hrs
Terrain	Tracks and paths over high-level moor; Kitty Tor extension can be wet and requires good navigation in low visibility
Maps	OS Explorer OL28
Refreshments	Dartmoor Inn (01822 820221) at the Lydford junction (A386)
Public transport	Buses between Tavistock and Okehampton stop at the Dartmoor Inn (A386)

From the car park the route heads north over Great Nodden before following part of the former Rattlebrook Tramway. After a quick visit to Sourton Tors for a view over Meldon Reservoir, the route rejoins the tramway. Then it's time to make a choice; either head directly to Great Links Tor or follow the loop over Kitty Tor, visiting Bleak House. Once at the top of Great Links Tor you are rewarded with a great view. The route then aims for Brat Tor and Widgery Cross via Arms Tor before heading back down to the car park.

Go through the gate at the north end of the car park and continue north-eastwards alongside the wall (left) for 600 metres. Turn left over a ladder stile and head northwards through the field to a path junction on the left-hand side. Stay in the field to the corner and turn left through a gate.

WALK 35 – GREAT LINKS TOR AND WIDGERY CROSS

Immediately turn right through another gate on to the open moor at Nodden Gate.

Turn left, then – with a wall (King Wall) on the left – head north-north-east towards Great Nodden. Cross straight over a track and follow the path up to the two

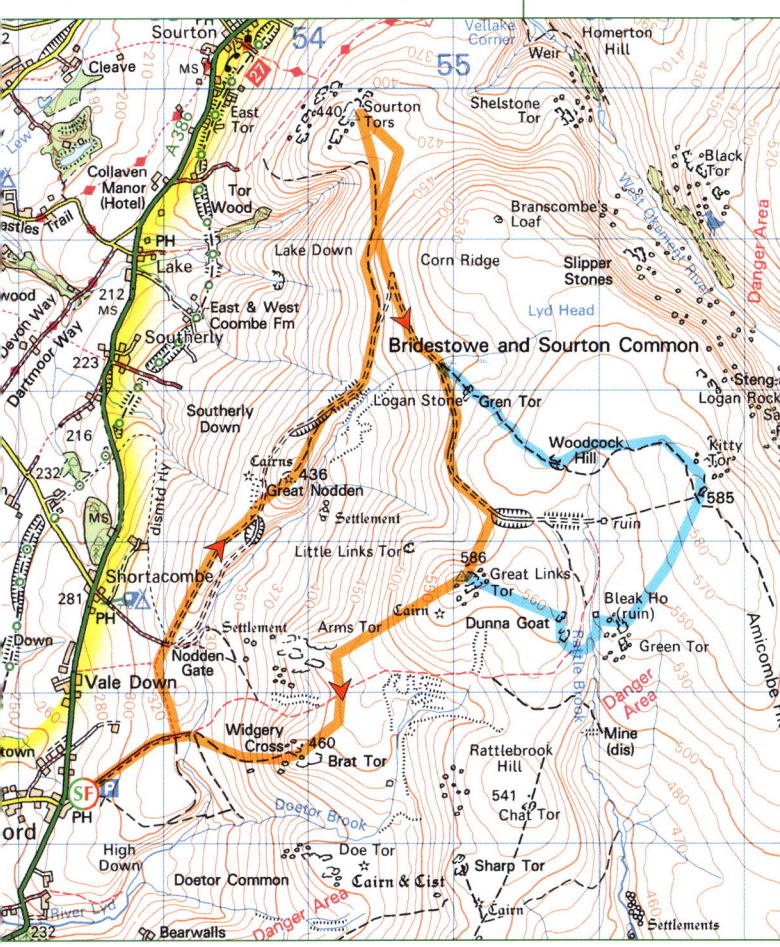

This is the trackbed of the 19th-century horse-drawn tramway that ran between Bridestowe Railway Station and the Rattlebrook Peat Works (see later).

Look left to catch sight of the Lake Viaduct on the former railway line that ran between Okehampton and Bere Alston, part of which now forms the Granite Way cycle route.

cairns on the summit of **Great Nodden** (436m). Keep ahead slightly downhill and bear right along the track. ◄

Follow the track for 700 metres to a junction (SX 544 883) on Coombe Down and fork left down the bank aiming for Sourton Tors; to miss out Sourton Tors stay on the main track to a hairpin bend and turn sharp right to rejoin the main walk (reduces walk by 2.4km/1½ miles and 50m ascent). Follow the wide, level path northwards to a slight cross-junction. Take the left-hand fork slightly downhill, heading north to an earthwork in the dip. ◄ Continue up to **Sourton Tors**.

> Views from **Sourton Tors** (440m) include the rolling farmland of Cornwall (west) and Devon (north), as well as views north-east across Meldon Reservoir and east to West Mill Tor, Yes Tor and High Willhays. Some 350 metres to the north-east of the trig point are the remains of the Ice Works, a late-19th-century venture to make ice in shallow rectangular ponds, which only lasted for 10 years.

Views from Great Links Tor include the Dunna Goats and distant Fur Tor

WALK 35 – GREAT LINKS TOR AND WIDGERY CROSS

Turn around and head south-east (slightly left of the outward route) to a junction at an earthwork. Bear right (south) to the cross-junction passed earlier and fork left, shortly rejoining the old tramway track at a hairpin bend. ▸ Take the left-hand track uphill. Where the track crosses a stream you have a choice to make about whether or not to follow the extension to Kitty Tor. To continue on the main walk keep ahead up the track for a further 1.2km (¾ miles), then turn right on a path up to **Great Links Tor**.

> The shortcut rejoins here.

> **Great Links Tor** (586m) sits majestically on Dartmoor's north-western flank with several impressive granite stacks. This high vantage point offers a great 360-degree view. To the west lies Cornwall and Bodmin Moor, to the north a patchwork of Devon fields. Moving clockwise are High Willhays (north-east) and Hangingstone Hill (east); then Cut Hill and Fur Tor (south-east); then – in the south-south-east – the mast near Princetown; then Great Mis Tor, Sharp Tor and Hare Tor (south); then the sea at Plymouth and the distinctive outline of Brent Tor and its church (south-west).

Kitty Tor extension

Some 50 metres after crossing the stream, fork left on a vague track (path) up past **Gren Tor** heading south-east up Woodcock Hill to arrive at Hunt Tor (560m). Bear left and contour round the slope, heading slightly north of east, then curve right to the two military huts at **Kitty Tor**.

> **Kitty Tor** (585m) consists of two rocky outcrops close to the summit of Amicombe Hill. From near the military huts there are good views across the West Okement River valley to Yes Tor and High Willhays (north-east), and to Lints Tor (east). The second outcrop has a flagpole; to the east of here is the Okehampton Firing Range.

Bleak House (ruins) beside the Rattle Brook

Head south to the second outcrop (military flagpole) and bear half right (south-south-west) for 1km slightly downhill across rather wet ground to Green Tor (541m). Turn right (west) down to the ruins of **Bleak House** beside the Rattle Brook.

The late-19th-century **Bleak House** was built for the site manager of the Rattlebrook Peat Works. Peat was extracted from Amicombe Hill and processed to the west of Kitty Tor before being transported off the moor on the Rattlebrook Tramway.

The views, which are better from Lower Dunna Goat, include Fur Tor (south-east). Higher Dunna Goat has a boundary stone marked 'L' for Lydford and 'BS' for Bridestowe and Sourton Common.

Turn left downstream for 100 metres, then turn right, crossing the clapper bridge over the Rattle Brook. Follow a good path off to the left, keeping to it as it soon swings right and climbs. Then turn right up to **Dunna Goat**, the first outcrop is Lower Dunna Goat (557m), the second is Higher Dunna Goat (562m). ◄ From Higher Dunna Goat turn left (west-north-west) to **Great Links Tor** and rejoin the main walk.

WALK 36 – HIGH WILLHAYS VIA YES TOR AND BLACK-A-TOR COPSE

Main route

To continue the main walk, looking to the south-west from Great Links Tor, there are two paths; take the right-hand one (west-south-west), passing just right of an outcrop. ▶ Continue down the clitter slope to **Arms Tor** (457m) then head south, passing a couple of earthworks, and cross over the bridleway. Keep ahead for 150 metres and bear right (south-west) along a path to Brat Tor and **Widgery Cross**.

> The left-hand one, which passes to the left of the outcrop, heads directly to Widgery Cross, passing just right of a Bronze Age burial cairn on the way.

> **Widgery Cross**, sitting majestically on top of Brat Tor (460m), was built by William Widgery to commemorate the Golden Jubilee of Queen Victoria in 1887. From here views include Sharp Tor and Hare Tor (south-east), and west into Cornwall.

Head west on a path steeply downhill (later this levels out) and then cross the River Lyd via the footbridge or stepping stones. Keep ahead alongside the wall (right) back to the car park.

WALK 36
High Willhays via Yes Tor and Black-a-Tor Copse

Start/finish	Meldon Reservoir car park (SX 561 918)
Distance	14km (8¾ miles) or 10.5km (6½ miles)
Ascent	470m or 445m
Time	4¼hrs or 3½hrs
Terrain	Good low-level paths and tracks; paths over the remote high-level moor are less defined; very good navigation required in low visibility
Maps	OS Explorer OL28
Refreshments	None on route; choices in and around Okehampton
Public transport	None
Note	Parts of the walk lie within the Okehampton Firing Range – check that the range is open before walking

From Meldon Reservoir it's a steady climb up to the summit of Yes Tor. From here the route heads south to High Willhays – the highest summit in both Dartmoor and Southern England. A quick visit to Fordsland Ledge gives a great view of the valley before heading down to Lints Tor via Dinger Tor. The walk then heads northwards along the valley following the West Okement River, passing the magical Black-a-Tor Copse on the way. The final section follows the southern side of Meldon Reservoir back to the car park. A shorter walk missing out Dinger Tor and Lints Tor is also described.

Exit the car park via the steps beside the toilets, go through the gate and turn left along the access road towards Meldon Reservoir. Continue to the far side of the dam and turn right, keeping beside the fence on your right.

Meldon Reservoir was formed by the building of Dartmoor's youngest dam in 1972. From the dam there is a view of the Meldon Viaduct, built in 1874 for the London and South Western Railway

Meldon Reservoir

WALK 36 – HIGH WILLHAYS VIA YES TOR AND BLACK-A-TOR COPSE

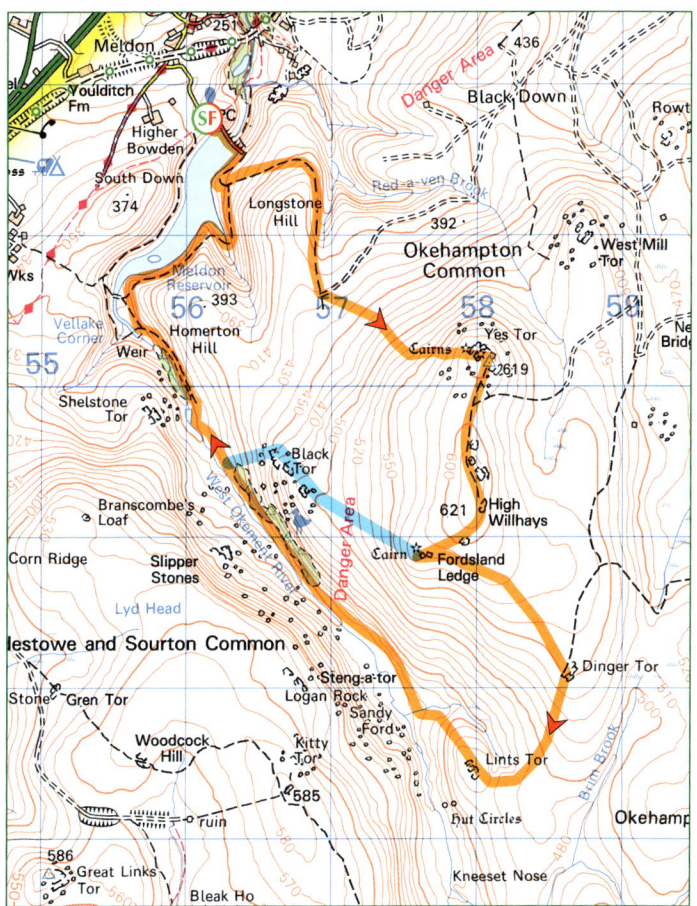

Company; the viaduct now forms part of the Granite Way cycle route between Okehampton and Lydford.

At a small gate on the right (which gives access to some picnic tables) turn left (east) following the grassy

WALKING ON DARTMOOR

> The path following the reservoir is the return route.

track uphill. ◄ Keep to the track as it swings right (south), still climbing up Longstone Hill. Keep left at two forked junctions to reach a cross junction (SX 569 906). Turn left and immediately fork right on a path heading south-east, soon passing into the Okehampton Range; you must check that the range is open before undertaking this walk. The vague path continues steeply up across the boulder-strewn slope to the summit of **Yes Tor** and then heads south along the broad ridge to **High Willhays**.

> **Yes Tor** (619m) is crowned by a trig point along with a military hut and flagpole; on a clear day, views stretch northwards across North Devon. **High Willhays** at 621m (2039ft) is both the highest point in Dartmoor and the highest point in Southern England. Views include Yes Tor to the north with North Devon beyond, Cosdon Hill (east), southwards to Cut Hill, Great Kneeset and Fur Tor, and Great Links Tor (west).

Looking south from the most southerly outcrop there are two paths; take the right-hand one heading west-south-west to reach **Fordsland Ledge**. ◄ At Fordsland Ledge you have to decide whether to follow the shorter walk or continue with the longer walk.

> The left-hand path heads south-east directly to Dinger Tor.

> **Fordsland Ledge** (582m) is home to the remains of a Bronze Age stone cairn, a couple of military huts and a flagpole. However, the reason for visiting is for the view: to the north along the valley lies North Devon; to the south-west is Kitty Tor, Great Links Tor and Amicombe Hill; and to the south is a great view along the valley, home to the West Okement River, with Great Kneeset, Fur Tor and Cut Hill beyond.

Shorter route variation
For the shorter walk: head west-north-west down to **Black Tor** and, after passing the outcrops, turn left down to the

Walk 36 – High Willhays via Yes Tor and Black-a-Tor Copse

West Okement River at the northern end of Black-a-Tor Copse; turn right to rejoin the main route.

Main route
To continue the longer walk, turn sharp left (east) and contour round the slope as it curves right to join a track beside **Dinger Tor** (550m). ▶ Turn right for a short way to the end of the track and then continue on a path heading south-south-west downhill, keeping above the stream heads on the right. Curve to the right heading west, pass a dip and continue curving right to head north-west up to **Lints Tor** (496m). From here there is a good view along the West Okement River valley.

Continue past the outcrops heading north-north-west and start descending into the valley. At the stream bear left, then bear right to cross the stream. Continue along the valley, keeping the West Okement River on your left and staying close to boulders on the right, picking the

Although slightly overshadowed by its higher neighbours, views include Great Kneeset and Fur Tor (south), Fordsland Ledge and High Willhays (north-west), and Cosdon Hill (north-east).

Passing Black-a-Tor Copse, with its moss- and lichen-covered oak trees and boulders, on the way down to Meldon Reservoir

The shorter walk rejoins here from the right.

driest route. Continue past Black-a-Tor Copse, with Black Tor above. ◄

The **West Okement River** rises near Cranmere Pool and flows north-westwards to join with the East Okement River at Okehampton to form the River Okement. **Black-a-Tor Copse** lies on the steep west-facing slope of the valley below Black Tor. The National Nature Reserve is home to ancient stunted English oaks growing among granite boulders clothed in moss and lichen. This is one of three high-altitude oak woods in Dartmoor, the others being Wistman's Wood (Walk 26) and Piles Copse (Walk 18).

Keep ahead with the river still on your left to a stone wall. Follow this on your left and then continue down the track, still with the river on the left. Later keep to a path along the bottom edge of the slope on your right to a footbridge on the left. Do not cross this, but turn right and follow a path slightly uphill, keeping the fence on your left. The route now follows the path beside the fence on your left for 1.6km (1 mile) with a great view over Meldon Reservoir, crossing a footbridge in a side-valley on the way. Keep left (straight on) at the junction visited earlier in the walk and soon turn left, retracing the route back over the dam and along the access road back to the car park on the right.

Yes Tor – Dartmoor's second highest

WALK 37
Belstone, Cullever Steps and West Mill Tor

Start/finish	Belstone car park (SX 621 938)
Alt start/finish	Rowtor parking area (SX 596 922)
Distance	14.5km (9 miles)
Ascent	435m
Time	4¼hrs
Terrain	Mostly on paths and tracks; high-level remote moor requires good navigation in low visibility; some steeper sections and stream crossings
Maps	OS Explorer OL28
Refreshments	The Tors pub (01837 840689) and the Old School Tearoom (01837 840498) in Belstone
Public transport	Bus links to Exeter, Okehampton and Newton Abbot stop on the B3260 (Tongue End Cross), 1.1km (¾ mile) north of Belstone
Note	Parts of the walk lie within the Okehampton Firing Range – check that the range is open before walking

From Belstone the route heads to Cullever Steps, crossing the East Okement River before heading up to East Mill Tor. After enjoying the views it's off across the Black-a-ven Brook to visit West Mill Tor for another great view. After passing Rowtor the route leaves the open moor and heads through Halstone Wood before crossing the East Okement River on the way back to Belstone.

Shorter route variation

For a much shorter route missing out Belstone, start from Rowtor parking area (SX 596 922) and head south-east along the tarred track for 450 metres to a junction and keep ahead; the main walk joins from the left (7km/4½ miles, 230m ascent).

Main route

Turn left from car park at Belstone and keep right at the junction to the village green. Continue along the

WALKING ON DARTMOOR

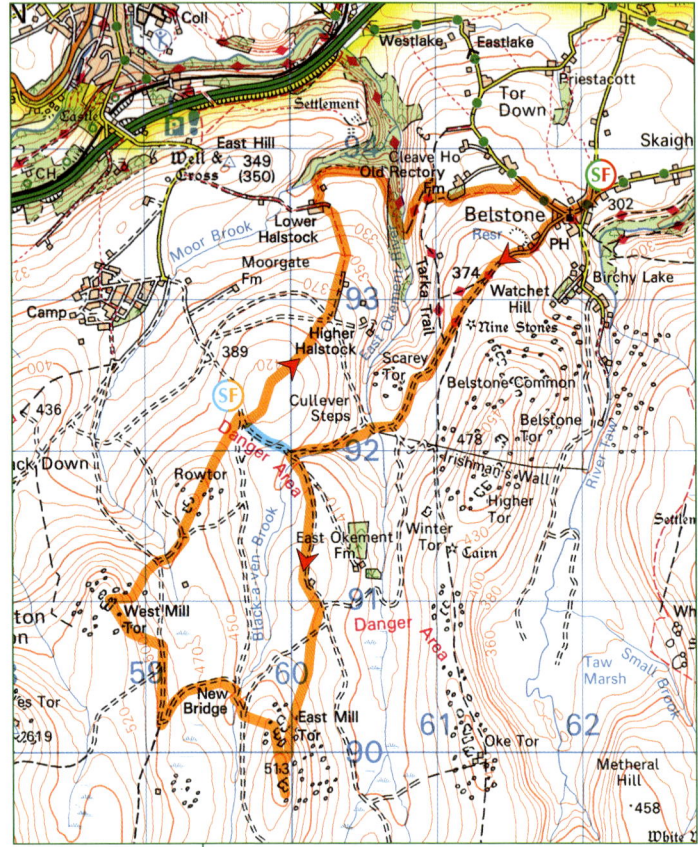

right-hand side; over to the left is the tearoom. Keep right at the next junction – the Tors pub is to the left – then fork left at the split (the next left leads to the church) and continue up to the end of the lane.

> **Belstone** is home to the Tors pub and the 15th-century Church of St Mary the Virgin; go inside the church to see the early medieval (7th- to

WALK 37 – BELSTONE, CULLEVER STEPS AND WEST MILL TOR

Church of St Mary the Virgin at Belstone

9th-century) Ring Cross carved on a granite slab. Huddled round the triangular-shaped village green are the old village stocks, the Belstone Pound (now a small garden) and the Old School Tearoom.

Go through the gate on to the open moor and continue up the track with a wall on your right. Where the wall goes right, keep ahead ignoring a track off to the left to follow the stony track south-south-west for 1.2km (¾ mile), keeping left of **Scarey Tor** to a track junction. Turn right and cross the bridges over the East Okement River and Black-a-ven Brook at Cullever Steps.

The **East Okement River** joins with the West Okement River at Okehampton to form the River Okement. **Cullever Steps** refers to the stepping stones across the river beside the stone-cobbled ford, just up river from the modern military bridge. Some 120 metres downstream is Cullever Steps Pool, a popular picnic and swimming spot.

As the track swings right, turn left (boundary stone on left) and keep left at the split following a grassy path up alongside the picturesque Black-a-ven Brook. Then keep ahead along the track to a T-junction. ◀ Turn left along the tarred military track for 850 metres (½ mile) heading southwards. ◀ Follow the track up to a military Observation Post (OP22) just after passing the small outcrop of Hart Tor to the left of the track; from here the track becomes unsurfaced and enters the Okehampton Range.

> Or follow the track as it swings right to a junction and turn left up to a T-junction.

> If you started from Rowtor you join from the right.

Keep ahead for 150 metres and then fork right (just west of south) on to a narrow path over the grass aiming for **East Mill Tor**. Cross straight over the track and continue uphill, weaving through the clitter to the summit.

> **East Mill Tor** (513m) offers a great view: looking west are Dartmoor's highest tops, Yes Tor and High Willhays; moving clockwise is West Mill Tor, then Rowtor and North Devon (north), Belstone Tor (north-east), the domed outline of Cosdon Hill, Oke Tor (east), Steeperton Tor, Wild Tor and then Hangingstone Hill (south-south-east). On the south side of the main tor there is a stone wall. This was once Observation Post 10. Originally there were 22 Observation Posts within the Okehamptom Range; now only 7 are in use.

After admiring the views head north to the last outcrop and bear left (west-north-west) down through the clitter to a track junction. Take the second track on the right, heading just west of north and cross Black-a-ven Brook at **New Bridge**. Continue to a track junction and turn left up to a T-junction. Turn right (north) to a junction (track joining from left) and keep ahead for a further 100 metres then fork left (north-westwards) up a vague path to the top of **West Mill Tor**.

WALK 37 – BELSTONE, CULLEVER STEPS AND WEST MILL TOR

West Mill Tor

West Mill Tor (541m), the highest point on the walk, offers a great view similar to that from East Mill Tor (although this time you can also see East Mill Tor to the south-east). If you look east as you descend, you can see the remains (including the engine and trolley shed, and the safety embankments) of the narrow-gauge Rowtor target railway, built in 1959.

From the gap between the two main outcrops head east downhill, soon bearing left (north-east) down to a 3-way track junction. Keep ahead following the track east-north-east, soon fording a stream, and continue to a Y-junction. Fork left for a few metres, then turn right (north-north-east) on a path to the summit of **Rowtor** (468m), which, although lower than its neighbours, has a number of granite outcrops to explore and some lovely views.

Continue north-north-east downhill, later keeping right at a split to reach a tarred track junction beside the Rowtor parking area. ▶ Pass the red/white range marker, turn right (south-east) for a few metres and then turn left (north-east) on a track over the slight hill to a track junction. Keep ahead on a narrow path aiming for a barn (the right-hand track goes to a range flagpole).

Cross two tracks and continue with a wall on your right. Go through the gate and follow the track

This car park can be used as an alternative start for a shorter walk missing out Belstone (shorter route variation instructions are at the start of the route).

Looking east to Belstone Tor from Rowtor

(bridleway) past the barn at East Bowden. Continue to a signed three-way junction at **Lower Halstock**. Turn right along the track (footpath) and, shortly before the house, turn left down between the walls. Go through a gate and follow the path as it swings right (east), with a river down to the left. The path swings right again (south-south-east) and shortly starts descending through an oak wood (Halstock Wood) to a path junction. Bear right (Dartmoor Way), with the East Okement River on your left, and then cross over the river via the footbridge.

Turn left (north) up a path (not the steep one straight up from the footbridge) to a track and turn sharp right (south) to the corner of a wall. Turn left alongside the wall (which is on your right), go through a gate leaving the open moor and follow the bridleway. Pass a line of mature trees and follow the left-hand field edge. Go through a gate and continue along the enclosed track before going through another gate. Keep ahead to join a minor road and turn right towards **Belstone**. Keep left at the junction and retrace your steps back to the car park.

WALK 38
Steeperton Tor, Hangingstone Hill and Oke Tor

Start/finish	Belstone car park (SX 621 938)
Distance	18.5km (11½ miles) or 13km (8 miles)
Ascent	535m or 350m
Time	5½hrs or 3¾hrs
Terrain	Long walk on tracks and paths which are indistinct higher up; sections over high-level remote moor require good navigation in low visibility; some river and stream crossings
Maps	OS Explorer OL28
Refreshments	The Tors pub (01837 840689) and the Old School Tearoom (01837 840498) at Belstone
Public transport	Bus links to Exeter, Okehampton and Newton Abbot stop on the B3260 (Tongue End Cross) 1.1km (¾ mile) north of Belstone
Note	Parts of the walk lie within the Okehampton Firing Range – check that the range is open before walking

From picturesque Belstone the walk heads south along the River Taw valley before heading up Steeperton Tor. After admiring the views the route heads to Hound Tor – from here you can detour to White Moor Stone Circle – before heading south to Wild Tor and Hangingstone Hill. The route then goes north to Oke Tor and follows the ridge past Higher Tor to Belstone Tor. Then it's off down to Nine Stones cairn circle before heading back to the start. A shorter walk, missing out Hound Tor, Wild Tor and Hangingstone Hill is also described.

Turn left from car park at Belstone, keep right at the junction, and then take the left-hand fork at the village green. ▶ Keep left at the next junction with the Tors pub over to the right and continue south along the lane for 500 metres. At the split, shortly after the lane swings left past some houses, fork right uphill. Go through a gate onto the open moor and follow the track southwards along the valley for 1.6km (1 mile), with Belstone Tor up

On the left, after passing the old stocks, are Belstone Pound (where stray animals used to be impounded) and the Old School Tearoom.

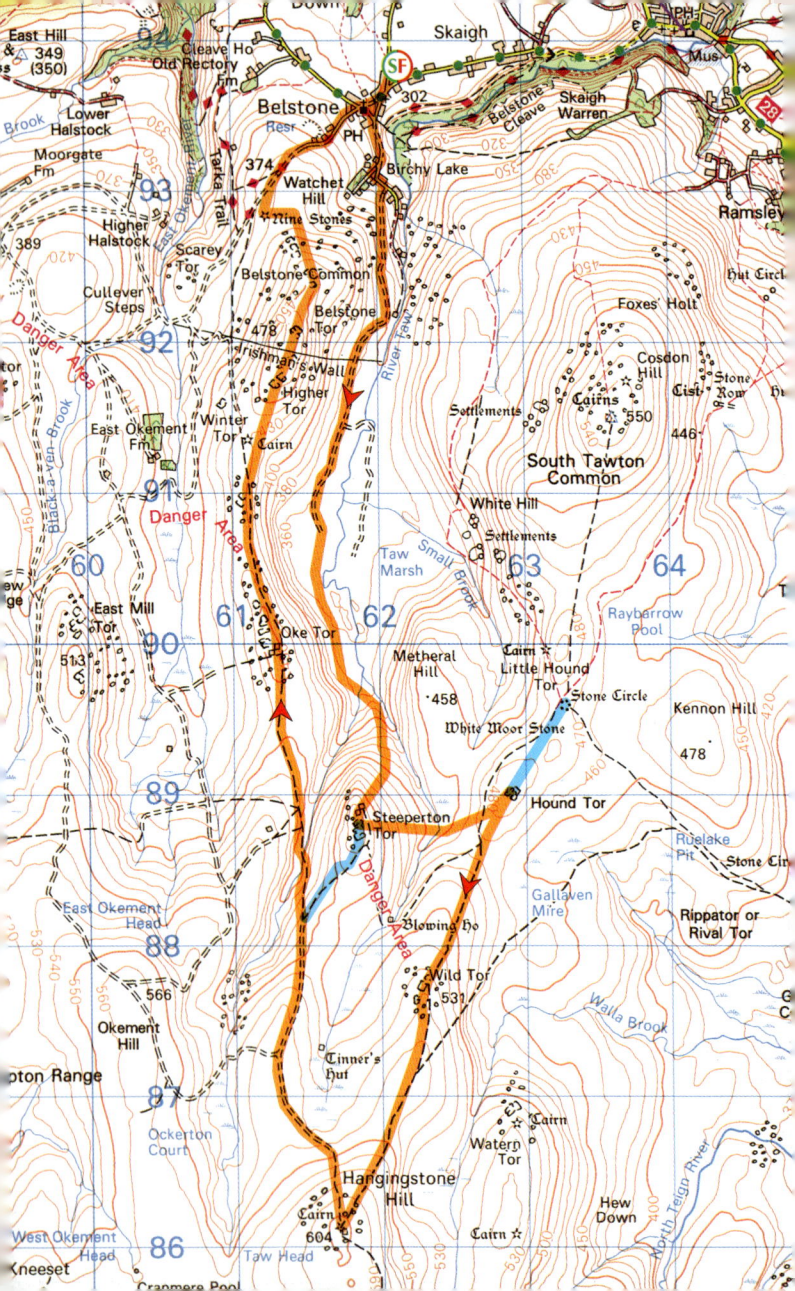

WALK 38 – STEEPERTON TOR, HANGINGSTONE HILL AND OKE TOR

to the right and the River Taw on the left, to a track junction. Go straight on along the valley with the conical outline of Steeperton Tor ahead. As the track fades continue along a less defined path, still following the valley but staying close to the base of the slope on your right.

On nearing the entrance to Steeperton Gorge bear left and cross the River Taw (stream). Head south-east and then south up a narrow and at times indistinct path to the military hut and flagpole on the summit of **Steeperton Tor**, passing into the Okehampton military range; you must check that the military range is open before undertaking the walk. Here the long and short walks separate; the longer walk turns left, the shorter walk keeps ahead.

Steeperton Tor (532m) offers a great view: looking north is the Taw valley (along which the route came); moving clockwise is the large dome of Cosdon Hill, then Hound Tor, Wild Tor and Hangingstone Hill (south) – all visited on the walk; continuing round are High Willhays and Yes Tor (west), and then Oke Tor and Belstone Tor (both passed later in the walk).

A sheep on Wild Tor

Shorter walk variation

Keep ahead (south) past the outcrops of Steeperton Tor, then bear half-right (south-south-west) down to a junction with a track (SX 614 882) and turn sharp right, now following the longer walk downhill towards the River Taw. ◄

> The shortcut rejoins the walk just after the main route descends from the summit of Hangingstone Hill; continue the instructions from this point.

Main route

Stand beside the hut and head south-east for 100 metres then east downhill, leaving the military range on the way. Cross Steeperton Brook and fork half-left (east-north-east) up to the top of **Hound Tor** (495m), which offers another great vantage point. The onward route turns sharp right (almost doubling back). Before continuing, you can make a detour to the White Moor Stone Circle (adds 1.5km/1 mile return).

Stone circle detour

From Hound Tor follow a path north-north-east to the **White Moor Stone Circle** and then retrace your steps. The remote White Moor (or Little Hound Tor) Stone Circle dates from the late Neolithic/early Bronze Age and consists of 18 stones. About 150 metres south-east is the White Moor Stone, a boundary marker that lies at the junction of three parishes.

Main route

From Hound Tor head south-south-west to a slight saddle and continue up to **Wild Tor** (531m), passing back into the firing range. ◄ Continue in the same direction for 1.7km (1 mile) to the military hut and flagpole on the summit of **Hangingstone Hill**. The onward route turns sharp right (almost doubling back).

> Views from here include Hangingstone Hill (south) and – moving clockwise – High Willhays and Yes Tor (north-west), then Steeperton Tor and Belstone Tor, with Cosdon Hill to the north.

> **Hangingstone Hill** (604m) is a fairly plain, rounded hill crowned by a military observation hut and flagpole; however, it is Dartmoor's joint third highest top and, from the summit, there are good views.

Oke Tor looking north

Head north downhill and keep ahead along the stony track. Where the main track turns hard left (west) go straight on (north), soon descending into the valley, then keep left at the split. ▶ Cross the River Taw at the ford (if required look either side for a suitable crossing point); just upstream are some ruins and spoil heaps from a 19th-century tin mine known as Knack Mine or Steeperton Tor Mine. Follow the track uphill and keep right (straight on) at the junction following the track north towards **Oke Tor**. Later, fork slightly right on a grassy route aiming just to the right of the tor.

The right-hand fork is the shorter route which has come down from Steeperton Tor and rejoins the main walk here, following the track downhill.

From the summit stack of **Oke Tor** (466m) there is another great view looking over High Willhays and Yes Tor (west); north along the ridge is Belstone Tor; and further round is Cosdon Hill (north-east); to the south is Steeperton Tor and Hangingstone Hill.

Continue northwards on a path just right of the tor for 900 metres (½ mile) following the ridge. Pass just right of an outcrop (Knattaborough Tor), leaving the firing range, and fork slightly right following a path north-north-east up to **Higher Tor** (471m). Keep ahead, passing Irishman's Wall (an east–west stone wall built around 1820) to reach **Belstone Tor** (478m) – another great place to sit and admire the view. Continue along the ridge to Belstone

Walking on Dartmoor

Common Tor (460m) then head northwards down through the clitter, passing to the right of Tors End Tor (429m) to a flat area; ahead is a military flagpole on Watchet Hill. Turn left (west) along a wide grassy path to **Nine Stones**.

> **Nine Stones**, also known as the Nine Maidens, which consists of 16 stones, is the remains of a Bronze Age burial cairn circle, rather than a stone circle. Folklore has it that the stones are actually nine maidens cast into stone for dancing on the Sabbath.

Turn right (north), soon keeping ahead along a track (Dartmoor Way and Tarka Trail) with a wall on your left, heading downhill. Go through a gate and continue down the lane, keeping ahead at the junctions until you reach the village green. ◄ Pass the village green (tearoom to right) and retrace the outward route back to the car park.

The first right after the gate heads to the 15th-century Church of St Mary the Virgin. Inside is the early medieval (7th- to 9th-century) Ring Cross carved slab. The second right heads to the Tors pub.

WALK 39
Cosdon Hill and Belstone Cleave

Start/finish	South Zeal car park off Shelly Road (SX 652 934)
Distance	14.5km (9 miles)
Ascent	470m
Time	4½hrs
Terrain	Paths, tracks and lanes; steep descent; high-level moor sections require good navigation in low visibility and can be very wet in places; wooded river valley section
Maps	OS Explorer OL28
Refreshments	Kings Arms Inn (01837 840300) and Oxenham Arms (01837 840244) in South Zeal; Taw River Inn (01837 840377), Devonshire Inn (01837 840626), Sticklepath Store and Tearoom (01837 840359) and National Trust café at Sticklepath
Public transport	Buses between Newton Abbot and Okehampton stop at South Zeal and Sticklepath
Note	The section skirting past Raybarrow Pool can be very wet; do not stray into the mire

WALK 39 – COSDON HILL AND BELSTONE CLEAVE

From South Zeal the route climbs steadily along tracks on to the open moor to visit an ancient triple stone row before skirting past the infamous mire of Raybarrow Pool to visit White Moor Stone Circle. Then it's uphill to the summit of Cosdon Hill for a great view before heading down towards Belstone. The route then heads along the wooded Belstone Cleave to the sound of the River Taw, crossing the Tarka Bridge on the way. The final stop is Sticklepath, home to the Finch Foundry, before heading back to South Zeal.

Exit the car park and turn right along the road, keeping right at the split, and head up to a junction. ▶ Cross straight over and follow the surfaced track (bridleway) uphill. At a right bend, fork left up a path before rejoining the surfaced track and turn left to a track junction. Take the left-hand track (bridleway) uphill, heading generally southwards for 1.4km (1 mile). On the way, pass a sign for 'Cawsand and the moor', ignore a path to the left and then keep left (bridleway) at a track junction. Cross a stream and continue between the stone walls. At the end of the left-hand wall, bear right (south-west) following a faint track over the open moor to reach a stone row. ▶

To the left is the bus stop.

For a shorter walk you can head due west from the stone row steeply up to the summit of Cosdon Hill (reduces the walk by 3.7km/2¼ miles).

Following an old track (bridleway) towards the open moor

231

WALKING ON DARTMOOR

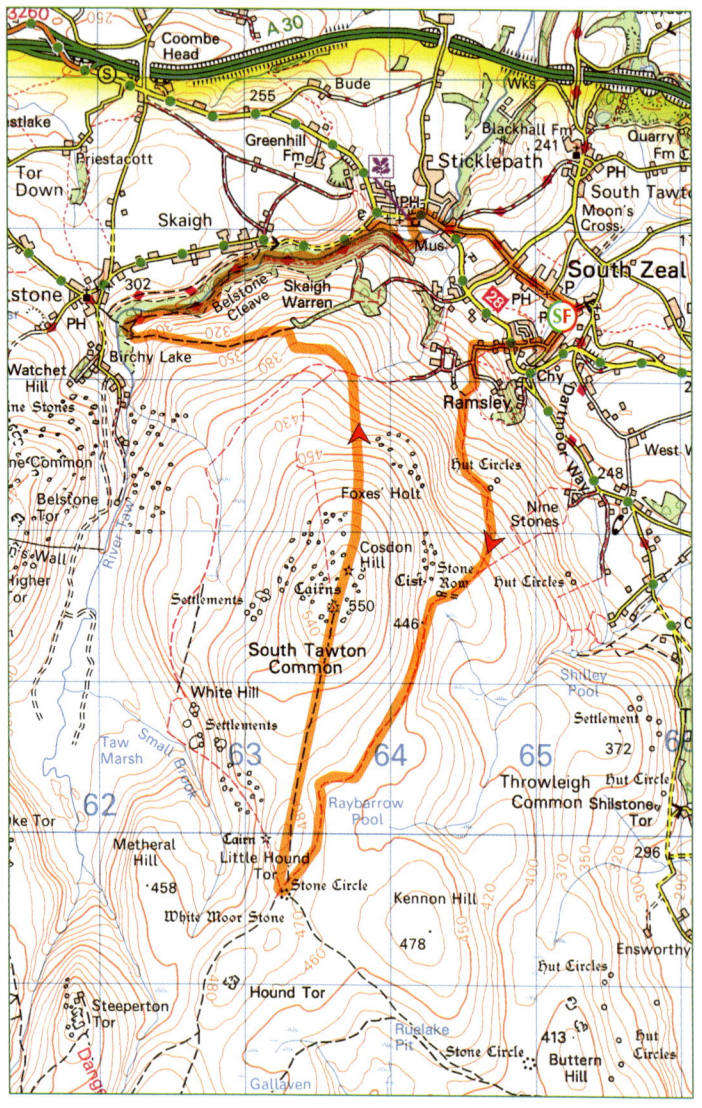

Cosdon Hill Stone Row, known locally as 'The Graveyard', dates from the Bronze Age and consists of three parallel rows of standing stones, with the remains of a double cist, or burial chamber, at its western end.

Cosdon Hill stone row – also known as 'The Graveyard'

Keep left of the **stone row** and follow a banked way that curves left to head south and then south-southwest uphill; distant views include Haytor (south-east) and, much nearer, Raybarrow Pool (a mire that must be avoided). The route then reaches a boggy area (SX 638 905 to SX 638 904) – care required – and soon swings right (west) and then left (south) above a mire. If the route is too wet, retrace your steps back towards the stone row a short distance to SX 639 907 and then head west uphill to find drier ground and the path that leads up Cosdon Hill; either turn left down to the stone circle or turn right uphill, missing out the stone circle. Having passed the boggy area, the route skirts round the side of Little Hound Tor to reach a slight saddle and a **stone circle**; from here the route swings hard right towards Cosdon Hill.

Cairn and trig point on the summit of Cosdon Hill

The remote White Moor (or Little Hound Tor) **stone circle** dates from the late Neolithic/early Bronze Age period and consists of 18 stones. About 150 metres south-east is the White Moor Stone, a boundary marker that lies at the junction of three parishes.

Continue north-north-east over Little Hound Tor and up to the large cairn and trig point on the summit of **Cosdon Hill** (550m). ◄ From the trig point keep ahead to a **cairn** and then descend generally northwards for 1.3km (¾ mile) to a junction of routes (SX 637 930). Ignore the track down to the right (this leads directly back to South Zeal and reduces the walk by 3.7km/2¼ miles) and ignore the route up to the left (west) alongside the disused leat; instead take the level route half-left (north-westwards) that contours round the hill for 400 metres to a cross-junction (SX 633 932). Turn right for 120 metres down to a large boundary stone and path junction.

From this lofty position there are some great views, including of Dartmoor's highest tops, Yes Tor and High Willhays, to the west.

Turn left (westwards) downhill, crossing Ivy Tor Water on the way then descending more steeply with views of

WALK 39 – COSDON HILL AND BELSTONE CLEAVE

Belstone ahead to reach a walled enclosure. Continue, keeping the wall on the right, and soon fork right to follow the wall as it swings to the right. ▶ The walk now heads east along the tree-shaded Belstone Cleave following the Dartmoor Way for 2.3km (1½ miles).

After 900 metres cross the River Taw via a footbridge up to a track and turn right. Then, just after the fork on the left, bear right down through the trees to re-cross the river via another footbridge. Known as Tarka Bridge, you can read the inscriptions by Tarka the Otter author Henry Williamson as you cross; part of his classic tale is based along the River Taw. Here the path splits; keep left along the riverside path, which is rocky at times, passing a weir and heading through Skaigh Wood – later the route swings to the right to a signed junction. Turn left, go through a gate and follow the track to a footbridge on the left. ▶

Go over the footbridge and follow the path through the trees. Bear right, go through a gate and follow the

The left fork heads to a footbridge over the River Taw and then up to Belstone (see Walks 37 and 38).

To miss out Sticklepath keep ahead to the road and take the lane opposite.

Tarka Bridge across the River Taw in Belstone Cleave

In its heyday, the 19th-century, water-powered Finch Foundry (National Trust) was making 400 tools a day, ranging from scythes to shovels.

narrow hedge-lined path; on the right is the Quaker Burial Ground. Turn right along the tarred drive (to the left is a car park) past the Finch Foundry and the 19th-century, thatch-roofed summerhouse to join the main street in **Sticklepath**. ◀

Turn right passing the Taw River Inn and the Sticklepath Stores and Tearoom. Fork left at the junction immediately after crossing the bridge over the River Taw and follow the lane (Dartmoor Way) up to a crossroads. Keep ahead following the main street down through **South Zeal**, passing the thatch-roofed Kings Arms Inn, then St Mary's Church next to the fine 14th-century cross. Continue past the Oxenham Arms to a junction at the bottom of the hill and turn right back to the car park.

> South Zeal is home to a 5000-year-old, late Neolithic menhir, or standing stone, located within the **Oxenham Arms**. In the 12th century, Benedictine monks built a monastery incorporating the menhir, and in the 14th century this became a manor house. Later it was acquired by the Oxenham family and became a coaching inn – the Oxenham Arms – in the late 15th century; you can still see the standing stone inside.

White Moor (or Little Hound Tor) stone circle

TEN TORS

Stunning Watern Tor and the Thirlstone (Walks 32 and 40)

WALKING ON DARTMOOR

WALK 40
Ten Tors two days

Start/finish	Belstone car park (SX 621 938)
Alt start/finish	Okehampton rail station (SX 592 944)
Distance	58km (36 miles)
Ascent	1600m
Time	2 days
Terrain	A long walk over very remote, high-level moor with poorly defined paths that can be rather wet; several river crossings; very good navigation required in low visibility
Maps	OS Explorer OL28
Refreshments	The Tors pub (01837 840689) and the Old School Tearoom (01837 840498) at Belstone; Okehampton has a range of facilities; village shop and East Dart Hotel (01822 880213) at Postbridge; Two Bridges Hotel (01822 892300) at Two Bridges (off route)
Public transport	Bus links to Exeter, Okehampton and Newton Abbot stop on the B3260 (Tongue End Cross) 1.1km (¾ mile) north of Belstone; rail station and good bus links at Okehampton; Postbridge and Two Bridges have bus links to Tavistock, Yelverton and Newton Abbot
Accommodation	Wild camping (see text); campsite at Beardown Farm (detour – see text; 01822 890287/07816 149366); East Dart Inn (01822 880213) at Postbridge; youth hostel (0345 371 9622) at Bellever (off route); Two Bridges Hotel (01822 892300) at Two Bridges (off route)
Note	The walk passes through all three military ranges – you must check they are open for two consecutive days before setting out; take care with all river crossings, as they may be impassable after heavy rain

The Army-organised Ten Tors, first held in 1960, is designed as both a physical and mental challenge, a test of endurance, teamwork and navigational skills. Teams of six teenagers are given a different selection of 10 tors – the tors are changed from time to time, meaning that there is no set route – and, depending on age, a set distance to cover, namely 35 miles

(14–15 years), 45 miles (16–17 years) and 55 miles (18–19 years). The event starts at 07.00 at Okehampton Camp on a Saturday and ends at 17.00 on the Sunday. Teams are not allowed to go further than their 8th tor on the 1st day; to find out more about the official Ten Tors event visit www.tentors.org.uk.

For this alternative Ten Tors style two day walk I've opted for a 58km/36-mile route, visiting 10 tors that have been used on previous Ten Tors events. However, the route takes in several more tors along the way and, to increase the challenge, you can easily visit a few extra ones. The walk as described can be started from Belstone or Okehampton Railway Station and could also be done as two linear walks. There are suggestions about where to look for overnight wild camping; however, it is up to you to choose a good site away from streams and rivers. A detour to Beardown Farm campsite is also described.

The route chosen (note that tors which have been used recently for Ten Tors challenges are shown in bold): Belstone or Okehampton Station – **Oke Tor** – **Steeperton Tor** – Wild Tor – **Watern Tor** – Quintin's Man – **Sittaford Tor** – Hartland Tor – Postbridge – **Rough Tor** – **Crow Tor** – White Barrow – Ger Tor – **Hare Tor** – Chat Tor – Green Tor – **Kitty Tor** – **Great Kneeset** – Dinger Tor – **High Willhays** – Rowtor – Belstone or Okehampton Station

Okehampton Railway Station start/finish

The Okehampton Railway Station start/finish adds 2.8km/1¾ miles and 150m ascent. Exit the station and turn left to a cross-junction. Turn left under the railway bridge and follow the lane uphill for 130 metres to a gate on the left where there is a choice. ▶ The right of way keeps ahead up the track past houses, before bearing left and then right to a footbridge over the A30; to follow the alternative route, turn left through the gate and follow a path (signed Permitted Path to Dartmoor) through the trees before swinging right up to the footbridge. Once across the footbridge turn right alongside the fence for 100 metres, then turn left up across the field and through a gate to join a minor road at a corner. Follow the road uphill for 150 metres and turn left along the farm access track to **Lower Halstock**. Follow the track as it curves right past buildings and rises. Go through a gate beside a barn and continue alongside the wall on the left to the corner. Bear left to a cross-junction and keep ahead (south-south-east) along the track for 700 metres. Ignore a track to the right at SX

> On the way, the track on the left gives access to the Granite Way Café, youth hostel and campsite.

605 922 – this is the return route – and shortly turn left crossing bridges over the Black-a-ven Brook and East Okement River at **Cullever Steps**. Continue to a junction and turn right; the route from Belstone joins from the left.

Day one

From the car park at Belstone turn left, then keep right at the junction and continue along the right-hand side of the village green (tearoom on left). Keep right at the next junction (the Tors pub is over to the left) and fork left uphill at the split to the end of the lane. Go through the gate on to the open moor and continue up the track with a wall on your right. Where the wall goes right, keep ahead, ignoring a track off to the left to follow the stony track south-south-west for 1.2km (¾ mile), keeping left of Scarey Tor to a track junction near **Cullever Steps**. ◄

If you started from Okehampton Railway Station you join the route here and turn right.

Continue southwards and almost immediately fork left up the track to a junction and turn right. Follow the track southwards for 950 metres up to an outcrop

Summit of Steeperton Tor looking north

(Knattaborough Tor, 438m) and keep ahead along the ridge to **Oke Tor** (466m, Walk 38). Pass to the left of the outcrop and keep ahead; later cross the Taw River at a ford at Knack Mine. Continue up the track for 300 metres to a junction and turn sharp left (north-north-east) up to **Steeperton Tor** (532m, Walk 38).

From the summit look south and, of the two paths, take the left-hand one heading just east of south to a ford beside the ruins of a blowing house. Cross Steeperton Brook, bear left and then turn right (just east of south) to **Wild Tor** (531m, Walk 38). Head south along the outcrops and then bear half-left (south-south-east) downhill. Cross the Walla Brook and head up to **Watern Tor** (536m, Walk 32).

Turn right and follow a path southwards alongside the military range poles, passing to the left (east) of Hangingstone Hill and Whitehorse Hill. Dip down to cross a stream and continue alongside the range poles up to **Quintin's Man** (Walk 32). Turn half-left (south-east) downhill and then continue alongside a wall on your left. Cross a couple of streams that form the North Teign River at Little Varracombe; you may have to detour upstream to a find a suitable crossing point after rain. Continue up alongside the wall towards **Sittaford Tor** (537m, Walk 32) and bear left (east-north-east) to cross a stile. Continue alongside the wall on your left down to a junction.

Turn right (south) to the **Grey Wethers Stone Circles** (Walk 32). Keep ahead (south) on a wide route for 400 metres and then fork left to follow a path along the left side of the valley for 1.3km (¾ mile) to a stone wall. Cross the stile and keep ahead to **Hartland Tor** (409m).

Continue down towards the trees, keep ahead through two gates and follow the river. Go through a third gate and turn left. Continue along two sides of the field and pass through two sets of gates to reach the B3212; to the left is the East Dart Inn. Turn right to cross the **East Dart River**. ▶ Continue past the village shop/tearoom and visitor centre (car park, toilets and bus links to Exeter and Tavistock) to a junction on the left signed to Bellever

> Just downstream is the impressive old clapper bridge.

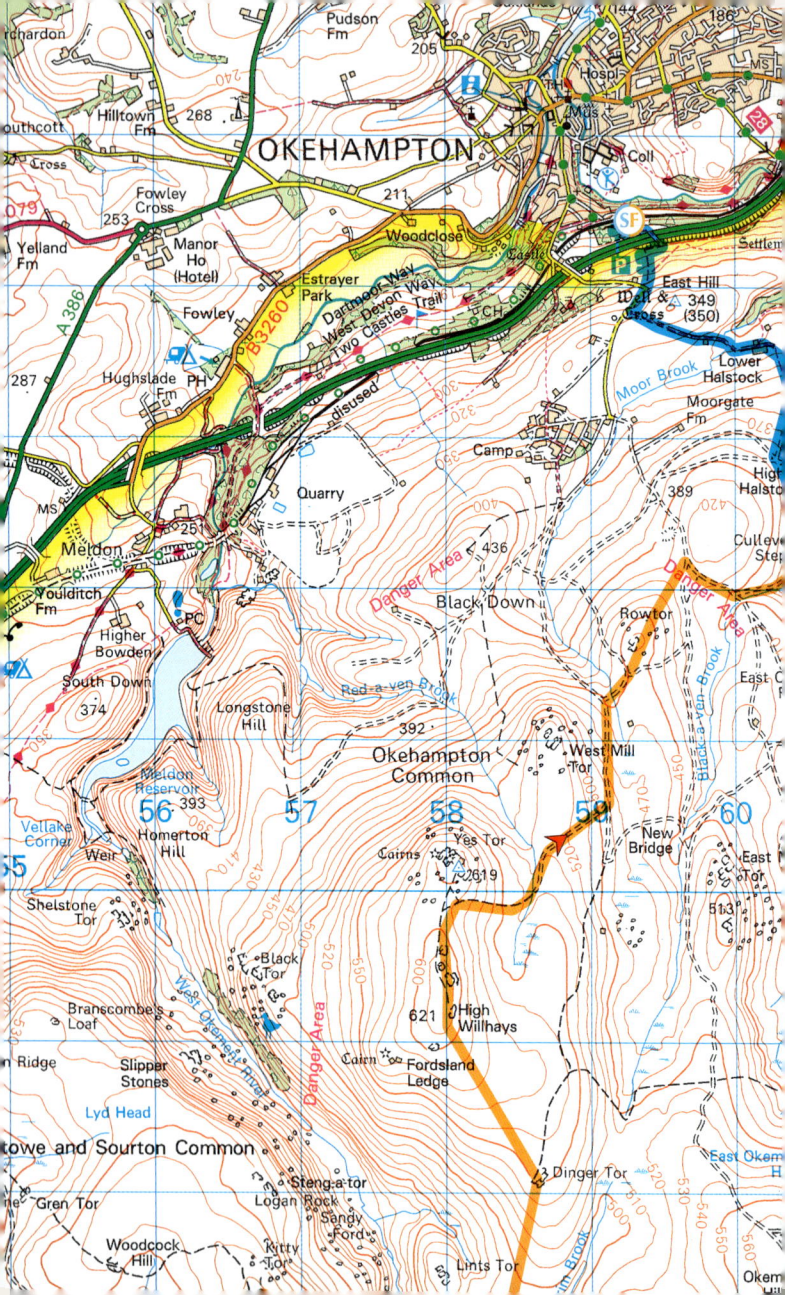

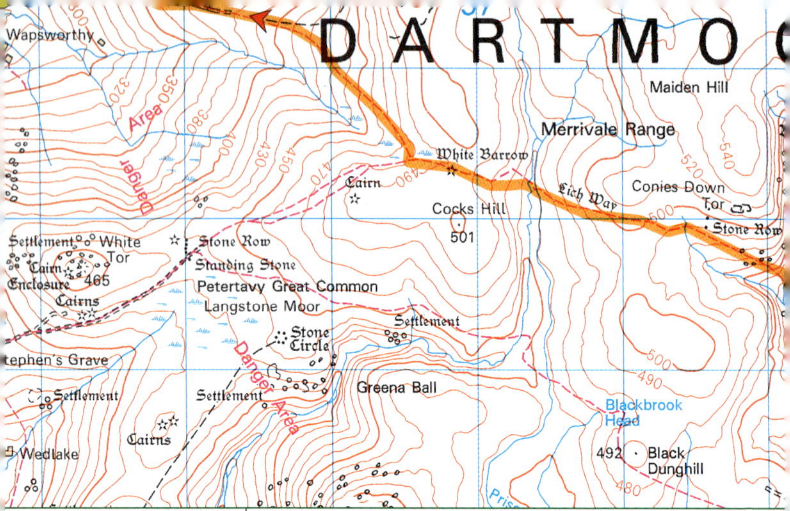

where there is a youth hostel; (www.yha.org.uk/hostel/yha-dartmoor; adds 3.6km (2¼ miles)).

Turn right and follow the gravel path (Drift Lane) for 600 metres. Go through a gate on to the open moor and start rising, later following a wall on your right. Dip down

Brown's House (ruin) looking west to Rough Tor

to cross Braddon Lake (stream) before continuing, keeping the wall on the right. Go through a gate and continue beside the wall for 250 metres, then fork left (north-north-west) up to a wall. Cross the stile and turn left (south-west) following the wall on your left, later passing an outcrop and descending to the corner of the wall. Cross the stream and turn right (west-north-west) to **Brown's House (ruin)**.

Continue westwards slightly downhill and cross the infant West Dart River; this may cause problems after heavy rainfall. Continue westwards up to **Rough Tor** (547m, Walk 26). Turn left (south) downhill following a path alongside the military range poles. Later, fork left to **Crow Tor** (494m, Walk 26) before heading back to the path alongside the poles. Follow the path across the stream at Foxholes, head uphill and bear left to cross a ladder stile at the wall. Continue south-westwards to a junction (SX 602 780) and bear right on a path passing to the left of **Lydford Tor**. ◀ Continue north-westwards down to a wall, go through the gate and continue down to the Cowsic River at Broad Hole; the route is now following the Lich Way (Walk 25).

The route to the south leads past Beardown Tors to Beardown Farm (see below for camping alternative).

WILD CAMPING SPOTS

Wild camping spots along the route include Crow Tor, Broad Hole near the Cowsic River (beware of rising river levels), Conies Down Tor or further on at Lynch Tor (off route) after passing White Barrow (visit www.dartmoor.gov.uk/about-us/about-us-maps/camping-map to find out where wild camping is currently allowed and follow the latest advice. If you are ahead of schedule, or if you are planning to make the first day much longer, continue with the Day Two route. However, the next available wild camping is around Sharp Tor and Chat Tor, slightly off route at Doe Tor or near Dick's Well (south of Great Links Tor).

Detour to Beardown Farm Campsite

Beardown Farm offers wild camping (no facilities) and a camping pod (with facilities); booking is essential via www.dartmoor-camping.co.uk. To reach the farm, head south past **Beardown Tors**, go through a gate and continue down Beardown Hill. Keep ahead along the track between the plantations, go through a gate and continue to cross a bridge over the Devonport Leat. Keep ahead and, just before Beardown Farm, turn right over a stile beside the gate. Continue along the track as it soon swings left to a junction and turn right; the camping area is on the right just before the bridge over the Cowsic River. ◀ Retrace the route back up past Beardown Tors to

A path on the left just after the bridge leads to the B3357, the Two Bridges Hotel and bus links to Exeter and Tavistock.

the junction (SX 602 780) and turn left, passing to the left of **Lydford Tor** (adds 5.8km/3½ miles and 140m ascent).

Day two
With care, cross the Cowsic River at the ford (Travellers Ford); you may have to look upstream for a suitable crossing; if the river is in flood, there is a footbridge downstream at Holming Beam (SX 594 770). Continue west-north-west uphill passing below Conies Down Tor (520m), keeping Conies Down Water (stream) to the left. Pass over the brow and head downhill, cross a bridge over the old Prison Leat and keep ahead to cross the River Walkham at a ford; you may need to look upstream to find a suitable crossing point. Head north of west uphill and pass just to the north of **White Barrow** with Cocks Hill (501m) further south. Some 300 metres after White Barrow fork right (north-west) aiming for the corner of a wall. Continue alongside the wall on your left. Later, a wall comes in on the right-hand side, head across to this and follow it, heading slightly north of west.

Go through a gate leaving the open moor, pass a building and follow the track ahead with Bagga Tor (372m) to the right. Where the track turns left through a gate (Bagga Tor Gate) keep ahead still following the boundary wall on your left. Pass **Brousentor Farm** and follow the track northwards to open ground. Fork left, following the Baggator Brook on your right towards the River Tavy; shortly before the river there is a choice of either crossing the River Tavy via stepping stones or using the footbridge and a permissive path.

If the river levels are low, you can keep ahead and cross the River Tavy via the Cataloo Steps (stepping stones) and continue north-north-west along the path to join a track; the permissive route joins from the right. To follow the permissive route, shortly before the River Tavy turn right and cross the footbridge over the Baggator Brook. Continue northwards (river over to the left), cross a stile and continue through a wall gap, then turn left to cross the footbridge over the River Tavy at Standon Steps. Keep ahead along the track; soon the route via the

Cataloo Steps joins from the left. Continue past Higher Willsworthy to join a lane at **Willsworthy**.

Turn right to **Lane End** and keep ahead past the parking area, heading north-east and entering the military range. Go through a gate, cross the bridge over Mine Leat and continue north-eastwards up to **Ger Tor** (445m). Head north-north-east over flat ground and then up to the top of **Hare Tor** (531m, Walk 34). Continue along the path in the same direction up Rattlebrook Hill (passing to the right of Sharp Tor, 519m) to **Chat Tor** (541m). ◄

> On the way over to the left is Sharp Tor (519m, Walk 34); there are wild camping areas around here, including Sharp Tor, off route at Doe Tor or near Dick's Well (south of Great Links Tor).

From Chat Tor continue in the same direction (slightly east of north) aiming for the twin tors of Higher and Lower Dunna Goat to the right of Great Links Tor. On reaching a junction, keep ahead towards Lower Dunna Goat and, at the split, fork right on a path heading east and cross the clapper bridge over the Rattle Brook. ◄ Head east to Green Tor (541m) – just upstream are the ruins of **Bleak House** – and then head north-east up over wet ground to **Kitty Tor** (585m, Walk 35).

> To visit Great Links Tor (586m, Walk 35) head to Higher Dunna Goat and then bear west-north-west.

Turn sharp right (south-south-east) down Amicombe Hill for 1.6km (1 mile) to a large boulder (SX 5733 8590) and then turn left (eastwards) down to the watershed col of Broad Amicombe Hole. ◄ Continue eastwards on a path up to the tor on **Great Kneeset** (568m). Turn left (east of north) to the northern outcrop and then head west of north down to Kneeset Nose at the confluence of the West Okement River and the Brim Brook. With care, cross the West Okement River (SX 586 868) and head up west of north and then bear right (east of north) on a vague route to **Dinger Tor** (550m). With the stony military track ahead, bear half-left (north-north-west) on a path to **High Willhays** (621m, Walk 36).

> To the south, the water heads for the Amicombe Brook and River Tavy, to the north water drains to the West Okement River.

IMPORTANT

If the West Okement River is in flood, try further upstream or head back to Kitty Tor then north-north-west down to a footbridge at SX 556 903. Once across, head upstream to Black-a-Tor Copse, then left up past Black Tor to Fordsland Ledge and turn left to High Willhays.

High Willhays – the highest summit in Dartmoor and Southern England

The main route continues northwards past the outcrops of High Willhays and, shortly before reaching **Yes Tor** (619m), bear right and follow a track downhill. Ford a stream and continue along the track as it descends to a junction. ▶ Turn left (north) and, at the next junction, turn right. Ford another stream and continue along the track to a Y-junction. Fork left for a few metres, then turn right (north-north-east) on a path to **Rowtor** (468m, Walk 37).

On the left is West Mill Tor (541m, Walk 37).

Continue north-north-east downhill, later keeping right at a split to reach a tarred track junction beside the parking area. Turn right and take the left-hand of the two tracks for 400 metres to a junction, then turn left down the track to another junction (SX 605 922). ▶ Turn right and follow the track as its swings left, cross the bridge over the Black-a-ven Brook and then the bridge over the East Okement River at Cullever Steps. Then turn left at the junction and retrace the outward route back to **Belstone**.

The return route to Okehampton Railway Station turns left at this junction and retraces the outward route.

APPENDIX A
Useful contacts

Dartmoor National Park Authority
Parke, Bovey Tracey, Devon, TQ13 9JQ
tel 01626 832093;
www.dartmoor.gov.uk

National Park Visitor Centres

Princetown
(PL20 6QF; 01822 890414)

Haytor
(TQ13 9XT; 01364 661520)

Postbridge
(PL20 6TH; 01822 880272)

Visit Dartmoor
www.visitdartmoor.co.uk

Local information centres
Ashburton
tel 01364 653426

Bovey Tracey
tel 01626 832047

Ivybridge
tel 01752 897035

Moretonhampstead
tel 01647 440043

Okehampton
tel 01837 52295

Tavistock
tel 01822 813946

Public transport information
For rail service enquiries contact
National Rail Enquiries
(03457 48 49 50;
www.nationalrail.co.uk).

For all public transport enquiries
(including buses and trains), contact
Traveline (0871 200 22 33;
www.traveline.info or
www.travelinesw.com)
or Devon County Council
(www.traveldevon.info).

Livestock incidents
All livestock, including ponies,
are owned by local farmers and
commoners. If you come across injured
livestock please phone the Livestock
Protection Officer: 07873 587561

Local wildlife
For injured animals or birds contact the
RSPCA: 0300 1234 999

Devon Wildlife Trust: 01392 279244;
www.devonwildlifetrust.org

Rights of way
Devon County Council
Rights of Way Office
www.devon.gov.uk/prow

Ramblers Association
tel 020 3961 3300;
www.ramblers.org.uk

Databases on Dartmoor tors and sites
The Tors of Dartmoor
www.torsofdartmoor.co.uk

The Dartefacts
www.dartefacts.co.uk

APPENDIX B
Glossary

Adit	horizontal tunnel made by miners
Ball	a rounded hill
Beehive hut	small stone hut that used to have a domed roof, used by tin miners for storage
Blowing house	building where miners smelted tin ore
Cairn	ancient burial mound made of large stones
Cist	form of ancient stone coffin (see kistvaen)
Clapper Bridge	a bridge, typically medieval, made of large slabs of granite usually resting on stone piers
Cleave	steep-sided valley, typically wooded
Clitter	boulders lying around and below a granite tor, caused by erosion
Combe	small valley closed at one end
Drift	the rounding-up of ponies on the open moor
Featherbed	an area of marsh that wobbles when walked on, typically with bright green vegetation
Fen	areas of peat bog and bog-grass on north moor
Hut circle	remains of a circular stone hut, usually Bronze Age
Kistvaen	stone coffin for human remains, Bronze Age
Leat	man-made watercourse used to direct water to mines and farms, built to follow the contours of the land but also sloping gently downhill to aid the flow of the water
Logan stone	a stone eroded in such a way that it rocks if pushed
Menhir	tall standing stone (typically Neolithic)
Mire	Dartmoor marsh
Moorgate	gate usually at the end of a lane or track leading on to the open moor
Newtake	reclaimed land taken from the open moor
Peat	decomposed and compacted moorland vegetation in areas of high rainfall
Peat pass/cut	path cut through peat for easier movement of animals
Pound	walled enclosure for keeping animals in
Reave	stone wall or bank marking the boundary of a field system
Tor	granite outcrop, usually on or near the summit of a hill
Warren	farms where rabbits were commercially bred for food
Waste	another name for 'newtake' but only found in south Dartmoor

APPENDIX C
Further reading

Collingwood, Josephine M *Dartmoor Tors Compendium* (Tavicinity Publishing, 2017)

Collingwood, Josephine M *Geology of Dartmoor* (Tavicinity Publishing, 2022)

Cooper, Andrew *Dartmoor National Park: A Celebration of Its People, Places and Wildlife* (Green Books, 2011)

Dibb, Michelle *Dartmoor into the Wilderness* (The History Press, 2011)

Haywood, John *Dartmoor 365* (Curlew Publications, 2020)

Newman, Phil *The Field Archaeology of Dartmoor* (English Heritage, 2011)

DOWNLOAD THE GPX FILES

All the routes in this guide are available for download from:

www.cicerone.co.uk/1108/GPX

as standard format GPX files. You should be able to load them into most online GPX systems and mobile devices, whether GPS or smartphone. You may need to convert the file into your preferred format using a conversion programme such as gpsvisualizer.com or one of the many other such websites and programmes.

When you follow this link, you will be asked for your email address and where you purchased the guidebook, and have the option to subscribe to the Cicerone e-newsletter.

www.cicerone.co.uk

CICERONE

Trust Cicerone to guide your next adventure, wherever it may be around the world...

Discover guides for hiking, mountain walking, backpacking, trekking, trail running, cycling and mountain biking, ski touring, climbing and scrambling in Britain, Europe and worldwide.

Connect with Cicerone online and find inspiration.

- buy books and ebooks
- articles, advice and trip reports
- GPX files and updates
- regular newsletter

cicerone.co.uk